MW00578408

write letter to Maya
anecdote of her
bulking God inside
to compassion

4/16/24 4PM

4

MYTH *and* MEANING

mythology as an organizational
schema to makesense of our
place in nature + the universe

THE COLLECTED WORKS OF JOSEPH CAMPBELL

Thou Art That: Transforming Religious Metaphor

*The Inner Reaches of Outer Space:
Metaphor as Myth and as Religion*

The Flight of the Wild Gander: Selected Essays 1944–1968

The Hero's Journey: Joseph Campbell on His Life and Work

*Myths of Light:
Eastern Metaphors of the Eternal*

*Mythic Worlds, Modern Words:
Joseph Campbell on the Art of James Joyce*

*Pathways to Bliss:
Mythology and Personal Transformation*

*A Skeleton Key to Finnegans Wake:
Unlocking James Joyce's Masterwork*

The Mythic Dimension: Selected Essays 1959–1987

The Hero with a Thousand Faces

Mythic Imagination: Collected Short Fiction

Goddesses: Mysteries of the Feminine Divine

Romance of the Grail: The Magic and Mystery of Arthurian Myth

Asian Journals: India and Japan

The Ecstasy of Being: Mythology and Dance

Correspondence: 1927–1987

Primitive Mythology: The Masks of God, Volume 1

Oriental Mythology: The Masks of God, Volume 2

Occidental Mythology: The Masks of God, Volume 3

Myth and Meaning: Conversations on Mythology and Life

More titles forthcoming

MYTH *and* MEANING
Conversations on Mythology and Life

JOSEPH CAMPBELL

EDITED BY STEPHEN GERRINGER

New World Library
Novato, California

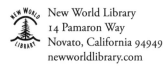 New World Library
14 Pamaron Way
Novato, California 94949
newworldlibrary.com

Copyright © 2023 by Joseph Campbell Foundation (JCF.org)

All rights reserved. This book may not be reproduced in whole or in part, stored in a retrieval system, or transmitted in any form or by any means—electronic, mechanical, or other—without written permission from the publisher, except by a reviewer, who may quote brief passages in a review.

Text design by Tona Pearce Myers

Library of Congress Cataloging-in-Publication data is available.

First printing, November 2023
ISBN 978-1-60868-851-7
Printed in the USA on 30% postconsumer-waste recycled paper

 New World Library is proud to be a Gold Certified Environmentally Responsible Publisher. Publisher certification awarded by Green Press Initiative.

10   9   8   7   6   5   4   3   2   1

CONTENTS

ABOUT THE COLLECTED WORKS OF
JOSEPH CAMPBELL

AT HIS DEATH IN 1987, Joseph Campbell left a significant body of published work that explored his lifelong passion, the complex of universal myths and symbols that he called humankind's "one great story." He also left, however, a large volume of unreleased work: uncollected articles, notes, letters, and diaries, as well as audio- and videotape-recorded lectures.

Joseph Campbell Foundation (JCF)—founded in 1990 to preserve, protect, and perpetuate Campbell's work—has undertaken to create a digital archive of his papers and recordings and to publish *The Collected Works of Joseph Campbell*.

The Collected Works of Joseph Campbell
John Bucher, Executive Director
Bradley Olson, Director of Publications

EDITOR'S FORWORD

"Whenever men have looked for something solid on which to found their lives, they have chosen not the facts in which the world abounds, but the myths of an immemorial imagination."

JOSEPH CAMPBELL, *PRIMITIVE MYTHOLOGY:*
THE MASKS OF GOD, VOLUME I

JOSEPH CAMPBELL IS THE AUTHOR of over two dozen books on mythology and the editor of ten to fifteen more (the exact number depends on whether one counts individual entries in multivolume sets as separate titles). His best-known work, *The Hero with a Thousand Faces*, details elements of a story arc Campbell identified across the myths of multiple cultures throughout history. Published in 1949, it influenced generations of writers, filmmakers, artists, musicians, and storytellers of every stripe, connecting Campbell in the public mind with what has come to be known as the Hero's Journey.

But Joseph Campbell's mythological perspective extends far beyond the solitary hero quest. For Campbell, the landscape of myth is the landscape of the human spirit. His consistent overarching theme is that through mythology, we can come to a broader understanding of ourselves and our common humanity.

"Mythology is no toy for children," Campbell wrote. "Nor is it a matter of archaic, merely scholarly concern, of no moment to modern men of action. For its symbols (whether in the tangible form of images or the abstract form of ideas) touch and release the deepest centers of motivation, moving literate and illiterate alike, moving mobs, moving civilizations."[1]

One could conceive of Campbell's books as falling into two categories. There are the deep, comprehensive, well-researched tomes, rich with reference notes, completed during his lifetime—works like *The Hero with a Thousand Faces* and the four volumes of *The Masks of God*, or the scholarly essays in *The Flight of the Wild Gander*—compelling, substantial reads that I think of as "written Campbell."

And then there's what I call "spoken Campbell"—works edited from interviews, lectures, and panel discussions. "Spoken Campbell" begins with *Myths to Live By* (Campbell's own edit of the lectures he delivered from 1958 to 1971 at the Cooper Union) and includes the companion volume to the televised *Joseph Campbell and the Power of Myth* interviews with Bill Moyers, as well as many of Campbell's posthumous compilations (e.g., *The Hero's Journey*, *Thou Art That*, *Myths of Light*, *Pathways to Bliss*, *Goddesses*, and *Romance of the Grail*). Though these cover the same themes as the written works and are just as profound, they are generally less detailed, lack exhaustive endnotes, and are more conversational in tone, conveying Campbell's personal wit and charm. The delightful nature of these spoken word offerings has helped make Campbell's ideas accessible to a wider audience.

The work before you, designed to reflect the broad sweep of Campbell's vision, falls into the latter category.

My participation in this project began in 2004, when Joseph Campbell Foundation (JCF) president Robert Walter invited me to assemble and edit a book compiled from multiple question-and-answer sessions with audiences following Campbell lectures, as well as a number of relatively obscure print and audio interviews conducted during the last seventeen years of his life.

This presented challenges far different from taking one or more lectures on a specific topic and rendering that material into a single chapter. Over the course of several years, I read and reread a broad array of transcripts and listened to countless hours of raw audio before ultimately settling on nearly three dozen separate sources. These conversations proved wide-ranging, covering a variety of subjects—and often, unlike his lectures, without any clear sense of organization. For example, on a book tour Campbell might speak with local reporters whose generic queries evince little interest in or understanding of myth; in such instances, Campbell sometimes barely references the original question before pivoting to answer what he felt should have been asked. On the other hand, in dialogue with a knowledgeable interrogator, he will often dive deep. Whether in formal discussions or informal conversations, Campbell regularly treats his listeners to enchanting, mind-bending tangents.

I then faced the question of how to organize this material. Naturally, it would be necessary to eliminate repetition, especially on subjects Campbell frequently addresses; occasionally, I'd find questions posed years apart by different individuals, in different locales, eliciting nearly identical answers. At the same time, it wasn't at all unusual to discover several sentences in one discussion that could serve as the perfect coda to flesh out an incomplete description culled from a completely different conversation.

Given that the idea behind this work is to provide a clearer picture of the man and his ideas, I opted to create a truly syncretic work—tickle out the constituent ideas, break them apart, and then braid them back together to form a more comprehensive, dynamic reflection of Campbell's mythological perspective.

A daunting challenge, indeed. The first few years I worked with this material, it felt at times as if I were trying to put together a twenty-thousand-piece jigsaw puzzle with no picture to guide me. Gradually, it dawned on me that Joseph Campbell's complete body of work *does* provide a picture to follow—what he referred to as "the One Great Story" of humankind.

And I had lots of helpers with this project. During the past quarter century, I've administered and/or moderated discussion boards across a variety of online platforms focused on Campbell and myth. I've had the opportunity to monitor thousands of detailed conversations and interact with countless individuals hungry to know more about Joseph Campbell's work, his mythological worldview, and its relevance—if any—for their own lives. Many such discussions over the years have revolved, either directly or indirectly, around what they would ask Joseph Campbell if they had the chance.

Now they do. Those questions form the through line to this book, the thread on which we bead Campbell's stories, his ideas, and the mythic imagery he shares.

The questions presented here are of three kinds. Some are inspired by questions that appeared in the original source material, though in much-abbreviated form. More than a few of the original questions, whether posed by an interviewer or an audience member, could consume half a page or more. Those asked in this book, however, are generally brief and to the point. The focus, after all, is Joseph Campbell and his ideas; the questions simply serve to get us there.

Many questions reflect the interest of the general public, collected over time from passionate participants on those discussion boards who might not have a string of letters after their names—from truck drivers, salesclerks, and pastors to filmgoers, video gamers, and musicians.

And then there are questions that are suggested by the material itself, created to bridge a gap between related ideas and move the conversation along.

The book is divided into seven chapters. The first, "The ABCDs of Mythology," covers the basics (What is a myth? Where do myths come from? What purpose do they serve?). In the second chapter, "An Outline of Everything," the accent is on the historical development of mythology. Chapter 3, "A Mythology Taken Seriously," examines the relationship between myth and religion, including the question of God.

"Yes All the Way!" turns from "the tangible form" of mythic images to "the abstract form of ideas" as Campbell discusses developments within philosophy, starting with Kant, and moving on to how those ideas have influenced literature and psychology.

"An Inward Turn" considers the Hero's Journey arc (How did Campbell arrive at this idea? What is its relevance to contemporary life? And how does it influence writers and filmmakers?), followed by a discussion of art and the creative moment.

In the sixth chapter, "To Complicate the Plot," Campbell considers the contemporary world, including the relationship between science and myth, the mythological underpinnings of democracy in the United States, the mythology of war, and whether we can anticipate the emergence of a new, authentic, living mythology in our future.

And, finally, in chapter 7, "The Course Has Gotten Wider," Joseph Campbell discusses his own life and career from a mythic perspective.

As you read, it helps to bear in mind that Joseph Campbell was born in 1904; his speech patterns reflect the tenor of his times. There are occasions where his phrasing sounds old-fashioned, even socially insensitive by today's standards. In Campbell's day, *cult* wasn't a pejorative, but an anthropological term referring to a specific system of religious worship (e.g., "the cult of Mithra" or "the cult of Christianity"); the terms *man* and *mankind* were thought to refer to all humans without regard to gender—and without conscious awareness of how that default setting devalues women; similarly, the *Occident* and the

Orient were standard usage by scholars oblivious to their own Euro-centric perspective.

By the end of Joseph Campbell's life, a major shift was under-way in academia and in the public square. In one late talk I listened to, he acknowledges making a conscious effort to refer to indigenous cultures as "primal," in deference to friends in the Native American community who had recently made him aware of how painful it was to hear anthropologists, historians, and other scholars refer to their people as "primitive"—a thought that had not occurred to Campbell before; nevertheless, it's no easy task to change a lifelong pattern.

There aren't many such instances, but if you do come across a word or concept that might sound jarring to the modern ear, be gen-tle; judge Campbell not by today's evolving standards, but in relation to the time in which he lived.

Much of what Campbell shares here has not previously been published. Readers new to Joseph Campbell will be enchanted by his perspective, but even those long familiar with Campbell's work will discover new insights and further depths.

I would like to acknowledge former JCF president Robert Walter for the original vision behind this project and for his never-flagging confidence and encouragement; David Kudler for editorial guidance; Jimmy Maxwell for assembling the audio; Lynn Tucker, Timothy Hallford, Terry Lupton, and Helen Maxwell for their contributions preparing transcripts from often fuzzy and muffled recordings; Ilya Smirnoff and John Bucher for feedback and suggestions that have proved invaluable; my wife, Destiny, for her support and understand-ing; and, of course, Joseph Campbell, for the decision to spend a life-time following his bliss and share the results with us.

Stephen Gerringer
Joseph Campbell Foundation Community Coordinator
and author of *Myth and Modern Living:*
A Practical Campbell Compendium
October 30, 2022

here's journey = circle of security

CHAPTER ONE

"The ABCDs of Mythology"

A common perception is that myths belong to the past—a dry and dusty field of study best left to scholars—and yet, decades after _The Hero with a Thousand Faces_ was first published in 1949, your work continues to find a popular audience. How do you explain this interest in mythology?

Well, I've been doing a lot of lecturing around the country since I retired from teaching, and I find an enormous interest wherever I go. I can say from my own experience—for I have been teaching this subject for some fifty years—that when a mythic dimension is opened to people, happiness, joy, and a sense of what might be called self-potentiality are opened to them as well. They have been given the saving image of human self-confidence and a new appreciation of the value of being a human being.

How would you define myth?

Myth is a universal language that takes on its own local forms from society to society. It is not just the fantasy of this, that, or another person. A myth is a dreamlike symbol—a legend that's part of other legends which together form a mythology. A mythology is an organization of symbolic images and narratives metaphorical of the possibilities of human experience and fulfillment in a given society at a given time.

Mythologies put the members of a culture in touch with deeper concerns than those of everyday economics and politics. Cultures emerge from their mythologies, not from economics. A culture is determined by the dynamics of the human spirit, and these dynamics are activated and called into supreme statement by things that transcend those economic concerns. You can actually see these fields of economics and politics as themselves manifestations of the spiritual potentialities of the human being.

When you realize that every one of the early civilizations was based on a mythology, you can realize the force of this great, great heritage that we have.

Economics always takes a back seat to mythology?

Well, the economic values of a society are determined by the mythology of the society. What you're going to sell and make your money on is a function of what the people want. And what they want is an expression of their values. If what people want are crucifixes, well, make crucifixes. And if what they want are television sets, make television sets. The mythology provides the orientation of the people's lives.

Just look at India. Here are people starving. They won't eat meat. Meat is walking all around them, cows all over the place eating the food that these people are interested in. Explain *that* in economic terms.

What leads you to characterize recurring mythological motifs as elements of a universal language?

Living with these things all the time, I can see how there are certain universal patterns for these manifestations. A shaman among the Navaho or in the Congo will be saying things which sound so much like, say, Nicolaus Cusanus or Thomas Aquinas or C. G. Jung that one just has to realize that these ranges of experience are common to the human race.

It's this recognition of a constant recurrence of certain themes and motifs throughout the literatures, mythologies, and religions of the world that has fascinated me all my life. And these motifs are metaphors for the mysteries and energies of the human psyche.

Can you offer an example of a universal image?

Well, the myth of the flood turns up practically everywhere, with the exception of some very small areas. I could give some examples from widely spaced peoples.

First, from America, the Blackfeet Indians of Montana. They have a story of the flood which has been told from years long before the coming of the white man. The hero of this particular story is the creator himself, whom these people called Old Man. He appears in their tales as a lonely, wandering, shadowy figure moving over the earth in the first years of its existence, shaping the mountains and the river valleys, creating animals and giving them their names. Shortly after his work began, a flood wiped out the whole creation. He took the animals on a raft with him, and for weeks they floated on the boundless waters.

His problem was to create a new earth because the water wasn't going down. So he decided to send a little animal down to try to find some mud from the bottom. He sent down the muskrat. The muskrat was gone a long, long time. And then the muskrat came floating up, quite exhausted, and said he hadn't been able to find any bottom.

So Old Man sent a diving bird down next, and this little bird came up dead. Then he sent down a turtle. The turtle was gone a very, very long time, and he too came up dead. But when they looked in his little mouth, they found a tiny bit of mud. Old Man took this, put it on the water, and pronounced a charm over it. He made his hand move so that the mud spun around. And then it grew bigger and bigger and bigger.

After a number of days he thought, "Well, now it's big enough." So he sent a fox out to see how long it would take him to come back. And the fox came back in one day. So he said, "Well, this isn't big enough yet." Then he spun the mud around some more, and when he sent the fox out three or four days later, it took him a week to come back. Finally, Old Man sent the fox out a third time and he never came back. So then Old Man said, "All ashore!" There was a new world, and life could get started again.

Couldn't this simply be a corrupted version of the Noah's ark story found in the Bible?

That story was here long before any influence from the biblical tales. The Indians are supposed to have first come to the American continent about 20,000 B.C., and there were continuous migrations throughout the succeeding centuries.

In this story the creator himself is the hero. And his own creation gets out of hand, goes sort of haywire on him.

But there are myths dealing with floods that overwhelmed human civilizations. And usually these bring in some sort of punishment for an offense against a deity or demon—a demon who the people made angry.

For instance, there's a tribe living in the Andaman Islands, in the Burmese area of the Bay of Bengal. And these people have a flood story. There's a prohibition among these tribesmen against making a noise when a cicada is singing. One day, one of their people made a noise when a cicada was singing. This angered the deities, and they sent a flood. So the crime wasn't a very great one from our standpoint.

But in this case the people had the problem of saving their fire because they didn't know how to make a new fire. A woman took the fire in a cooking pot and carried it up the top of a tall tree, and all the people went up the tree after her. It was the tallest tree in the world. The flood came up and only the top of the tree was above the water. Then, with the subsiding of the water, everybody came down again. And once again the whole civilization got going with a fresh start.

These are ancient stories that have been passed down over thousands of years.

From generation to generation.

Do you suppose they were embroidered as they go along?

The floods differ considerably from place to place, and they vary from teller to teller. Actually, there are all kinds of little variations. But even with that there remain fundamental patterns that continue throughout the whole tradition.

Do we know which flood myth was the earliest?

Well, the oldest recorded story was found on a broken clay tablet in one of the ancient cities of Mesopotamia, from the Sumerian civilization.[1] The story tells of a flood sent down by the gods of the upper world. Now, it's known that they were angry, but we don't know why; the tablet is broken, and that part of the story doesn't appear.

But then the god of the lower waters, whose name is Enki, took pity on mankind. He turned to a god-fearing, pious, humble king named Ziusudra and taught him how to make a great big boat into which Ziusudra took his family and all the animals around about.[2] And then they floated on the waters of the flood. After many, many weeks the waters went down, and the king and his family went ashore. They made offerings to the deities of the upper world who had sent the flood. These deities took mercy on them and made them actually immortal and gave them a place of eternal residence in the land of the rising sun.

Now, this story is over a thousand years older than the biblical story. It dates from about 2000 B.C. And many scholars think that the story of Noah and the flood is actually a derivation from this story. Instead of being based on a polytheistic theology with many gods in conflict with each other, the biblical story translates the whole theme into that of one deity becoming angry at mankind, but saving from among mankind the one good man who could then bring forth the world in a fresh way.

Does water always play a destructive role in mythology?

Most cycling myths end in a flood and begin again out of a flood. One after another, the myths tell us it all began with water. That's one class of myths about water. But in a desert situation where water is scarce—in a very real sense the water of life—cities are, of course, built where there is water. Water is the center, and water comes, furthermore, from the abyssal depths and thus is a powerful symbolic as well as economic factor.

Is there a mythological image or ritual in our culture that draws on this symbolism?

Christian baptism. This ritual can be traced back to ancient Babylonia—and still more ancient Sumer—to the rites of Ea, god of the watery abyss. The special rituals associated with him were water rituals, including baptism: going into the water and coming out again, a kind of reentering the womb and being born again.

A rather amusing observation about Ea is that in the Chaldean period of the sixth to fifth centuries B.C., his name had become Oannes; if you put a *J* in front of the *o* and an *h* after it, you have Johannes, or John. So John the Baptist is actually the inheritor of the role of Ea, lord of the watery abyss who gives you rebirth—birth into the spiritual life.

Jesus uses the same image in a very outright way when he says, "He who is not born of water and the spirit cannot enter the Kingdom of Heaven."[3]

Isn't there a risk that emphasizing universal patterns common to all mythologies ignores what is unique about a culture?

Well, in general, I would say that there are two apparently contradictory approaches to mythology. One is the historical approach. There one studies the local, ethnic transformations of the great mythological themes. That approach has certainly fascinated me all my life.

The second approach, however, has to do with the immediate psychological relevance of the mythological symbols. One asks, How do these symbols operate on us every day?

I've spent my life not only studying, but greatly enjoying—even enraptured by—the mythologies of different people in very different parts of the world. In my early boyhood American Indian myths entranced me. I was brought up a Roman Catholic, and already as a youngster recognized the same myth motifs in American Indian legends and the doctrines of the Roman Catholic Church. Then, in later years, I began studying Hinduism and Buddhism, and there they were again! Then turning from the study—years of study—of Hinduism, Buddhism, and Oriental thinking, to classical Greece, I found the same essential ideas. They *are* the same, and nobody can tell me that this is not so. They have been differently inflected and applied to very different social purposes. That is what the local *differentiating* factor is all about, and that is what anthropologists and historians properly study.

But from a psychological standpoint—trying to recognize where *humanity* is, in all of this—one sees everywhere the same symbols, and this becomes then the problem of first concern. And what transforms the consciousness is not the language but the image; it's the impact of the image that is the initiating experience.

If you get the point of mythology and see that what's being talked about over here is what's being talked about over there too, you don't have to quarrel about the vocabularies.

THE ROLE OF MYTHOLOGY

Why do these mythic patterns recur among different peoples throughout history? What role does myth play in a culture—and does it still play that role today?

Let's begin by trying to untangle the confused notion of myth.

Every mythology has grown up within a bounded horizon. In the past, the mythological system of any tribe or culture has served four functions.

One is the mystical aspect, which has to do with the opening up of the sense of a mystery dimension, that informs and transcends all. The second has to do with the cosmology, and that has to be brought constantly up to date—that is to say, to see this universe as it is now rendered by the science of the day (compared with that Bronze Age three-layer birthday cake cosmology in the Book of Genesis). And then the third aspect of a mythology is the sociological: every mythology has grown up within a bounded horizon, for a certain people. And the fourth addresses the pedagogical problem, guiding the individual harmoniously through the inevitable crises of the stages of life in his world today—in terms of its goods, its values, its dangers. These are the archetypes, the elementary problems, that everybody faces, no matter where.

Could you expand on each of these functions of mythology?

First is the mystical or metaphysical function of linking up regular waking consciousness with the vast mystery and wonder of the universe. This is the most essential service of a mythology, opening the mind and heart to the utter wonder of all being—arousing and maintaining in the individual a sense of awe and gratitude for the mystery of life, the mystery of existence, the mystery of the universe—which is the mystery of one's self.

Any part can be a symbol for the whole. For instance, for Dante, Beatrice's beauty leads to the realization of divine love as the moving power of the universe. Unless the panorama of the world—and the experience of your own presence in it—opens back into that mystery zone from which the energies come that inform the body and shape the universe, you don't have a mythological structure.

Second is the cosmological function of presenting some intelligible image or picture of nature. In primitive cultures, the relationship between man and woman is frequently seen as a mirror of nature: the universe is created by a union of Father Sky and Mother Earth, say.

This second, cosmological function would be closely entwined with the first?

Yes. The first is the mystical function of awe. And the second is presenting an image of the cosmos through which that awe will be communicated, so that the whole universe itself will be experienced as a holy picture. Every aspect of it will open up in the back into this mystery dimension in such a way that its mystery can be experienced, so that we can relate to it with gratitude.

When one becomes too blasé about making use of things, then you forget the privilege of using them and of their being there at all. And the great mythologies were concerned to keep that sense. For example, you sit down to eat, you eat your meal, and put it away again. But if you say grace before meals, you realize it's a miraculous gift that has come to you. And if you'll think, as the primitive person does, of the animal who gave his life to be eaten here and become *your* life, you are in a very wonderful harmony and accord with something beyond yourself.

That function of myth doesn't seem fully supported in modern society.

I'll tell you why. The society is not teaching us how to relate ourselves to the transcendent—to that which lies outside of the phenomenal world of facts. And the clergy aren't doing it either. They're translating their metaphors into facts all over the place, and each is stuck with his own tradition. They're hanging onto prose.

Not only does a mythology open up the transcendent; it also presents a certain picture of the universe. Of course, the one in our tradition is ridiculous. It belongs to about 2000 B.C. The cosmic imagery of a mythology must be up to date; otherwise, the mythology isn't working; you can't believe it. And if you have a lot of things that you can't correlate with contemporary nature, you can't handle it.

Go to any church or synagogue and you'll find the clergy there trying to support an archaic concept of the universe against the findings of science. Religion has been kicking against the findings of science ever since Hellenistic times. Just think, the first chapter of Genesis was composed at a time when the Greeks had already measured the circumference of the earth to within a couple of hundred miles! It presents a deliberately archaic notion of the shape of the cosmos and the way in which the cosmos came into being, and then the religious system is hung on that belief. Look what happened in 1543 when Copernicus published his formula for the heliocentric universe and the geocentric system seemed threatened. Since the religions had tied their faith to that system, a persecution of scientists set in.

Now, the individual has to feel comfortable in his universe, spiritually comfortable as well as physically, and if the religion does not relate one to the universe *as it is*, but is fighting against it, what does the individual do? The old system had the notion of special-species creation, so the emergence of evolutionary thinking in the late eighteenth and early nineteenth centuries seemed a destruction of religion. That we should be related to the animals was something that in our tradition wasn't acceptable, though in India, for example, it has long been taken for granted.

So these relationships to the findings of science do get into the mythological world. And it does make a difference to your concept of your role in life whether you think of man as a special creation superior to the animals or think of him as in accord not only with the animal world but also the plant world, the whole of the natural world. So that's the cosmological aspect of it.

And the third function of mythology?

Third is the sociological function of validating and enforcing a specific social and moral order. The example that comes to mind is the Ten Commandments and the Deuteronomic Law, which were believed to have been revealed directly to Moses by God.

This sociological function supports and maintains the moral or ethical system of the specific social group to which one belongs, so that when you define your social group, you define the margin of your mythological identification. It's an identification that one makes with a group, which is a mythological act. One person identifies with this group, and another person with that, and each acts in these contexts in ways that are not always rationally supportable.

This social order in traditional cultures is typically regarded as divine. The notion in a traditional culture is that the laws of the society are as fixed and divinely given as the laws that govern the universe. You cannot just sit down in a Senate or House of Representatives and design those laws. Rites, rituals, and also a moral order—what it is proper to do and what is improper to do—come from the eternal divine. In our world, where we have the idea of a God who created the world, that same God delivered the law. In India, where you don't have the idea of a God who created the world, but of a world that came forth like a flower and will go down again and come back again, the caste system is part and parcel of the impersonal rhythm of nature.

I don't see a mythologically grounded social order operating today.

I think it's a problem, and it's one of the most thrilling things about the contemporary moment. It's a kind of free fall we're in, and there's a thrill there.

Every mythology has been addressed to a certain group which had certain functions to fulfill. But the social order and the needs for society are changing so fast that to hang on to the virtues of yesterday can turn you into a sinner today. What was good day before yesterday is now a menace in many, many cases. And there's this tact for the moment now that's required of us, whereas in those archaic cultures the order goes on timelessly.

Earlier mythic rituals confirmed you in the responsibilities of the life role you voluntarily assume. Those responsibilities are not now mythologically imaged, and the thing is going to pieces. You can see, just in practical, immediate life, the need for some kind of knowledge that will relate you to the true nature of the situation that you have entered.

That has to do with that social aspect of myth that provides life models to live by. The pattern of the rancher, the pattern of the frontiersman—all grew out of actual life situations that don't exist anymore. What's happening is that the life models are changing very, very fast—as fast as women's fashions, actually: a new dress length every year. And you can't build a substantial mythos on such a basis. The frontier is all finished now. We have another environment, and what are the models for it?

Today, when you move into a life career, it isn't going to turn out to be the one you thought you were entering. The pattern of the teacher, the pattern of the writer—patterns that I experienced—are not at all what I thought they were going to be in the good old days when I was first thinking about them. And so I just don't think we are going to have, as we experience our careers, the sense of depth and spiritual dignity that the old mythologies used to give to the lives they supported and informed.

Where does the fourth function of mythology fit into the puzzle?

The fourth is the psychological or pedagogical function—guiding the individual through the inevitable stages of a lifetime: the dependency of childhood, the responsibility of adulthood, the wisdom of old age, and the ultimate crisis of death. Every culture has rites of passage and related myths that serve this need.

But those stages have to be experienced in terms of that particular society. It's no use having everyone try to be an American Indian. When people read the Tao Teh Ching, then they want to be Chinese. And all my friends are reading the Bhagavad Gītā; they're wearing turbans and things like that, and I can't bear it!

The first universal, existential reality is that of the mystery of birth. That's more than a biological phenomenon, believe me—the mystery of a new being coming in.

And the next—every culture, everywhere, forever, has had to bring that little nature phenomenon into relationship to a society. That's where the problem comes: into what society are you going to bring this nature phenomenon? And the local myths stress that you're coming into *our* society, *our* way. (That wouldn't be bad if the society didn't think of itself as the only one worth being incorporated in.)

Every society has had to guide this little biological phenomenon through the inevitabilities of growth, childhood, adolescence, then moving into marriage—adulthood—and then to move on from that to release of yourself from commitment to the world, and, finally, passing on. And in every traditional mythology, that isn't a loss, it's a gain, when you realize that you're gaining an inward life. Death is not loss. All you're losing is simply this passing phenomenon of a body. But the consciousness is becoming more and more of itself. Proper mythology tells you how to die.

These four functions are the elementary ABCs—or ABCDs, I guess you'd have to say—of mythology. When there is no medium around to serve these aims, one feels a certain lack.

Male coming-of-age rites in primal cultures then fall under the fourth function?

Yes. The problem with the boy is to break his connection with the mother absolutely and turn him into a man. Not only a man, but a man ready to perform very dangerous actions. On those levels, the male life is a very dangerous life. And so the rites take his little boy's body away from him.

I remember reading, I think it was among the Mandan Indians, where those young men had a hell of an experience. They said, "Our women suffer, we must suffer too." And the men's rites in Brazil, the tribes there speak of them as the men menstruating. That is to say they are losing their self-assurance and their self-determining power;

something has taken over. They become the agents for something. The women become the agents of nature. The men become the agents of that society which fixes the field within which the women bring forth life. Basically, that's a mythological thing.

Yet in many primal cultures women menstruating are considered "unclean." Isn't that intended to diminish and demean women?

No. All life is unclean. Anything that has to do with a vital moment is unclean.

Now, "unclean" must be understood in its mystical sense: that which is regarded as unclean and taboo is so full of power that it's dangerous to be in touch with it. And so menstruation is the first uncleanliness. But that's not a nasty, nasty uncleanliness—it's *power*.

Women's first menstruation is a serious affair everywhere. At that moment she is no longer in command of her body. She is no longer simply herself; she has now become the vehicle of a process. Nature has taken over.

Frazer makes this very clear in *The Golden Bough*. When a young girl has her first menstruation, she's put in a special hut and the women dance around it and all this kind of thing. And there are two reasons for that: there's power there and the community has to be protected from it, and she has to be protected from it herself.

But she also has to meditate on it and realize what she is.

The way I say it—and I don't think I would want to be quoted on this in a reckless way—is that life overtakes the woman. She doesn't have to do anything. God, there she is, she's a woman—menstruation has happened, and a few months later she's pregnant! She is a mother. She has become the mother that she didn't have to break away from— she *became* the Mother.

The boy has another problem. When it's time for the boy to become a man, he has to *do* something. Nature hasn't overtaken him at all. When a young man is initiated, the society overtakes him, the men's society, and says, "Look, kid, you are no longer what you thought you were." And the function of the male initiation rites is always rough compared to that of the woman. The male is told to take this, take that; he's smashed up, his body is changed, and he becomes then a vehicle of the social order.

What the woman represents is nature. What the male represents is society, and division—this society is against that society. He's in there for achievement and who's top man. There's nothing *well,* about who's top female in the same way at all; there's only one who knows more than another.

It's a tough problem in a culture where all living is so close, and so physical, to *break* this: to have to go away and just be in the men's ground for a while and find his place there and live there, no women around. And then he can return, but he has this other center.

And that's the beginning of turning the mother's boy into a man.

So, at least in earlier cultures, human biology has shaped gender roles?

The Goddess is a personification of that which is embodied in every woman. It is a whole structure of energies that comes through the woman's body. And since it is woman who gives birth and nourishment to that which has been born of her, the female is symbolically associated with the powers of the earth itself, which gives birth and nourishment to us. So, in the way of analogies, the female is associated with the planting and seed world. She is the transformer who transforms semen into life and blood, and that is the *mythological* role.

The woman's whole body is part of this function. The male's body is not. The male does not have that function. With that little package down there, he's really released from biology. The male is associated with protection, deliberate action—so typically the male, in a mythological context, is the one who protects the life force which is in the female.

When you think of society in millenniums of being, there's been war, there's been fighting, there's been heavy work, chopping out space, building buildings, and all that—that's been man's work. It's all he's had to do, and he's built for that. And the woman, she is not built for that. Meanwhile she's encumbered with children, and new ones coming, and all of this. Her action is not deliberate. She's overtaken by life. And so her role is that of facilitating life, bringing it forth, and fosterage. And the man's is that of protection and fashioning the field in which that can take place. *what?!*

The man has to be deliberate. And so he has to be trained to deliberateness. The woman has to be trained to accepting this thing which is happening, and which is what it's all about.

Hasn't modern culture moved beyond these traditional mythological roles?

Today we have what might be called a "contamination of fields." This is something that's avoided very strictly in early societies. Women are not allowed even to touch the men's weapons lest there take place a psychological contamination. The separate fields are very clearly defined.

Now, I remember my mother asking, "What's gonna happen?" Secretaries in business when I was a very little boy were men, not women. Then women began to come in with the typewriter, and they also were smoking cigarettes. My mother said, "This is the beginning of the end." And it was. There has been a contamination of fields in terms of the old structures.

Now, of course, we know that when one form dissolves, another form comes out. We may be in the birth of something else.

Every human still experiences these life initiations—birth, coming of age, relationships, family, growing old, and dying. Where do we look for the mythology to help us through this?

I don't think there can ever be a general, comprehensive mythology. For there to be a shared mythology, there must be a shared body of experiences. In small, horizon-bound societies, everyone was immersed in the same social and visual reality. If everyone lived with cattle or sheep, pastoral images were common. But our contemporary world is so heterogeneous that few people share the same experiences. Pluralism makes a unifying myth impossible.

The panorama of possibilities and possible lives and how they change from decade to decade has made it impossible to mythologize. The individual is just going in raw. It's like open-field running in football—there are no rules. You have to watch everything all the way down the line. All you can learn is what your own inward life is and try to stay loyal to that.

But if we cannot reinstate such a mythology—general and comprehensive—we can, at least, return to the source from which mythology springs: the creative imagination.

How do we do that?

By placing the emphasis on your own inward dynamic and then filtering out of the inheritance of tradition those aspects that support you in your own inward life. This means not being tied to this, that, or another tradition. See, I'm very much for comparative studies of mythology. I think one of the problems today is that society has moved into a multicultural relationship that renders archaic these culture-bounded mythological systems—like the Christian, the Jewish, the Hindu.

The sacred, *from a social standpoint*, is the object or system of objects that has been set up by the society to integrate the individual spiritual life into the functioning of the social system. But what is sacred *for the individual* is that which of itself has come to mean depth to him.

By getting to know your own impulse system and its images and the things you really are living for, then you can find support for universalizing and grounding this personal mythology in the other mythologies of mankind. In the multitude of myths and legends that have been preserved to us—both in our own Western arts and literatures, synagogues and churches, and in the rites and teachings of those Oriental and primitive heritages now becoming known to us— we may still find guidance.

The Origins of Myth

Where do myths come from?

It's the experience of death that I regard as the beginning of mythic thinking: actually seeing someone dead who was alive and talking to you yesterday—dead, cold, beginning to rot. Where did the life go? That's the beginning of myth.

That's what happened, I think, in the Paleolithic caves when burials came in. "I thought that was all you were, but now, my gosh, there's another dimension to this." And if that can be recognized after death, well—if we recognize it before death, look what it does!

In *The Flight of the Wild Gander*, that's what I called the mythological dimension.[4] It's a little shift of focus, so that you and I sitting here, we are in the foreground of something. Back behind us one life is living in both of us, isn't it? And consciousness—otherwise, we wouldn't be able to talk. That's what's taken for granted somehow, but in mythology it isn't taken for granted. The accent goes *there*, and then all of life takes on new perspective.

When did this shift occur historically?

In terms of mythological experience and mythological thinking, the earliest evidence we have is the Neanderthal Period burials and cave bear skull sanctuaries. They may go back as far as 100,000 B.C. or even pre-Würm (prior to the last glaciation in the Alps).

What this means—when you have a burial with grave gear—is that death is not the end. And it's interesting that, simultaneously, we have these caves, small caves—not the great big ones—on high mountains, where the veneration of cave bear skulls is indicated. The bear is very important—walks on its feet, looks like a man—probably the first worshipped creature on the planet. There are shrines with these set-up skulls and whole bins full of skulls with stones around them; the human being lives beyond life, and the animal does also. That's the beginning of myth.

A theme that still resonates today...

There's that wonderful picture of Death playing the violin to the artist, by a Swiss painter named Böcklin. The artist is there with the palette and brush, and Death is playing the violin. That means that the eyes should be open to something of more cosmic import than simply the vicissitudes and excitements of your own petty life. Hearing the song that is beyond that of your own individual life cycle is the thing that opens you to wisdom. You can hear it in your life, interpreting it, reading it, not in terms of the calamities or boons of your individual existence, but as a message of what life is.

Oh, it's a beautiful accent! *That's* mythological. That's the mythological dimension.

What do you think happens at death?

I think the consciousness disengages itself from the body.

And then what?

I don't know.

You don't worry about death? Do you believe in reincarnation?

When you're my age, death is no problem. I don't think about death. Reincarnation is a mythic image. I don't believe in literalizing mythic images. What the idea of reincarnation says to me is that the sense and dimension of my life are greater than would appear in the experience of a single lifetime. It's a very deep, mysterious mystery that we're participating in.

Would you say mythologizing about death, or anything for that matter, ultimately has its source in the human imagination?

I think of mythology as a function of biology.

Biology rather than imagination?

Oh, yes! It's biological. It is the translation of biological impulses into story form.

How does that work?

Fantasy and imagination are products of the body. The energies that bring forth these fantasies derive from the organs of the body.

Through the organs, the energies of life flow. These energies represent different thrusts. Each energy has a different impulse to action. Those different energies informing each organ move them. Now, these organs are not always in harmony with one another. The energies of one organ may be in conflict with the energies of another, so there can be conflicts between the energies inside.

Among these organs, of course, is the brain. And then you must think of the various impulses that dominate our life system—the erotic impulse, the impulse to conquer and all that, self-preservation—and then certain thoughts that have to do with ideals that are held up before us as aims worth living for, that give life its value, and so forth.

All of these different forces come into conflict within us. And the function of mythological imagery is to harmonize them, coordinate the energies of our body so that we will live a harmonious and fruitful life, in accord with our society and with the new mystery that emerges with every new human being—namely, what are the possibilities of this particular human life?

And mythology has to do with guiding us: first, in relation to the society and the whole world of nature, which is outside of us, but also within us, because the organs of our body are of nature; and then also guiding the individual through the inevitable stages of life from childhood to maturity, and on to the last gate. The mythological organization helps a person to know where he is. The energies that should dominate in early life are not those that are going to dominate in late life. There is an organic process of transformation. These organs dominate, now those, now another. These are the same in human beings all over the world, and this is the basis for the archetypology of myth.

You might say a mythology is a formula for the harmonization of the energies of life.

So mythological images still have value for us as individuals?

What I think mythology primarily does is put you in touch with dimensions of your own being and deep consciousness, which the purely earth-oriented, daylight-consciousness, economic, political, social orientation does not reach. But there are these other dimensions to which the symbols of mythology open up—they actually open up dimensions of our psyche.

After all, the myths originally came out of the individual's own dream consciousness. Within each person there is what Jung called a collective unconscious. We are not only individuals with our unconscious intentions related to a specific social environment. We are also representatives of the species *Homo sapiens*. And that universality is in us whether we know it or not.

I become more and more convinced that the study of mythology is, in a way, the study of biology, because the energies that produce dreams are the energies of our organs speaking to us, and it's from those that the myths come. When we go to sleep and dream, the dreams are our own little private myths.

The dream is a private myth, and the myth is a public dream.

MYTH, METAPHOR, AND MEANING

Is it possible for those of us who aren't scholars to understand mythology? Can anyone be taught how to read myths?

Yes, just as one can be trained to experience art. Many people come to art verbally trained, and as they look at pictures and visit galleries, they gradually open to it and learn how to experience the artwork. So also, I think, with these matters of the spiritual traditions of myth. There are some people who close themselves away from them, some people who open themselves to them. There are also some people who are gifted in opening themselves, just as there are people who are gifted in playing a piano. But I think the potential for at least clumsy piano playing is available to all of us.

Where would we start?

One has to understand that mythology is primarily a symbolic language. In order to read symbols, one must be instructed in the language, and instruction in the metaphorical language of myth is now lacking.

There are two attitudes toward religious and mythic images today. One is that they are references to facts, and the other is that they are lies. But they are neither facts nor lies; rather, they are *metaphors*. Mythology is a compendium of metaphors.

yes

I have found that some interviewers simply have not known what myth is about. And in one spectacular case when I explained that myth was metaphorical, just as poetry is, the person interviewing me said, "Myth is a lie." I found that he didn't know what a metaphor was. He didn't understand what myth and religion were really referring to; he thought they referred to facts, and consequently were lies.

If I recall correctly from high school English, both metaphors and similes are comparisons between unlike things, except a metaphor does not use *like* or *as*. How does that relate to myth?

Mythology is poetry. If you read poetry as prose, what have you got?

If I say to my sweetheart, "You are like a flower," well, she isn't a flower—I could even make a metaphor of it and say, "You are a flower, you are the joy of my life," or something like that. That's the way myth works. But then, if the next time I say, "You're like a swan, you're like a bird," and she says, "Well, make up your mind! Which is it?" then she's translating poetry into prose and doesn't know the reference.

That's like going into a restaurant and reading the menu, deciding what you're going to eat, and you eat that part of the menu. The menu is a reference to something transcendent of that piece of paper.

When you interpret the metaphor in terms of the denotation instead of the connotation, you've lost the message. But if you've been taught the message of a mythology and its set of metaphors, you go in and you know what to order.

This comes out in the idea, for example, in the first words of the

Lord's Prayer: "Our Father who art in heaven." Well, God *isn't* your father. He isn't even a male. To speak of the transcendent mystery as though it were a male or female, which is a biological thing—this is ridiculous. People are translating the poetic image into prose when what it means is that our relationship to what is transcendent is like that of a child to a parent.

It would be quite as proper to say, "Our Mother who art in the earth"; there you get the same child-to-parent relationship. There are mythologies that do speak of the Mother Earth; for instance, the mythologies of the American Southwest—the Pueblo, the Navaho, and the Apache people have the whole human race emerging from the womb of Mother Earth. Perfectly good image. Because we do in fact emerge from the earth. We're the eyes of the earth; we're the bodies of the earth, you know.

These images, whether they're female or male, call for relevant rituals and attitudes, and these will differ from one culture to another.

Why do you believe a literal rendering devalues mythology?

Scientific laws seem to discredit the imagery of myth. For instance, the theme that constantly occurs to me: in the Roman Catholic religion, it is dogma to believe that Elijah, Jesus, and Mary have all ascended to heaven. And you know what it means for a physical body to go up into the stratosphere! At the speed of light, they wouldn't be out of the galaxy yet. What are you going to do with that?

I think that the scientist is simply gathering facts, relating them to each other, and interpreting them in terms of the rules of science. But poets seem to have known what these myths have been about. The problem in popular religion is that they translate poetry into prose and lose the poetic reference, which goes past the image. People are losing faith because they think of these images as false. They don't understand that the image is not a reference to a fact, but a metaphor for what has been called a spiritual truth.

Any interpretation of myth that reads the symbols as though they were references to concrete historical events or personalities is off the rails. Myths refer to spiritual potentialities. Of course, they use historical and natural phenomena and events as their symbols.

The spiritual sense or value that a culture imputes to a particular historical event or character is expressed through myth. For instance,

Jesus, who taught the way of the spiritual life, is said to have had a special birth, "born of a virgin." Similarly the Buddha, who also represents the spiritual life, is said to have been born from his mother's side at the level of the fourth *cakra*, the level of the heart, signifying transformation.

In each case the person born, the physical person, was probably a normally born human being. These are symbolic births, symbolic readings of the importance of the characters.

If we are not to take them literally, then to what do these metaphors point?

You've got to translate these things into contemporary life and experience. *Mythology is a validation of experience*, giving it its spiritual or psychological dimension. What is connoted through these symbolic forms is *the spiritual potentiality of the human being*. The reference of these symbols is to spiritual values, *not* to fact, although the source of the image itself is the factual world.

In a living mythology, the factual world that supplies the images of the myth is the factual world here present. Myth cannot be exported into another land or another period. Our scriptures are from another land and another period. Therefore, in studying our scriptures, we are continually thinking about the sources of the images, and then the images themselves. We have lost the message. A mythology transmutes the world in which we live into an icon—the world becomes transparent to transcendence, and with that so do we.

I have found in general that people in religious circles do not understand that what they are devoting their thoughts to are metaphors, which point not to something that happened a long time ago somewhere else, but to something that ought to happen within themselves. These are all metaphorical psychological states. We call them in religion *spiritual states*—what the Buddhists call "Buddha realms," realms of spiritual functioning or realization and relationship to the world. What myths are dealing with are the powers of the psyche that are in you.

If myth is translated into literal fact, then myth is a lie. But if you read it as a reflection of the world inside you, then it's true. Myth is the penultimate truth.

Where, then, is heaven?

Heaven is not a place; heaven is a metaphor for that mystery zone out of which forms come.

In religious imagery, adventures into "outer space" really refer to adventures into "inner space." I would say, for instance, that the idea of a deity's ascension into heaven actually refers to the descent into that source within ourselves, recognizing within the powers that are those of the gods. All the gods are simply projections of human potentialities. They're not out there. They're in here.

In the Christian tradition, at least one version is represented by the thought, "The Kingdom of Heaven is within you." And who's in heaven? God is. So where is he? Look in here. The connotation of the metaphor refers to our own inward life—and, eternally, to the human condition.

You often quote your friend and mentor, the scholar Heinrich Zimmer, on this subject. How did he put it?

"The best things cannot be spoken, and the second best are misunderstood. The third best is the usual conversation—science, history, sociology."

If the "best things" are beyond words, why are the second best misunderstood?

Because the second best are metaphors for the best and are too easily read literally. The imagery that has to be used in order to tell what can't be told—symbolic imagery—is then understood or interpreted not symbolically but factually, empirically. It's very easy to make this mistake; in fact, it's quite normal. When a story is told to you, you think the story refers to facts. It's a natural thing, but that's the whole problem with Western religion. All of the symbols are interpreted as if they were historical references. They're not.

The ultimate mystery of being and nonbeing transcends all categories of knowledge and thought. This point of view, which is recognized in the Upaniṣads as early as the ninth century B.C., is something the West never caught on to until Kant. You can't talk about what transcends all talk. Yet that which does transcend all talk is the very essence of your own being, so you're resting on it and you *know* it. The function of mythological symbols is to give you a sense of "Aha! Yes, I know what it is. It's myself!"

Do you see what I mean? It's the experience you have of aesthetic arrest when you behold an art object that says, "Ah! *This* is *It*, and it's the radiance of my own being." You're putting yourself in touch with a plane of reference that goes past your mind and into your very being, into your very gut. This is what it's all about, and then you feel a kind of centering, centering, centering, all the time. And it helps you survive any accident of time to know that this thing, yes, comes and goes through time. And whatever you do can be discussed in relationship to this ground of truth. Though to talk about it as truth is a little bit deceptive, because when we think of truth, we think of something that can be conceptualized. It goes past that.

One of the problems with our Western religions is that God is made concrete, just as in popular religions. The Second Coming *will* occur as a historical event at some specific date in the future. There *was* a deliverance by God of a message to Moses. There *was* the virgin birth. There *was* the founding of the Church. This limits a religion's ability to interpret its own symbols mythically.

But the *same* symbols in other cultures are referring to one's own spiritual condition. And it doesn't matter at all whether these things happened elsewhere. What matters is that the symbol should awaken something within you and deepen your own sense of your own being.

So it comes back to our own personal experience?

There's a little verse by Angelus Silesius, a great German mystic of the seventeenth century:

Of what good, Gabriel,
your message to Marie,
unless you can now bring
the same message to me?

That is to say, can you awaken the Christ in me so that I live, as Paul says, "Now not I, but Christ in me?" That's the virgin birth, the birth of the God within the soul.

Why should it be a problem for the rest of us if some people choose to interpret their mythologies literally?

Take three of the world's great religions: Judaism, Christianity, and Islam; they can't even live in the same town. They're the same religion, just in three different inflections, and they can't even read their own metaphors! One group calls God *Yahweh*, another *God the Father*, another *Allah*, and so we go to war! I think the world's insane—at least, the people who are running the world.

Each of them is reading their symbols in terms of historical references, rather than in terms of mystical references. Just, for example, the idea of the Promised Land—to think that the Promised Land is a piece of real estate is to concretize the symbol. The symbols of religion in mythology are primarily metaphoric of human potentialities of experience and fulfillment and have nothing to do with action in the literal sense in the physical world. The Promised Land is the heart at rest and in harmony; this is not a place anywhere.

In this wonderful book by John Neihardt, *Black Elk Speaks*, Black Elk was a Lakota Oglala Sioux who had in his youth a mystical vision of the destiny before his people.[5] He saw "the hoop of his nation," as he called it, as one of many hoops, and all the hoops interlocking, and all of them expressing the same humanity. The hoop of his little nation had to be opened out and become one of many, many hoops of many, many nations.

Black Elk said, "I saw myself standing on the highest central mountain of the world. And so I saw, in a vision, all the nations as one people." He said, "The central mountain of the world is Harney Peak, in South Dakota." But then immediately he said, "The central mountain is everywhere."

What he's saying is that your spot, wherever it happens to be, is the central point of the world. That's a mythological as opposed to a religious interpretation. This is the same message as the one we find in a medieval alchemist book entitled *The Book of the Twenty-Four Philosophers*. There we read, "God is an intelligible sphere whose circumference is nowhere and whose center is everywhere."

That is the word of one who has waked up! He understands the function of the cult image—the cult focus on a specific image or idea of sanctuary. But that is not the final reference. That is but the finger pointing to the moon—the metaphor intending the Transcendent.

That's something that has been lost, I would say, in the Judeo-Christian tradition.

When you take *your* Harney Peak to be the central mountain, you have lost the reference to humanity and have become stuck with your particular ethnic or national group, and that's what we have with all of these religions. They are taking their symbols historically and concretely and not reading them as metaphors, and consequently they've lost the connection with humanity. If you think the central city of the world is Jerusalem, or you think the central city is Benares, and the central city is not everywhere, you are stuck with a cult. You haven't got the metaphor.

Then most don't understand there are real-world consequences that come from reading mythology as fact?

We're aware of it but we don't interpret it as mythological. Just consider the trouble spots in the world today and what's behind them. First, there's the conflict in India between Hinduism and Islam that goes on and on. These are two great mythological structures—the mythology of Islamic monotheism and Hinduism, which is perhaps the oldest high culture tradition still functioning in the world.

Moving further west, when one thinks, for example, of the state of Israel, it is difficult to think of mythology as having relevance only to a world of children. The state of Israel is a mythological institution. It is based on a mythological idea, on what is taken to be prophecy and a sign from God himself. It is on the beam of that trajectory that the state of Israel has been assigned to the Jewish people. And remember that the Middle East may very well provide the spark for the next world war, because there is another mythological tradition, that of Islam, opposed to the Old Testament mythological tradition.

And since we are now in a planet that is one people, one planet, interlocked economically and politically in such a way you can't speak of any horizon as being separate or a separate hoop, it's time to read all of these things in terms of the human reference, not of the local political one. So I think these three religions right now, with what's going on in the Near East, have refuted themselves for the future. They have to be opened out; the hoops have to be opened.

And this wonderful keeper of the sacred pipe of the Lakota, Black Elk, had the image for the future. One, the hoop of your nation is an interlocking hoop with many other nations; and two, your sacred mountain is simply your symbol for what is essentially of the human heart and universal.

What do you mean when you use the term *symbol* in relation to myth?

I'm calling a symbol a sign that points past itself to a ground of meaning and being that is one with the consciousness of the beholder. What you're learning in myth is about yourself as part of the being of the world. If it talks not about you finally, but about something out there, then it falls short.

There's that wonderful phrase I got from Karlfried Graf Dürckheim: "transparency to the transcendent."[6] If a deity is occlusive of transcendency and cuts you short of it by stopping at himself, he turns you into a worshipper and a devotee, and he hasn't opened the mystery of your own being. I call that the pathology of theology.

Then symbolic imagery in myth, more than just a literary device, is actually offering wisdom and insight relevant to the living of life?

Heinrich Zimmer was the first person I ever heard speak about myths who spoke about them the way I was thinking about them.[7] That is to say, not as curiosities for a curiosity cabinet, but as guides. Hearing Zimmer's lectures and the way in which these myths came out, not as curiosities over there somewhere, but as *models* for understanding your own life—this is what I had felt myths to be all this time.

Of course, Jung had it, but not the way Zimmer did. Zimmer was much more in myth than Jung was. Jung tends to put forms on the myths with those archetypes; the Jungians kind of cookie-molded the thing. None of that with Zimmer. I never knew anyone who had such a gift for interpreting a symbolic image. You'd sit down at the table with him and bring up something—he'd talk about the symbolism of onion soup. I heard him do it! I don't remember what it was, but he went off on onion soup....Oh, God! This was a genius! You know that kind of reading experience yourself, where you hit it, and you're building your own insides by pulling this stuff into you—that's the way he worked. He had an inherent talent for amplifying the imagery through his own experience.

I learned from him that one should not be afraid of one's own interpretation of a symbol. It will come to you as a message and will open out. The key to this is in that little preface that I built out of some scraps of his writing, "The Dilettante among Symbols," at the opening of *The King and the Corpse*. That's Zimmer! When an image had opened to him that way (and mind you, he knew one hell of a lot about symbols), he'd know just where to turn to validate his own interpretation in the experience of it. He would check it. But his interpretation of symbols always came out of him personally, reinforced by a host of clues from the East.

You also refer to symbols as "images."

A mythology is a system of *affect symbols*, signs evoking and directing psychic energies. It is more like an affective artwork than a scientific proposition.

The point I want to make, and the point that has interested me ever since I began writing, which was back in the 1940s now, is that the symbols are universal. It's the translation of these symbols into the circumstances of various provinces that is giving them the aspect of differences. But if one makes correct homologous analogies, it's possible to cross these barriers, because images are not language bounded. It's the interpretations of the images that are language bounded.

Here's where I set myself apart from the line followed by Claude Lévi-Strauss and Ernst Cassirer.[8] Language is secondary. It has to do with the communication of myth.

My own view is that the visual aspect of myth is what is primary. Myth derives, it seems to me, from envisionments, from visions, and vision is transcultural, translinguistic. The fact that we find the same myth motifs all over the world seems to me to break down the verbal, philological argument. The verbalization is then local, in terms of local interests and concerns, so that—although the local mythology has certainly been verbalized—the archetypes, out of which the verbalizations have been drawn as secondary formations, are preverbal.

The structure out of which the myths come, therefore, is the structure of the human body and of the relationships to each other of the energies of the organs of the human body as impulse-givers, whether in conflict with each other or in harmony.

Mythology bypasses intellectual understanding?

The logics of image thinking and of verbal thinking are two very different logics. I'm more and more convinced that there is, as it were, a series of archetypes which are psychologically grounded, which just have to operate, but in whatever field is available to them. In the myths, they are represented *pictorially*. There's a big distinction to be made between the impact of the image, and the intellectual and social interpretation and application of the image.

Now, when one begins philosophizing largely with the cerebral functions of the head, we can be pulled away from the body's nature. The body has a reason system of its own which the mind has to find out about, and the myth comes from the body system, which is the nature system.

Mythology talks through the image. And what transforms consciousness is not the language, but the image. The *impact* of the image is the initiating experience. So by understanding—or trying to understand—the communication of the imagery of myth, just as trying to understand the communication of the imagery of your dreams, you bring yourself into accord with your own deeper nature.

Are you speaking only of visual imagery? What about ritual?

Myths come from the same ground that dreams come from, the inspiration of the unconscious. A ritual is the enactment of a myth; by participating in the rite, one is participating in the myth, opening oneself to the mythic dimension of experience, and consequently activating the accordant structures and principles within one's own psyche.

Now, an important point to realize is that all the old, basic, historically grounded traditions were rendered effective through rituals. You can think of all rituals as originally life-structuring: the function of ritual is to organize the life of the society. Traditional societies are based on rituals, and every aspect of life is ritualized. That hangs over in our world, for example, with the marriage ritual. That really is a ritual; that is to say, at the moment of marriage, your character is transferred—if you really are married. You've given up being Tom Jones and have become a member of a larger unit—of the two that are one and the one that are two, in terms of a mythological idea.

But you have to be ready for the experience in order to have it. You can participate in a rite and not have the experience—so then, three days later, you're having a divorce. The ritual hasn't clicked.

How do rituals work?

Rituals of themselves are actually very boring. They go on and on, beyond your secular tolerance. In this way, they break open something in you, and the participation then is with the rite in its proper sense, and not as an entertainment. You are experiencing it as a ritual. And when experienced in this way, something is happening to you in the way of a transformation of your level of consciousness. Without some kind of ritual enactment, the whole thing fails to get inside the active aspect of one's system, unless one happens to be working through actual life problems in terms suggested by mythological considerations.

A well-rendered ritual works as an art object works when the artist no longer has to tell you why he made the picture and what it is about. In a ritual, as in a work of art, you are recognizing an aspect of yourself; through the enactment it brings to mind the implications of the life act that you are engaged in—and if you don't experience it that way, nothing has happened.

Now, people ask me, "What rituals can we have today?" My answer is, "What are you doing? What is important in your life?" What is important, they say, is having dinner with their friends.

That is a ritual.

This is the sense of T. S. Eliot's *The Cocktail Party*. A cocktail party is a ritual. It is a religious function in that way, and those people are engaged in a human relationship. This is the Chinese idea, the Confucian idea, that human relationships are the way you experience the *Tao*. Realize what you're doing when you are giving a cocktail party. You are performing a social ritual. You are conducting it. When you sit down to eat a meal, you are consuming a life.

When plane crash survivors in the Andes found they had to eat their friends, they made a ritual of it. At least they got the point: when you're eating something, this is something quite special to do. And it seems to me you ought to have that thought when you eat a carrot as well as when you eat an animal. But you don't know what you're doing unless you think about it.

That's what a ritual does. It gives you an occasion to realize what you're doing so that you're participating in the inevitable energy of life in its exchanges. That's what rituals are for; you do things with intention, and not just in the animal way, ravenously, without knowing what you're doing.

This is true also of sex. People who just engage in sex as a fun game, as something exciting like that, don't realize what they're doing. Then you don't have the sacramentalization. And the whole reason marriage is a sacrament is that it lets you know what the hell is correct and what isn't, and what's going on here. A male and female coming together with the possibility of another life coming out of it—that's a big act!

Rituals have to do with helping you realize what the hell you are doing, and that you're not simply an entity acting; you are the vehicle of the life process, an agent somehow of a life stream.

Are mythological images constant, or do they change?

The interior of man has been essentially the same for forty thousand years, since the first emergence of *Homo sapiens sapiens*. Myth has to do with the spiritual potentialities of this constant, this human being. But the images of myth must be derived from the environment of today and in this place. There is therefore a constant transformation of the imagery, but not of the reference.

In societies with different environments, the symbol changes to reflect local conditions. The deep, dark forest in myth is the realm of the unconscious where there are energies that people have not yet assimilated in their lives. In the folktales of Europe, the dangers of the unconscious are symbolized by the forest with the dangerous wolf.

In Polynesia, the ocean becomes dangerous, and the conger eel or the shark becomes the dangerous power. In Hawaii, the wolf is replaced by the *wereshark*—a man who has a shark's mouth on his back that he tries to cover and keep from notice. By day he's a man; by night he's a shark.

If mythology is metaphorical and, at the same time, a means for engaging reality, might reality itself be metaphorical?

That's really the point! When Goethe says, *"Alles Vergängliche ist nur ein Gleichnis"*—everything transitory, everything in the world, is a metaphor—our own lives are metaphorical of the spiritual state which we represent and incorporate. And what the myth does is pitch our mind to that realm of connotations which we are actually caught by and rendering in our lives.

So the point of these mythic and religious images is not the image, but the experience?

The experience, and the state of our own being, that it can point us to.

Now, just for example, we know from Freud and Jung that dreams are metaphorical. You have a dream; it is metaphorical of some condition that you're in. And you read the dream to discover what's wrong with you, what is it you are pushing for that you don't know about, and so forth.

Now, the difference between dream metaphor and the mythic metaphor is the mythic metaphor refers, like the dream, to the psyche, to states of the psyche, but at the same time it has what we would call a metaphysical reference. It is referring to the nature of the world. And since we are parts of the world, it is through the proper experience and interpretation of the metaphors of myth that we are brought to find our own deepest nature, to bring ourselves *into accord with* our natures.

The word in Sanskrit for the kind of revelation that is represented in the sacred books of India is *śruti*: "that which has been heard." The inner ear has opened to the song of the universe, the music of the spheres. The inner eye has opened to the informing Form of all phenomenality. The German poet Gerhart Hauptmann somewhere has written: "To write poetry means to let the Word resound behind words" (*Dichten heisst, hinter Worten, das Urwort erklingen lassen*).

That's what it's all about.

CHAPTER TWO

"An Outline of Everything"

Your work touches on so many areas: comparative mythology of course,
but also art, religion, psychology, literature, anthropology, mysticism,
evolution, and history.

Well, when I was in graduate school, I started what I called an "Outline of Everything."

Your theories about myth are an outgrowth of that?

I am not putting forth a theory. I'm trying not to speculate. I'll tell
you what I am trying to do—see, I really grew up as a historian, not
as a sociologist, and I'm intentionally accenting the historical way of
writing: this is what they were saying. I put down what I find in the
material. I'm not saying that "this is true, this is false," but "this is what
we find here, this is what we find there."

You have created two multivolume series grounded in the historical
manifestations of mythology: *The Masks of God* and, two decades later,
Historical Atlas of World Mythology. Have your views changed in the
years between?

I started *The Masks of God*[1] in the 1950s, and I used a standard division: *Primitive*, *Oriental*, and *Occidental*. The innovation there was
the fourth volume, *Creative Mythology*—that's a hell of a big volume!
Now, what has happened in my mind since is the division in terms of
what might be called stages of mythological development. It's a totally
different perspective and an immediately clarifying one, at least for
one who is involved in the whole range of mythological material.

But bringing these studies together in the *Atlas*, with a new organizing insight that suddenly came to me from classifying the material in terms of stages of culture—really basic, large stages—is exciting.[2]

The big organizing principle that I am using is historical and geographical—it's an atlas. In *The Hero with a Thousand Faces*, I was stressing the archetypes; the accent was psychological and therefore universal. Here, I am stressing the differentiations and the distribution of the differentiations. In a broad way, the concept out of which the whole work has grown is geographical. An innovation occurs in this place, and its influence spreads over the planet. Another innovation in another place, and *its* influence spreads over the planet.

This one also has a totally different format. I don't think there has been another scholar anywhere who has had the good fortune to have a publisher who said, "How many pictures do you need?" I think that actually mythology is image, and it's only because the publication of pictures is so expensive that we don't realize that in our reading. So this opportunity to have hundreds and hundreds of pictures, the ones I choose—and besides, those brand-new, beautiful maps—opens a whole new prospect to exposition. I can say things here you can't say without a visual accompaniment.

Myth is expression, not just reading. The reader has to see the picture and say, "Aha!" So the reference has got to be right there; the picture and text need to be on the same page. I just can't tell you what agony it is getting the illustrations into the book, though I love working with them. The discourse is really extrapolation out of the implications of the image. And to be able to have a book where my prose meets the image, right on the same page, is a marvelous privilege. It really is. The problem is not simply to communicate the idea; I want to communicate *the experience* of these mythic forms. That's the main thing. Not only the discourse, but the experience. Like a poem. Reduce a poem to prose, and you don't have it. Mythology is poetry.

That reification of the experience is right there. And the form of this book is something I'm very much interested in continuing through what is going to be four volumes.

The only other book I've done that was built on this principle was *The Mythic Image*, which is published by Princeton, and they have abandoned the book. They turned it into a smaller-format paperback, black-and-white, where the pictures don't do the communicating that they were meant to do. I was allowed only thirty-two color prints or

pictures there. Here I have hundreds. I mean, we're in another stratosphere. Really!

PRIMAL CULTURES

Where do you begin?

The first culture stage, that of the hunting and gathering people, is
one great story.

The Neanderthal is now regarded as *Homo sapiens*. *Homo neanderthalensis*—*Homo sapiens neanderthalensis*—had a considerable brain
capacity at 1,600 cubic centimeters; the average today is 1,550, so
he's certainly *sapiens*, but a different *sapiens*—the brain has different
forms from what comes up in 40,000 B.C. when Cro-Magnon man
(*Homo sapiens sapiens*) appears in Europe, and also in Borneo (not
Cro-Magnon, but still *Homo sapiens sapiens*). It is as though there were
a parallel evolution with human species appearing in different places
at about the same time. But it's only in Europe that we have the Paleolithic caves, those painted caves, and the little figurines; those are the
earliest manifestations of a systematic religious symbology.

And it *is* systematic; there are certain motifs that occur throughout. This is a period of 20,000 years that those damn things were
being held together and presented. There's a sweep from that area:
first the cave bear and bear worship out of Neanderthal times right
across the whole North; then a kind of skeleton or "x-ray art" where
through the animal you see the inner organs, and the course of that
right across into the Americas and down and across into Australia.
And, along with that, shamanism.

**Shamanism, one of the oldest ritual belief systems known to humans,
is still practiced today in some tribal cultures. But didn't modern Europeans consider shamans con men when they first encountered them?**

Arctic explorer Knud Rasmussen once received a profound answer to
a serious question he posed to an old shaman somewhere in the Arctic.
A shaman, of course, is in a very anomalous position with his people.
He is the one who has waked up, but he is in danger because people
are afraid of him and tend to blame him for anything that goes wrong.
So the shaman has to invent ways to hold the people off—ways that

often involve a lot of make-believe and fakery. Rasmussen asked this
old man up there in Alaska if there was anything he really believed in.

"Oh yes," the old man said. "I believe in the soul of the universe. I
hear it. It has a very gentle voice, like the voice of a woman. It's a voice
that you can't hear with people around. You can find it only in silence
and solitude. And what it says is: 'Do not be afraid of the universe.'"

That's big stuff! Some of those "old boys" really had it.

We have these two aspects, the popular belief and then the deep
realization. Now, it's because of that deep realization and the wisdom
that comes out of it that this man had power. One who has power
doesn't have to make believe.

This belief system is common in primal cultures?

It's the same story, the mythology that is characteristic of hunters and
gatherers all over the world. And I'm sure of it in its various inflections because, as the mythology moves from one area to the other, its
applications to the local life conditions change—there are transformations of great magnitude that take place—but there is an underlying
continuity.

How do you explain this continuity?

Every day, the hunter is experiencing vitally the essential problem of
life, which is that life lives by killing. If you didn't eat something that
has been killed, whether an animal or a plant, you wouldn't be here.
So there's that whole problem.

The animals that are killed and eaten are regarded by these people
not as inferior beings at all, but as equals to themselves. The relationship to the animal is of compassion, so the idea comes up of a covenant
between the human and animal communities. And the mythology
takes this into account all the time.

This motif of gratitude to the life that has given itself to you, in
terms of what is an inevitable principle of life—that it lives by killing and eating other lives—this is sometimes hard for people to take.
The first move away from it is vegetarianism, but you're killing things
there, too. Now that we know how plants understand that you're coming to cut them, just think: they can't run away. I think this is a very
brutal activity. You can't get away from it. You're living by killing. Life

lives on the burning point of that which has been alive now feeding what is to be alive. This is a basic principle.

This is reflected in their mythology?

A perfectly typical myth is that of the marriage of a human woman to the animal master, and then a covenant between the animals and the human community. If the human community performs the proper rites, the animals will become willing victims and give their bodies as the food for that community, with the understanding that the blood will be returned to nature and the animals will come back the next year. One kills animals, then, with respect and gratitude for what the animal is doing. It is a basic theme in this mythology, no matter which tradition you turn to; we have the appearance in Europe of this Paleolithic high mythology, and it is carried right across the planet.

In your writings you describe a whole cluster of elements related to this culture stage.

Yes—it holds up. For example, Lewis Morgan, author of *The League of the Iroquois* and *Ancient Society*, was an American anthropologist who recognized what is now called the classificatory system of relations: totem and clan relationships, where they called people who are not blood relation to them "grandpa" and "father" and "mother" and so forth, because of this classificatory relationship from the matrilineal sequence. He finds this in Australia, in America, and all over the place. That is a symptom of a continuity.

You say that, as the mythology moves from one area to another, "its applications to the local life conditions" will change. Such as…?

One is the development that goes along the tropical line in jungles— the equatorial belt. Those people live in a world where they never see a horizon. It's very close in, and it's vegetal, vegetal, vegetal.

Then you get up among these people I've just been talking about, the Neanderthals and Cro-Magnon, who lived up close to the glaciers. You are in a world of great plains, a totally different image world, with a horizon, the dome of heaven, and animal herds—ranging, ranging, ranging.

Colin Turnbull, in *The Forest People*, his charming book about the

Pygmies, tells of bringing a Pygmy in his car suddenly out of the forest on a height, so he can see the plains—total panic! Couldn't distinguish distance, didn't know how to understand perspective or anything, and just had to turn and run.

And so, we have these two worlds. They are quite distinct from each other, but with interactions.

Different myths?

You have the same myth. But it has to show itself through different environments. And one of the great things that you realize when you study primitive mythology is those people see the landscape in which they are living as the Holy Land. What they have done is see the whole thing in terms of mythological configurations. The different animals are playing mythological roles, the animals of *that* environment.

Now, what's happened with us is our Holy Land is somewhere else a long time ago, so the place where we're living is no longer the holy place. You make pilgrimages all over there to that place which has nothing to do with your life. The environment has been desanctified by our mythology.

Mythologies mirror the relationship between religion and nature?

People whose myths are grounded in nature ground their religion in nature. Those whose myths are grounded in society ground religion in society. These are radically contrasting attitudes. One divorces you from nature, a nature that is corrupt, and the other unites you with it.

You've recognized this cultural stage among the indigenous peoples of the North American plains, who seem to have had a much deeper connection to nature than we do across the same geography today.

The loss of this is one of the disasters of the conquest of the Americas by Western powers. It's a dreadful story, the way the white race pushed ahead, and out in front of them went our diseases—measles, smallpox, and others—decimating populations before the white people ever got to the area. They did not respect the mystical dimension of the cultures of this land; they didn't respect the land itself.

As a result, there is this quality in America of a concrete high-way laid across the land. It doesn't matter whether you're in Iowa or

Pennsylvania, you're on the same road with the same stores. There's no sense of place. It's a violation of the land, I think, that we represent in this continent.

Now, I'm not saying that this could *not* become mythologized, but it hasn't. It hasn't. There's no reverence. There's a sense of "we are dominant here," rather than becoming an agent of something.

We are just now—especially among the young people with their ecological consciousness—just now beginning to have a sense of what the land can tell us, and along with this has come a respect for the American Indians and their myths, teachings, and religious rites.

SEEDS OF CHANGE

What culture stage follows?

The first period, hunting and gathering, goes from the beginnings up to the emergence of agriculture. Well, the emergence of agriculture involves a mystery. Here we had people in the world for three and a half million years, and suddenly, in three totally different spots around 10,000 B.C., you have agriculture coming in: Middle America to Peru; Southeast Asia, Thailand, and then into Oceania; and in Southwest Asia, Mesopotamia, which is the place where it was first recognized archaeologically.

And so the next stage is that of the early planting cultures, with the whole shift to agriculture, which transformed the total mythology. It's women's magic—birth and nourishment. They are cultivating the food that you're going to eat. You're not out killing wild things. The myth shifts from the male-oriented to the gestation-oriented, and the image is of the plant world—out of death and rot comes life. You put the seed in the ground, it dies, and new life comes out of it.

The basic myth is of an earthly paradise, like the Garden of Eden, where there is no distinction between male and female, between men and animals, and no movement in time. Then a killing takes place, the bodies are planted, and out of that come the food plants. So begetting and death come together. You see in some ritual sacrifices the repetition of that original mythological act: you go back to the beginning and get a renewal of energy.

You're sacrificing an animal. Well, the hunt is a form of sacrifice too; their problem is they're sacrificing all the time, and they're living on it. Now, when you have societies that are nomadic and have to do with animal food, killing animals and so forth, the male predominates.

The woman is associated mythologically, ritually, and psychologically with the plant world. And the move to the planting world, with this highly sophisticated sacrament of sacrifice and eating the animal sacrifice—do you see where we are? It's a purchasing animal. They offer an animal with the thought that they are going to get a benefit from this: "I give that thou shouldest give." A totally new mystery comes in with this agricultural tradition, and there is a frenzy of sacrifice.

This life-out-of-death motif becomes an *extremely* important theme there. At the same time, animal domestication comes in, so you have sacrificial rites where the domesticated animal plays a role, and this whole theme of sacrifice, a kind of sacrifice you don't get in the primitive world—namely, where what you are sacrificing is an incarnation of the God.

When you're in the planting culture, you are at the ground base of St. Patrick's Cathedral. You're in the communion meal, the sacrifice of the God, cannibalism associated with the sacrifice—and this isn't nourishment cannibalism at all; this is sacramental cannibalism that comes right up in the Roman Catholic Mass. You can play echoes from New Guinea to Mount Calvary, and they're valid and they're strong: there's a temporal, geographical, spiritual continuity that runs right through these traditions.

Do we develop a more hierarchical form of religion with the transition from hunting and gathering to planting cultures?

Oh yes! It depends on the structure of the society. You won't get hierarchical structures in myths of the very simplest hunting and gathering peoples.

The planting people are village-bound, really. The hunter, inevitably, is outside the village. He's on his own most of the time, or with a small team, a hunting team, and then he comes back. The shaman goes off on his own flight, whereas the priest is the agent of a village system of gods. There is a pantheon of which he is the ordained minister. But the shaman goes off to have his own experience; he has his own familiars, his own personal guardians, and they are the ones that carry him on these distances. Quite different.

What mythological development follows this stage?

The problem of an enlarged social unit, ground-rooted—the village, and its growth into the town. This third stage comes around the fourth millennium B.C. with the rise in Mesopotamia of the first cities in the history of humanity. We have an enlargement of the culture domain with dynastic families, kingship, and established priesthoods. Writing and mathematics are invented for recording gifts to the temples. The temples become observatories, and the priesthood is concerned with systematic observation of the heavens for omens and festival seasons. And when the astronomical observations can be recorded, as they can when you have writing, and the mathematically ordered movement of the seven visible spheres through the fixed stars can be measured, a totally new concept comes into play in activating the human imagination: a cosmic order illustrated in the heavens.

This is a total transformation of the mind. So interest shifted up to the heavens—and we still say, "Thy will be done on earth, as it is in heaven." The royal court began to organize its own ceremonial patterns to reflect the order of the heavens. There is a whole regulation of society from above.

In the earlier animal and plant mythologies, it was the exceptional situation that drew attention and received religious regard—an extraordinary tree, or something that happens in this particular pond or neighborhood, or this strange little animal. Now, in this new, Bronze Age mythos, the exceptional is of no interest; what's of interest is the ever-recurring cycle, and we begin to get what might be called sacred mathematics. Certain numbers begin coming in. An important one is 43,200: it's the number of years in a *yuga* in India, the number of warriors in Wotan's Hall in Iceland, the number of heartbeats in twelve hours, the number of seconds on your watch in twelve hours.[3]

The notion there is that the cosmic rhythm is echoed in smaller but analogous cycles. In the life of the individual, you get the macrocosm (the universe) and microcosm (the self), and then you have the high cultures, all of them based on this, where there's the mesocosm (society), so you've got a three-level ground.

Are there ancient cultures that weren't organized around cyclic myths?

Primitive cultures do not have them, but the Mayans and Aztecs did.

In very early myths, there is no real concept of future. The future extends only through, say, your grandchildren. Then there were the

great cycling myths of the four ages—maybe gold, silver, bronze, and
iron. The future here is a declining one, which will finally decline so
far that it will be wiped out and a new cycle will return.

What does the appearance of this new mythological imagery achieve?

I'd say the basic mythology of the high literate civilizations from the
time of the first emergence of such civilization in Mesopotamia, during the fourth millennium B.C., was concerned to coordinate, into a
single, organically conceived social unit, the disparate types of men
who were functioning in that developed world. In the earlier period
of foraging in these little tribes, all of the adults were in control of the
whole cultural heritage. When the cities began to evolve with specialized vocations (priests, governing people, trading people, peasants,
and so forth), the problem arose of coordinating these disparate types
of human life.

This mythology imagines the social unit as an organism in accord
with the cycles of the seasons, as our ritual festivals still do (Christmas
and the Festival of Lights at the time of the dawn of light in the winter
solstice, spring festivals, fall harvest festivals, and so forth).

The purpose of religion in these archaic cultures was to break the
ego, to break the feeling of individual responsibility, and submit to the
great Cosmic Round. We find in their lives and art an elaboration, an
elegance, a festival spirit, an imposed order, and individual submission in accord with the observable laws of the cosmos. All of the basic
mythology revolved around that which put the society in accord with
the world of nature, and then the individual, who was also a product
of nature, was put in accord with nature—his own nature—through
participation in those rites.

Elements of this stage are still with us?

City life grew up on the basis of agriculture. You had a single form of
society from about 4000 B.C. until the industrial revolution: agricul-
turally based cities whose nourishment depended on agriculture.

We govern our social order by the seasons. At the time of the
winter solstice, we celebrate Hanukkah and Christmas, but this is a
moment that has been celebrated all over the world as the end of the
agony of going down into darkness, and the beginning of the coming
of light again: the coming of life out of death, which you get with

the breaking up of the seed and out of it comes the plant. Out of rot comes life. This notion—out of death comes life—is fundamental to these mythologies.

And the point that's coming through to me more and more as I work on these materials—and I've worked on them all my life—is that most of our great traditions derive finally from the Bronze Age. And the Mother Goddess is the principal divinity of that time.

The Mother Goddess predates the emergence of the masculine hero theme in mythology?

The earlier tradition, so far as my findings go, is the one where the sun is feminine and the moon masculine. The moon is the image of the sacrifice that dies and is resurrected. The moon dies in the light of the sun and is again born from the light of the sun. And so the sun is the mother of the moon.

That makes the sun feminine. The fire of the sun and the fire of the womb that converts seed into life are equivalent. Also the fire on the sacrificial altar consumes the victim. These are all associated with a mythic consciousness that dates at least from the early Bronze Age. Here there is a deep sense of the melancholy and tragic quality in life, since the moon, the symbol of life's death and resurrection, carries its own shadow within itself, as we all do.

You can see something of the influence of myth on language when you consider the Indo-European family of languages. Here nouns have genders, but it's strange how these change. In German they have a masculine moon and a feminine sun: *der Mond, die Sonne*. This accords with a myth that extends all the way from the River Rhine to the China Sea, where in Japan the goddess Amaterasu is the sun, her brother being the moon god. Then there's a myth about the moon brother and sun sister that is known to practically all the circumpolar peoples of the North.

When did the dominant mythological image change from a feminine to a masculine sun?

This is heroic mythology. It comes in around 2500 B.C. with the Fifth Dynasty in Egypt. It was built up throughout the Near East and elsewhere. There the image is of the rising sun in the morning, a hero dispelling darkness and shadows. So there is *Sol Invictus*, the

unconquerable sun, the masculine hero. The sun hero, then, becomes
a very important figure.

In French, the sun is masculine and the moon feminine—*le soleil,
la lune*—and this accords with another myth context. Apparently, this
mythic orientation came by way of the Mediterranean into France but
not into early Germany. So at the Rhine these two mythic traditions
confronted each other. In my estimation, that's why the French and
the Germans will never understand each other. The French language
has a sunny, bright quality. There are deep, mysterious things you simply can't say in French.

From Goddess to God

**What explains the shift from goddess-oriented cultures to patriarchal
traditions accenting masculine gods and heroes?**

Nomadic herding peoples—the Mongols, the Indo-Europeans, and
the Semites—came smashing in on those city areas and you have the
period that we know, the heroic age.

When did this happen?

In the second millennium B.C.—actually, it begins earlier than that—
with the invasions of these great cultures in Egypt, Mesopotamia, the
Indus Valley, and the Huang Ho, by the Semites coming out of the
Syrio-Arabian desert, the Indo-Europeans from the northern grasslands (their base seems to be just north of the Black Sea), and then,
later, the Mongols going into China.

You have the picture in the Near East of the people in the river
valleys—the ancient Egyptians, the ancient Canaanites, the ancient
Mesopotamians, Sumerians, and so forth—planting people. And then
the hunting and the fighting people from the plains and from the
desert come in. One has a Mother Goddess accent, the other has a
Father God accent, and they come into collision. You had then the
coming together of these two worlds and the beginning of the world
we still know.

"The world we still know"—how so?

The powerful male-oriented warrior peoples actually picked up the
material of the earlier Bronze Age traditions and inverted it to the

celebration of their own male rather than the female divinities. I think the Old Testament, particularly the Book of Genesis, is very clearly an inversion of earlier materials. And we now have those earlier materials from the old tablets of Sumer in Mesopotamia. And when one compares the treatment of the female divinities that we find in the mythologies of India, for example, where the Goddess recovered her strength long, long ago (from about the seventh century A.D.), we can really see what's happened in our own tradition.

And this makes our mythologies a little bit complicated to appreciate. On the one hand, the images speak definitely of the Mother all the way through—and I think they speak that way to our hearts and guts—whereas intellectually we're being told that it's Daddy that we're reading about, and it makes us a little bit neurotic, I think.

What is happening in Northern Europe around the time of the Indo-European and Semitic invasions?

What was happening in Europe was very, very interesting. You can start the real history of Europe with the ice ages, in the period of the Neanderthal. Then, as the glaciers move upward, they leave behind them a tundra, and grazing on the tundra are animals like the wooly rhinoceros, wooly mammoth, and saber-tooth tigers. Over time the tundra gives way to grasslands, and there's a period called the Solu-trean,[4] of herds and hunters of herds—the hunting and gathering stage we talked about earlier—and then gradually, from Southeast Europe, forests begin to take over. The first forest lands consist of evergreen and then deciduous trees; that reduces the animal herds, and the animals go north. Many hunters followed them, so that all of those people in the north are residual of the early Paleolithic period.

But a whole new kind of life then built up in the forest area. And with agriculture coming in, the forest begins to be cleared and you have vast parklands that are being created.

Then, around 7000 B.C., we have the appearance of a quite developed neolithic mythology based on the Mother Goddess. There's a very, very fine book by Marija Gimbutas called *Gods and Goddesses of Old Europe* (her original title was *Goddesses and Gods*, but the publishers turned it around), covering the period from 7000 to 3500 B.C. You don't have that celestial accent. You have the Mother Goddess; this is her great period in Europe. This terminates, then, with the Cretan world, from 3000 B.C.

Was there a flow, then, between Eastern Europe and Mesopotamia?

This is earlier than that, than Sumer and Egypt. The figurines that Marija Gimbutas brings up are 7000 B.C. That's Neolithic stuff, the Mother Goddess in relation to the early planting cultures of Eastern Europe. Sumer doesn't get going until 3500 B.C. By that time the goddess thing in Europe has been overwhelmed by the incoming Indo-European peoples. The invasions come in at the fourth, third, second millennia B.C. That's another set of problems.

In Europe, then, follows the Age of Bronze, and bronze is an alloy of copper and tin (or copper and arsenic, but the more important combination was copper and tin). Now, wherever there were tin mines, there were settled communities bringing the tin out and shipping it to the big Bronze Age centers—Transylvania in the Balkans was one area, and Wales and Ireland another—so that all the way up to Great Britain and Ireland you have connections with the Egyptian world. You have Stonehenge, built in stages between 3000 B.C. and 1500 B.C., and earlier than that there's Newgrange in Ireland, that great tomb there. That's a marvelous period for Europe. But it's still Neolithic earth-based, not heaven-oriented.

But what about the sun and moon and stars? Weren't these worshipped long before cities arrived on the scene?

There are certain celestial phenomena that play roles even in the very simplest mythologies. The rising of the Pleiades, for instance, and some of the more vivid spectacles in the heavens. But that's very different, that kind of optical observation, from the mathematical. It's the mathematics that gave a whole notion of the information of the universe.

It took mathematics and writing before they would be able to calculate precisely the movements of the heavens. And they then recognized these movements as being mathematically predictable, so that mathematics becomes the key to the order of the universe.

The knowledge of mathematics gave priests their power?

No, priests have power without mathematics.

But didn't that give them the ability to "predict" events?

Yes, but I just don't go with this whole idea that the priests are intentionally nasty and they just want to have power. They have it anyhow, because they know things. And earlier than that the shaman had power.

So Mesopotamia really is "the cradle of civilization"?

Mesopotamia! Almost no doubt of that now. By "civilization" I mean city-states—and with kingship, writing, and mathematics, unless some further evidence comes in, it's Mesopotamia, about 3200 B.C., in the period that used to be called Uruk B. That's when we get the first writing.

Did Mesopotamia influence Egypt?

No doubt about it. This was the whole problem in the 1920s. That was a marvelous period of archaeological work in the Indus Valley and the Mesopotamian and Nile areas. It went back and forth on the question which was the earlier. We are now completely sure the earlier system is the Mesopotamian.

Didn't writing emerge separately in Egypt and in Sumer?

The earliest Egyptian writing comes following a very strong influence from Mesopotamia into Egypt; the Mesopotamian is a couple hundred years earlier.

But cuneiform and hieroglyphics are so dramatically different!

Totally different. It's a totally different writing. The cuneiform was written on clay. You know the mud there, that's about all they have. And then these little styluses that made marks in the clay, so you have those very complicated things. It looks almost like Chinese writing. The Egyptian starts with papyrus, and with the murals that they were creating. When you go into one of those Egyptian tombs in the Valley of the Kings, it's incredible—in the tomb of Seti I, every inch of the wall is sculpted—and those tombs were shut up; no one was ever to see it. Fantastic—the magic power of writing!

What is diffused is the *idea* of writing, not the writing.

In the early Egyptian, for instance, there is a tomb in a place called Hierakonpolis that appears around 3000 B.C.[5] The images in the mural on the wall of that tomb are very much like those from Iran. Yet within a few years, you've got the Narmer palette, commemorating the unification of the Upper and Lower Kingdoms of Egypt, and it's carved in the familiar Egyptian style that would remain for three millennia. There was a big movement there.

This is one of the interesting things about the study of culture. New influences come in, but the old ground takes over and assimilates it and grows on. It's a dialogue. It doesn't mean that Mesopotamia is what we get in Egypt. Not at all. Rather, we get *Egypt activated*, brought into a new level of realization through these influences. Just as in Japan today—when you go there and see Japan as an industrial nation, you are not in New York. It's another spirit, a totally different ethos that's there. But it has assimilated this Euro-American lifestyle and moved on through; that's the way it has always gone in culture transformation.

The Indo-European and Semitic invaders of those earliest civilizations both have thunder-and-lightning sky gods. Is there a connection between them?

Well, they come from two different places. There have been attempts to relate the Semitic languages to the Indo-European languages, but as far I know they haven't pushed through. I don't think a relationship has been demonstrated.

Is it then just a coincidence both have male gods?

Well, it comes out of the fact that nomads are nomads, and the masculine hunting and fighting accent is emphatic. A totally different psychology goes with killing than planting; they're really different. The male deity predominates, the thunderbolt hurler—Yahweh, Zeus, and so forth.

And these are tough people. They're not ground-rooted; they're going over the territory—so you get mythologies that are associated with deities or powers that are the same wherever you are: the Wind, the Sun, and Moon, but not *this* tree, *this* rock, *this* pond. It's a different thing.

Also, they're living a tough life, and they're lusting after the ease of the valleys. When the valley people become too soft, the invaders come in, and then you have the interaction of two mythologies. One is ground-based, and where you have planting it's the Goddess who is the primary figure; and then there are fighting, male-oriented powers where the God himself is a fighter throwing thunderbolts around. The interaction of these two differs greatly in the Semitic and Indo-European fields.

How so?

When you have such a contrast as between the Semitic and the Indo-European people, you find the same motifs going through, except the accent, interpretation, and social application greatly differ. But the same themes prevail.

These societies come in as conquerors to settled areas, and there are two attitudes. One, the male god marries the female. So this is a kind of genial conjunction of the two societies. This is what you get in Greece. In a society like the Greek, you have a very interesting combination. You have the Homeric tradition of the warriors, and you have the tradition of Eleusis, of the two great goddesses, Demeter and Persephone, in the soil. I think a healthy society has to have the two.

How does assimilating (or co-opting?) the goddess affect the evolution of Indo-European mythologies?

Well, what I see is that where the Goddess mythology prevails or continues, there is a beautiful accord, at least intended, in the relationship of man to the world of nature—to the nature of his own body and to the nature of the world around him (the two being one nature). So the Indo-European gods marry the goddess. They're all really nature powers.

Among most of the peoples of this world the primary powers are the powers of nature. Insofar as that is so, the deities that personify different nature powers are equivalent. Greeks and Romans were quick to recognize such analogies. Hindus have done this as well, and also Buddhists. This is syncretism. And when your deity is the personification of a power that's operative in nature—and being operative in nature, it is operative in you—it's very easy to say, "He whom you call Indra, we call Zeus."

What happens in the Semitic realm is something quite different. The principal deity among the Semitic tribes is the tribal ancestral deity. These are two different kinds of God.

Where the male orientation predominates, the references primarily are to society and its laws. And you have a strongly ethical accent (and in-group ethics) in these mythologies. In Semitic myths—and that includes not only Hebrew myths, but also Babylonian, Amorite, Assyrian, and so forth—the tendency has always been to make the tribal deity the top deity of the universe. You can't have syncretism across lines like that. There is an exclusiveness inherent in every aspect of the myths of the Semitic world.

How is this influence felt in our culture today?

It's rather difficult for a person brought up in a tradition like our own to recognize the analogs in what we call the nature religions to our own system of pantheons and divinities. This makes a big difference, actually; it cuts the individual in a patriarchally oriented culture off a bit from his own nature and commits him specifically to the culture systems of that particular society to which he belongs.

If Semitic gods don't marry the goddesses of the Mesopotamian and Canaanite cities they conquer, how does their culture handle this collision?

In the Semitic societies the female was wiped out, particularly with the Hebrews. You get an exclusivism and, along with that, a violence.

Why is this so?

Why is it that the Semites are so violently anti-goddess? At least the Jewish Semites, though not all of them—the Canaanites and the Amorites and so forth were not.

No other people did this. Other cultures recognize the nature divinities as the great powers and the tribal deities as inferior. The main thing about the Jewish myth was that it had no trust in nature. In the Old Testament, Yahweh was in perpetual conflict with the fertility cults and the nature goddesses.

The only answer I can suggest is the clue which I got from Frankfort and Frankfort in their useful little volume called *Before*

Philosophy[6]—and I notice that later editions have removed this part. They make the point that Semitic people came from the desert, and in the desert, you can't rest on nature. Goddess Earth in a desert isn't giving you much help. You rest, rather, on society. Society is what supports you, and so the high deity of the society is really the Lord of your life; Mother Nature is barren sand.

Is that violence really so different from what happened in the Indo-European sphere?

It goes further than anything the Indo-Europeans represent. It's a violence that involves total annihilation of the enemy. Just read Joshua and Judges. The Bible tells you to kill everyone in Canaan, right down to the mice. You don't get anything like that in the Indo-European invasions.

The Hebrew tradition in the beginning is the tradition of a hunting warrior people, not of a settled, tilling-the-land, trading people. And it's from the latter that the origins of higher civilization stem—agriculture, animal husbandry—and not the wandering hunter. The hunters are all male-oriented: the male brings in the food. The planters are mother-oriented: the woman is the analog of the producing, nourishing earth. And throughout the Old Testament days, as soon as the Hebrews get into Canaan, they begin to plant also, and, immediately, the local cult takes over! You read the Book of Kings: one king after another is worshipping on the mountaintops, building altars on the mountaintops, and he did not do right in the eyes of Yahweh.

Do we find echoes of this conflict between planting and herding cultures in the Bible?

There's a very amusing Sumerian dialogue that appeared about fifteen hundred years earlier than the Cain and Abel story, of a herder and an agriculturalist competing for the favor of the Goddess. The Goddess chooses to prefer the agriculturalist and his offerings.

Well, the Hebrews come into this area, and they're not agriculturalists; they're herders. And they don't have a goddess, they have a god. So they turn the whole thing upside down, and make God favor the herder against the agriculturalist.

Throughout the Old Testament, it's the younger brother who overturns the older brother in God's favor. It happens time and time again. This is simply a function of the fact that the Hebrews come in as younger brothers. They come, as barbaric invaders, from the desert into highly sophisticated agricultural areas, and they're declaring that although the others are the elders (as Cain was—the "founder of cities"), they are God's favorite. It's a form of sanctified chauvinism.

The Semitic tribes (Hebrews, Amorites, Arabs, etc.) erupted out of the desert over the course of several centuries. Might those desert origins explain why, in Genesis, God created everything except the water?

You've put your finger on it. What happens in the Old Testament is that the masculine principle remains personified, and the female principle is reduced to an element. The first verse of Genesis says when God created, the breath of God brooded over the waters. And the water *is* the Goddess.

Can traces of the ancient goddess still be found today?

Yes—the Madonna is one aspect of that great Bronze Age cosmic Goddess.

What makes you say so?

The Goddess, in her early manifestations, is a total Goddess. But then she becomes, in various aspects, specified to this, that, or another role. The goddess Artemis, for instance, is a magnificent figure. But she becomes specialized; in the late literary Greek tradition, she becomes the goddess of wild animals, and so the huntress, and is also patron goddess of young, adolescent, virgin girls—but in another aspect, she is the Great Mother as well, and that mother aspect of the Goddess is the one that is represented in the Madonna.

Now there are a couple of very specific deities that are models for the Christian Madonna, and one of them, probably the most important, is the Egyptian Isis. She is the mother of Horus and consort of Osiris. Osiris is the dead-and-resurrected god; his mythology is one of the models for the Christian myth of the dead-and-resurrected Savior.

In Egypt, with respect to Isis, she is the throne on which the pharaoh sits. She is the support; the pharaohs come and go, but she is there. And so also, in the Byzantine Madonnas, she is not the nursing mother that she is in the Italian tradition. She sits there and the little

Christ child is on her knee, as the world emperor, with the woman as
the ground base.

That's good old Bronze Age thinking. The king becomes associated with the sun and the lion in either case—either as the child of
the Mother Goddess and her lions, or as the solar god himself, so that
the lion becomes associated with kingship. (The lion is the ruling animal—in Aesop's fables, it's King Lion, and so forth.)

So these mix up, particularly in the late Hellenistic and Roman
periods in the Eastern Mediterranean. There was a whole galaxy of
mythologies that influenced each other in that period, back and forth,
leading to the Christian recovery of the Goddess. She was wiped out of
the Old Testament tradition; the Goddess just isn't there really, except
in a very secret way in the figure of Wisdom: Sophia. She appears in
Ecclesiastes as having been present with Yahweh at the creation. But,
otherwise, she's wiped out.

Then, with the Christians in the first centuries, she comes back
very strongly. There are certain aspects of Catholicism, for instance,
where Mary is more important than either the Father, Son, or Holy
Ghost. In all of the great cathedrals of Notre Dame, she is the guardian, protecting, mediating Mother. See, the god image as it is in our
tradition is a pretty heavy one—he's a kind of savage deity—and the
mother is a protective, intermediary screen. When she's wiped out in
Puritanism, God becomes really a ferocious figure, as you read in some
of those Puritan sermons.

In the Bible, life is corrupt, and the Goddess is the abomination,
whereas in India, you have this sense of the Goddess as the ground of
all things. She is the principal image of devotion now—Kālī, Durga—
in her various modes and aspects.

When you have a cult, whatever the cult,[7] there has to be a speci-
fication, a concretization, so that the attitude of worship and devotion can find a place to play. And since all things are Buddha things
(in Buddhism, we are all incarnations of Buddha consciousness—the
only difference between ourselves and the Buddha is that we don't
know it; we're ignorant of our own Buddha nature), any individual,
and any thing, can be recognized in a ceremonial way as incarnating
that consciousness.

I was at a charming ceremony in Calcutta at the time of the worship of the Mother Goddess as slayer of the buffalo monster.[8] Well, a
little girl, maybe about three years old, was consecrated as the goddess,
as Kālī, for that ceremony. They gave her candy to make her happy, and

there were the prayers to her and chants and garlands put on her neck and so forth. That's a lovely thing in India, because everyone is a goddess, but in a secular way you can't be paying attention to that detail all the time. This gave you a chance to address your devotion to the mystery of the Goddess through a little girl. And then she was desanctified, you might say—she gets up and trots off with her mother.

Now, in the Roman Catholic tradition, they sanctify a wafer. Anything can be recognized for its mystery. I've seen people take just a stone, a rock, put a red circle around it and regard it not as a rock, but as a mystery—which everything is, believe me. It's just unfortunate when a certain tradition thinks that its particular concretization is *it*, you know.

What the Goddess represents is the movement of time. She is what the Hindus call *māyā*. And transcendent of *māyā* is *brahman*, which is just energy and unconsciousness—undifferentiated, uncommitted consciousness. Ramakrishna, who was the really important saint of the nineteenth century, said that when energy is thought of or experienced as at rest, we call it *brahman*. As soon as it is in movement, that is *māyā*. So James Joyce plays on this in *Ulysses*. Molly Bloom has shifted all the furniture around in the room, so that when Bloom comes home a little after midnight, he's bumping into things all the time.

I notice that women do like change. And the male sort of likes just to have things as they were. When Jean and I go to a restaurant, all I have to do is walk into a restaurant that I've been in before and they already know what I'm going to order. But Jean has to try something new—though she's usually disappointed, and I'm not.

This interest in life, in movement and change, is *māyā*.

So that stream, that running stream which is the running stream of time, the River Ganges, the River Liffey, the River Jordan, whatever river you want, becomes symbolic of the flow of time. And so it's given commonly a feminine name. And when you go into the water in baptism and come out again, it's like going into the mother womb and coming out in rebirth.

The water *is* the Goddess.

Is the serpent in the Garden of Eden evil?

Yes, but that's because we have rejected nature. You set man up against nature and say nature is good *and* evil, and you mustn't go into accord with nature. You've got to fix it. Then you can't say yes to the serpent. This is a peculiar ethnic transformation of an elementary idea that is characteristic of our culture.

Why would you want to say yes to the serpent?

Well, the serpent is the energy of nature. Now, it depends on how you're going to think about the energy of nature. If you think of the energy of nature as culminating, you might say, in the flower of the spirit, then there is a continuity from the ground of nature to the flower of the spirit.

But if you conceive of nature as antagonistic to spirit, then you have a duality there. And when nature is antagonistic to spirit, then you have the winged angel who suppresses and puts down or slays the serpent. But when you have the other view, the serpent rises, puts on wings, and we have the winged serpent. That is the serpent of the Buddha tradition. He rises from the naive levels of the world of earth and nature to the flowering of the spirit.

These are two totally different notions: the spirit as the flower of nature, and this tradition of a conflict. In the myths, you have very clearly expressed this totally different orientation to the world of nature.

The serpent isn't necessarily evil in every mythological tradition?

The serpent is always a shocker; I mean, monkeys and horses respond negatively to the serpent. I remember the first serpent I ever saw as a kid: it was a real shocker. You knew about serpents, but *mmm*, this thing! It has a fluid movement and yet its tongue is always flickering like fire, so it unites fire and water. And it represents the earthbound power of life. Life-bound earth.

Also, a serpent is nothing but a traveling esophagus. It's there to eat, and you feel there's no argument with this. All of these basic symbolizations of the ruthless quality in life are right there in the serpent. And they strike people that way. You find in the culture of this place, that place, and the other place, the serpent that is dominant in their symbolism is the most dangerous serpent. For instance, in the Americas it is the rattlesnake. In other cultures you have the python, and in India it's the cobra. (Oh boy, have you seen cobras? They're really something—really horrendous animal!)

But now the same serpent sheds its skin to be born again, suggesting the power of life to throw off death, so it becomes associated with the moon, which throws off its shadow to be born again. The serpent signifies immortality in the field of time: the energy of life in the field of time is what we are, and it represents that aspect of our existence.

The Old Testament spends a lot of time on rules of behavior—I think of the commandment against graven images or the ban on pork.

Pigs were the first animals to be domesticated, and the most important animal becomes sacred. In the Middle East pork was sacred. Frazer points out in *The Golden Bough* that what was sacred very often was thought of as impure; the pig had too much *mana* in it, too much sacred power. There is a taboo against it, and this is associated with impurity. So in Egypt as well as in certain parts of the Near East, people who were swineherds were impure—a sacred impurity, you might say. This apparently comes over in the Jewish taboo against pork. As Frazer points out in *The Golden Bough*, the Greeks couldn't figure out whether the Jews worshipped the pig or abominated the pig. But he notes also that a sacred object is not to be touched.

Now, it has been suggested that pork was sacred to the Hebrews at a certain time, and it may well be. The pig then would be eaten only on the occasion of a sacred meal. Judaism, like every other religion, has different cult directions in its great days. And there is evidence that there were Jewish cults in which there was a special eating of pig meals.

But it may also be that the Jews were setting themselves against eating what was the sacred animal of the people whom they despised—which was everybody else in the neighborhood.

The pig was sacred to the wrong god?

For the Jews, yes, but for the Egyptians, no. The pig was associated with Set, actually. Set was represented by a black boar at one time. Adonis is slain by a boar. Diarmuid Ua Duibhne, in the Irish tradition, is slain by a boar. Attis is slain by a boar. The boar that kills the god is the animal aspect of the god himself. The god kills himself. It's a self-slaughter that is symbolized there.

How many people know how the Buddha died?

Spoiled food, yes?

Spoiled food? *Potent* food. And what was it? Pork.

This story is in the Pāḷi Canon, which is the earliest life of the Buddha we have, first written down around 80 B.C.

When the Buddha was invited by Cunda the smith to dinner, he and his disciples were served succulent pork.

The Buddha says, "Do not serve this to my disciples. I will eat it, and what I do not eat, bury in the ground." He eats the pork, and then is overtaken with a terribly deadly indigestion. He knows he is going to die, and he says to Ānanda, who is his Saint Peter, "Now listen. When I die you must tell Cunda that he must not regret this that he has done. There are two meals that a Buddha eats which are the greatest. One is the meal immediately before his achievement of illumination (this is the meal by a little farm girl who served him milk rice), and the second is the meal that he eats before his *parinirvāṇa* (his leaving of the world forever). So see to it that our host does not regret what he has done. He has done a wonderful thing."

This is the Being killed by the boar, the pig, which represents the ultimate power of the spirit that is being striven for by the devotee: Adonis, as I say, is killed by the boar—he represents the symbol of the way to eternal life—and so Osiris and other gods, right across the board.

This pig is a very interesting thing. Now, when you have a man possessed by the spirit, by a devil, and Jesus casts it out into the herd of swine and the swine go into the sea and drown, well, the swine is the thing that's there with the spirit that you can't hold, that's too big for you. The devil is simply a god that you can't assimilate.

I had not realized the central role the pig plays in so many mythologies!

Whenever I see a mention of pigs, I get excited because this is that first sacrificial animal, and Christ is the last sacrificial animal. And the bull comes in between, and the horse comes in between: the swine sacrifice, the bull sacrifice, the horse sacrifice of the Aryan princes, and then the symbolic sacrifice of Jesus, who in the Christian tradition has terminated the need for sacrifices because this is the total sacrifice. So he himself is the terminal figure representing the same thing that that pig represents.

As I said, in India they won't eat beef. Sacred bull, sacred cow—that animal became symbolic actually of the mystery of the cosmos itself. The moon is the dying-and-resurrected God, and the cow then is Mother Earth as consort of the moon. There are three main sins in India, unforgivable sins: killing a Brahman, killing a woman, killing a cow. They are all carriers of high-powered mythic content. And I think this has to do with the pig in the Jewish tradition.

I might confess that when I began looking for the Campbell family crest, I found it was a boar's head on the top of a shield. So perhaps I have a certain affinity that's very deep.

What does the bull represent?

The horns of the bull are associated with the horns of the moon, the crescent moon. Also, the bull is an animal that represents sexual vitality—and the moon is associated with the *eros*, the second *cakra*. The bull is killed, representing the triumph of death—but then the bull's descendant comes, the little calf, and the next bull comes. The death and resurrection of the moon are symbolic of life throwing off death and coming through again, just as the serpent shedding his skin. Just as the serpent is associated with the moon in one system of imagery, the bull becomes associated with the moon.

It's the same thing. The bull becomes linked to the lunar forms, as the lion is linked to the solar forms; the serpent is linked to the lunar forms, as the eagle is linked to the solar forms. The sun jumping on the moon then every month, the eagle pouncing on the serpent, and the lion pouncing on the bull—these are images that are being mythologized, signifying the eternal aspect of consciousness overwhelming the temporal.

When did the bull become a sacrificial animal?

When bulls came in—it has to do with herding cultures, where you have domesticated bulls.[9] Before that, you have domesticated swine,[10] and the boar plays that role. The boar's tusks become the two crescent moons, and the black face between is the dark between them. And this is what you find in Melanesia, and also in very early Aegean and European systems associated with the swine culture before the herding of cattle became dominant.

Jane Harrison speaks about this in her wonderful book *Prolegomena to the Study of Greek Religion*. The bull's horns turn up, and the bull cult is addressed to the deities of heaven; the boar's tusks turn down, and the pig cult is addressed to the powers of the underworld. And people who have sinned are cleansed by being washed in the blood of the pig. Orestes was cleansed of the guilt of his matricide by being washed by a heavenly pig cut open: washed in the blood of the pig.

So we have these two worlds—the underworld, the world of biological energy, and the upper world, the world of the light of consciousness—and the two rituals are associated with these two animals.

There seems an inherent tension in the Genesis tale between the serpent and the winged angel in Eden who casts humans out of the Garden, as opposed to the union of those conflicting forces in the image of the winged serpent (or dragon) in Eastern traditions. Whether in opposition or harmony, how do the images of serpent and bird relate to each other?

The serpent signifies immortality in the field of time. The serpent is bound to the earth. The bird is released from the earth. These two figures represent the tension between the earthbound and the spiritual flight—and man, the mammal, the animal, is between the two. It's fascinating that both of these—the bird and the serpent—are related. They go back to the dinosaur time: the bird's feathers and the serpent's scales have common origins; they're both also egg-laying, not yet placental animals. And here *is* the placental man who identifies himself with the other placentals, the mammals, between these two extremes. The bird then represents the power to throw off the bindings of the earth and fly.

You don't believe in a literal seven days of creation?

Of course not. That has nothing to do with the actual evolutionary story as we now get it.

Is there a way to reconcile the creation story in Genesis with what we know from science?

Why should one bother to, any more than you would try to reconcile the Navaho story?

It's about time we stopped feeling that we have to believe in the Bible. It's the most overadvertised book in the world. It's very

pretentious to claim to be the word of God, or accepting it as such
and perpetuating this tribal mythology, justifying all kinds of violence
to people who are not members of the tribe: "There is no God in all
the world but in Israel."[11] That leaves out everybody else. This is one
of the most chauvinistic views of morality.

**Aren't you splitting hairs here? Hasn't your work justified violence in all
sorts of primitive societies?**

Did I say anything quite like that? No, I said that was the way it was.
And this kind of thing *has* maintained the structure of society, hasn't
it? But I didn't say it was all right.

The thing I see about the Bible that's unfortunate is that it's a
tribally circumscribed mythology. It deals with a certain people at a
certain time. The Christians magnified it to include them. It then
turns this society against all others, whereas the condition of the world
today is that this particular society that's presented in the Bible isn't
even the most important. It's not the dominant society in the world.
It isn't. And this thing is like a deadweight. It's pulling us back because
it belongs to an earlier period. We can't break loose and move into a
modern theology.

HUMANITY TRANSCENDENT

**After the emergence of those first cities around the fourth millennium
and the shift heavenward to mythologies based on recurring cycles,
what stage of culture comes next?**

This happens around 500 B.C., which is the date of the Buddha, of
Confucius, of Lao-tzu, of Zoroaster. Pythagoras is in there, Heraclitus
is in there—and the great thing in Greece, of course, is the tragedies,
so Aeschylus is in there also. That's a terrific period right across the
board.

All of those Bronze Age cultures had about a thousand- or fifteen-
hundred-year period to yield what they're in now—a period of the
thing getting out of hand, more than they can handle, with infighting
within the culture itself, and disintegration. You then have these philosophers arising, trying to define how to pull this together.

Confucius comes after the "Period of the Contending States."

The Buddha comes along following the period represented in the Mahābhārata, of the great battles of the families; the Greeks are on the brink of the Peloponnesian War and the fighting with the Persians. Here comes an intellectual intention to recover the knowledge of the principles that coordinated the society in the days of the youthful, mythological enthusiasm of the culture. It's a marvelous period!

How does the mythological imagery mirror this transition?

If you look at the mandalas, the visible designs which symbolize world-views characteristic of different ages, you can trace the progression of human self-consciousness. When man was a hunter, he considered the animals divine and he wore animal masks, created animal totems, and took animal names to signify his accord with the world around him. On the level of early hunting people, the two great societies were the human society and the animal society. And the mythology takes this into account all the time.

But next comes the problem of the plant world. And you have mythologies dealing with the plant. Then comes the notion of the sun and the moon and the signs of the zodiac all determining human existence, and there come the mythologies associated with those great spheres. In agricultural societies, the cycle of the season and the process of death and rebirth become central.

The mandala first appears when these cultures become complex.[12]

The earliest structured mandalas that I know are from about 4000 B.C. in the Near East, in the ceramicware known as Samarra and Halaf, from Tel al-Halaf and Samarra, in Iraq. Villages had become cities, held together by a cosmological analogy: a center and the four directions; the patron god and the four castes. The mathematical pace of the planets moving through the fixed constellations became the center of wonder, and man projected the gods in the form of solar deities who wore the crown of the sun.

Still later, the Christian symbol of the cross became the center of the mandala.

But now our nearest neighbor is not the animal or the plant or the sun or moon, but man. And the main problem before our mythology now is man to man. In psychology, the mandala is employed as a structuring form to coordinate the disparate functions and interests of an individual life. You can pull your life into order through mandala

meditation. Jung noticed in the mandalas of his patients, the human
figure has become the focal point.

Mankind—I and thou—must now create the world. And so we
turn from the heavens, we turn from the plants, we turn from the
animals to the psyche of man, and all of the myth moves over into
philosophy at that time—in Buddhism, in Confucianism, in Taoism,
in the various Greek philosophies.

What does this philosophizing produce?

The realization that all the gods, that all of the manifestations of myth,
are manifestations of the psyche. There is the translation of all of this
outside mythology—animals, plants, and the stars—into the power
of man himself, philosophy, and the inward life. It's one great song
that comes.

Now, it's my feeling that what has been called the *Philosophia
Perennis* (or "Perennial Philosophy"), the Gnostic theme that occurs
throughout a certain range of philosophies, is a carryover into verbal
discourse of this archetypology of symbol in myth. Before that you
had the images but not the text.

This major shift happens in all these places at roughly the same time?

Yes. This starts in India actually with the Upaniṣads. But there's a difference between the way that happens in the Orient and the way that
happens in the West.

In the Orient, the key theme is *tat tvam asi* ("thou art that"). This
appears in the Chāndogya Upaniṣads around 900 B.C. in India. There
is a wonderful, wonderful passage there where this old sage, Aruni, is
instructing his young son, Svetaketu. And he says to his young son,
"Bring me a fig from yonder tree," and the boy brings the fig. The
father says, "Cut it in half, split it, divide it." The boy says, "That is
done."

"What do you see there?" "I see these tiny seeds." "Take one of
those seeds." "I've done it, sir." "Split it, cut it in half." "I've done so."
"What do you see?" "Nothing." "Well, Svetaketu, out of that nothing has come that great big tree. Out of that nothing has come the
universe. Out of that nothing has come you. *You* are that nothing. *Tat
tvam asi*, Svetaketu."

This is the beginning of turning inward to find the divine within.

Then you get into the Bṛhadāraṇyaka Upaniṣads: "Worship this God, worship that God, worship another; those who speak that way do not know. The source of it all is in oneself, the *ātman*." And there is the footprint of eternity. So this is the shift that takes place.

Does this reach the West?

After Alexander. When Alexander crossed Persia and went into India in 327 B.C., that's the beginning of enormous changes.

I am going slow on theorizing. I really am. I'm trying to show, simply, Alexander went to India and, by gosh, next thing we hear, King Aśoka is sending Buddhist missionaries to Alexandria and to Macedonia and Cyprus and so forth, and the old Platonic philosophy comes along. And pretty soon even Christianity, you know.

Where else does this surface?

It appears in the Book of the Dead in Egypt, the whole passage of the soul through the underworld to the throne of Osiris. As the soul goes through this, it is eating back the gods. And there are passages that are thrilling to read: "My arms are the arms of Thoth. My mind is the mind of Osiris." This, that, and the other: "All of my body is of a god. It will not be taken from me."

The recognition here is that the gods are manifestations of the essential energy of the human being. And it comes to a culminating moment, the moment of the opening of the mouth, and opening of eyes to light in the underworld: "I am yesterday, today, and tomorrow. I have the power to be born a second time. I am that soul which is the source of the gods." You recognize your identity with that transcendent energy of which all phenomenality is a manifestation.

Now, when you transfer that into philosophy, you get a metaphysical rather than an ethically based philosophy. "Good and Evil," Aeschylus says, "are one." Heraclitus says, "For God, all things are good and right and just. For men, some things are right and others not."[13]

But this does not take hold in the popular philosophy of the West.

Now, in the West, we've had the address to objective fact (rather than the metaphoric reading of the universe, seeing the mystery behind it), becoming fixed on the objects of measurement and desire and fear. This short-circuiting leads us also to an ethical emphasis:

good against evil. Our religions are largely ethical and not metaphysical. And so it's just about at the period of 500 B.C. that this distinction begins to break in.

GNOSIS: BEYOND GOOD AND EVIL

What triggers that split?

It's at that time that a different turn is taken in Persia. The Persian empire was founded by Cyrus, 529 B.C., and he is followed by Darius, whose dates are 521 to 486 B.C. Darius gives as his prophet, Zoroaster. His dates are variously argued. Some place him as early as 1200 B.C., others around 600 B.C.

You have a totally new mythology with Zoroaster. His mythology is basically an ethical tradition, with the notion that good and evil are absolutes—not just relative to the position you're in, but that there is absolute Good, absolute Evil—and these are symbolized in two deities: a deity of light and virtue and justice and wisdom named Ahura Mazda, and then, contrary, the god of darkness and hypocrisy and misinformation and malice, named Angra Mainyu. Ahura Mazda created a good world; Angra Mainyu threw evil into it, so you have the Fall. And this world is *not* good.

The world that we are living in is a world that is compounded of these two principles. The other traditions ask you to put yourself in accord with nature. This tradition says, "No. Nature is mixed of good and evil. You do *not* put yourself in accord; you correct it." Now, that is a deep, fundamental distinction, which, as far as I know, nobody else has even pointed to.

The focus on good and evil in religion begins with Zoroastrianism?

I think so. It's in the Persian tradition. Everything that has come out of the Near East now has it. That also comes through in the biblical tradition: with the Fall in the Garden, nature becomes corrupt. You get it in the Dead Sea Scrolls: the Sons of Light against the Sons of Darkness. And you get it in the whole Christian tradition. The teachings of this great prophet of the Persian Achaemenid house of Darius the Great have come down through the Bible into Christianity.

How does this dynamic differ from the cycling myths?

In the Zoroastrian myth, a great cataclysm is going to occur when the power of evil and darkness is finally destroyed. Christianity was born at a time when there was a great rush of such cataclysmic myths in the Jewish world. In the first century B.C. and the first century A.D., this idea of a coming world end was very strong. It underlies the tradition of the Dead Sea Scrolls. The Qumran community was expecting an end of the world and the coming Day of Yahweh. They were preparing themselves to survive the event. Baptizing only a few miles up the Jordan was John the Baptist with a similar apocalyptic expectation.

So then, instead of endless recurring cycles, history becomes linear, with a finish line in sight?

And now everyone is called upon to participate in this mixed world where good and evil are in conflict. We are exhorted to put our weight on the side of the good powers and restore the world of perfection. We have inherited this in a secularized form in our notion of progress leading toward a golden age.

And this is in contrast to the Gnostic tradition of the Perennial Philosophy?

Gnosis is the psychological crisis of seeing everything as God. In Sanskrit this is called *bodhi*—enlightenment—and he who has attained it is called the Enlightened One, the *buddha*. The Kingdom of God is not a historical event yet to come—it's here, it's happening, *iti iti* as they say in Sanskrit. The only thing holding you back from seeing it is your attachment to the hard physical thing you are. So kill that attachment. When you do, when you see, then it really doesn't matter if you die this minute.

In Christianity you get a concretization of everything. God is concretized. Not only God but the Devil. Heaven and Hell are fixed poles. When you have a polarity, you are still in the world of phenomenology, and God is a fact and has a name. He represents something—and anything that represents something is this side of *māyā*, isn't it?

I suggest you get hold of Elaine Pagels's book *The Gnostic Gospels*.[14] She deals with some of these problems and gives references there to help understand how and why the Byzantine notion of Christianity came down full force and wiped out everything else.

The whole Gnostic tradition is wiped out. When you go to India, you find that there are ninety-eight different ways of thinking about the deities. There were ninety-eight different ways also in early Christianity. But then, by military power and violence, all ways, except this one of the Byzantine throne, were called anathema, heretical, and wiped out. That's a choice of which Christianity you are going to develop. This is a specific, historically determined choice.

Why, I cannot answer. You don't get that kind of thing elsewhere. Well, you do in Islam, and I think in Judaism also—you can see it in the Old Testament: the Yahwist group were the ones who gained control. And when you read Elijah, for instance, my God! It's a bloodbath of people who are on the other side of the fence!

Then, as you read in the books of Samuel and Kings of the lives of the different Jewish kings, you find that about four of them did well in the sight of Yahweh. All the rest were worshipping on the hilltops, worshipping the Goddess. Then Josiah in 621 B.C. went in and cleaned up the temple. He found in the temple prostitutes, a horse of the sun god, a serpent that was being worshipped named Nehustan, which Moses was supposed to have molded in bronze in the desert, and all that kind of thing. It was quite a moment there. This history of the dominant pushing out the other varieties comes right through our own story.

But there were other Christianities, a secret Christianity. This is the Christianity that was buried in the Egyptian desert, in the Nag Hammadi Gospels of Gnostic material.[15] Read that, or read Thomas Merton,[16] and you would think that you are reading an Oriental text. It's a very important and interesting fact that Christianity was developing during the first three centuries A.D., and so was Mahāyāna Buddhism in northwest India, fifteen hundred miles apart on two ends of a road that had run through the Persian Empire and was viable; there were camel trains and elephant troops on this road.

Intriguing, though, that the central icons of these two religions are so utterly different. The crucifix is the epitome of suffering, while the Buddha would seem to signify the transcendent peace and serenity of enlightenment. Can you speak to that difference?

That's a very interesting question that I've thought about a good deal. I don't have an answer, but I do have a suggestion.

The West is a world where the seasons are accented. So you have an accent on time and death and resurrection. And it's in that area that the dead-and-resurrected god is a very important deity that goes way, way back to very ancient times—to Mesopotamia with Dumuzi, the one who dies and is resurrected, or Osiris in Egypt, Adonis and Attis, and Christ. They are all associated with lunar powers.

And then in India you are in a tropical, jungle zone where, as Goethe says, you have the blossom and the fruit at the same time. Time seems to be just the same time all the time. There the accent is on the stillness.

In Europe what you have in the imagery of the savior is an accent on the passing of time and the crisis threshold of death and rebirth. But in the Buddhist mythos, the accent is on the still point. Now, when the Buddha drops his hand and quits the world, that is the counterpart of the crucifixion. That is leaving the world to go to the father—psychologically, leaving the world of the body: he drops it.

Then, when he comes back with the boon-bestowing gesture, that's the counterpart of the resurrection on Easter Sunday. *Easter Sunday is the counterpart of the Buddha. And Buddha touching earth is the counterpart of the crucifixion.*

But you see what's happening. In the West the agony aspect has been accented; in Buddhism, it's not.

Now, with the image of the Bodhisattva in Buddhism, that's where Christ comes in closer connection. The Bodhisattva is on the cusp of Buddhahood, but willingly comes back to the world: "joyful participation in the sorrows of the world." You can almost speak of Christ as a Bodhisattva. If you want a vivid representation of joyful participation in the sorrows of the world, Christ crucified is it. We read in Paul's Epistle to the Philippians that wonderful passage, which is now thought to have been a prayer or a credo that was already formulated at the time Paul wrote the letter, around 60 A.D. or so: "For Christ did not think Godhood something to be clung to, but gave it up and took birth in the form of a servant even to death on the cross."[17] That is, out of love for the world, coming into it—*joyful participation* in the sorrows of the world. And that means suffering the sorrows yourself.

They glue together very well. But the essential difference between the authorized traditions is the unique godhood of Christ. We do not participate in it, except by imitation. In Buddhism, we are all Buddha beings, and the only problem is that we don't know it. We don't act as though we were.

The point I'm trying to make is the Christian symbology does not have to be thrown out. It is susceptible to this kind of reading.

How did the Gnostics read the Fall in the Garden?

The Serpent did his best to turn them away from that god who was an ethical god, a righteous god, full of vengeance. That's why the Orphic cults—the Gnostic, snake-worshipping cults—saw Jesus as the Second Coming of the Serpent. Because with Jesus, the law of Yahweh, the Old Testament, was transcended—we finally got rid of it. But then the Christians went right back. Their tradition is the Old Testament tradition all over again! Good and evil, right and wrong, sin and atonement.

In Western philosophy, the Perennial Philosophy carries these notions on. But the Aristotelian and Cartesian philosophies have taken more interest in the actualities of the time-space phenomenality, discussing them in those terms rather than in terms of these great, great, mystical references. And this has determined a contrast between the Occidental interest in the external phenomenon and the Oriental in the underlying rhythms and mysteries that inform all phenomena.

These are the two philosophies that are in contrast in the modern world.

CHAPTER THREE

"A Mythology Taken Seriously"

religion

Is there a difference between mythology and religion?

A religion is really a mythology taken seriously and interpreted in a specific, provincial way. The basic images of mythology are, for the most part, universal images—what Adolf Bastian called *Elementargedanken*, or "elementary ideas." However, each culture-world takes its own individualized inflection of these universal images to be the best, to be true, in a way that the others are not. Often, societies become so fixed on their own specific symbols that they lose sight of the universal message embodied in their myths. When that happens, one culture cannot relate to another.

I've been interested all my life in what we might call comparative mythology. And you see that what these people are saying in that language, these people are saying in this language, and they're getting mixed up simply because their language is different. If you go into a bakery shop here and say in French you want *pain*, they'll say, "Oh, we don't have that." But you're asking for bread, which is what they have. And that's the way it is, across the lines.

What is the value of religion in an individual life?

The problem of the religious life is to open the ego system to the grace of transpersonal energies and influences. Then the question is, where do those transpersonal influences and energies come from? They come—from the psychological standpoint—from the depths of the psyche, which is deeper than the ego system. If one has faith in nature, then one can let come whatever springs from the depths of the psyche and see what is coming as one's own nature's communication to one's own limited ego consciousness.

Spiritual truths are taught through religious images. The relationship of this mortal, passing, phenomenal vehicle of consciousness to the mystery of consciousness, finding this more enduring aspect of your life in yourself—that's what the religions are talking about. They personify that mystery.

Perhaps in an esoteric sense, but your description seems at odds with how most people understand their religion.

Popular religion believes its deities concretely, rather than reflecting back to the great unknown. In popular religion, it doesn't matter what the god's name is. The people turn to their gods for only three things: health, wealth, and progeny. "Please make the corn grow, please make my daughter well, or I will never burn another candle on your altar." In Sanskrit they call this manifestation of divinity the *deśī*, or folk belief.

But there is another term, *mārga*, which is borrowed from the hunter's vocabulary and means "the trail left by the footsteps of an animal." This is the elementary or universal idea of a religious myth, the trail that leads you to the chamber of the heart where the treasures of enlightenment reside.

In traditional societies, the first part of life is properly spent engaging oneself with society, through the *deśī*, the folk beliefs. Then, when society disengages you in the middle of your life—and it will—the *mārga* takes you into yourself, as is proper to the second part of life.[1]

But our culture is not mythologically inspired; it is not leading people into depth. Today our meditation time is spent on newspapers reading about rape, murder, politics, and stocks. You might say we're being emptied. That's why today you find the unprecedented withdrawal of young people into meditation and so on.

Western religions don't make up for that?

Jung says religion is a defense against the experience of God. I say *our* religions are.

I think one might define mythology as a projection of metaphoric images, telling of the possibilities of experience, action, and fulfillment of the human spirit. There's a mystery dimension in myth—there always is, and you can't put a ring around it. It's the difference between drawing a circle on the ground and dropping a pebble into a pond from which circles go out. The myth drops a pebble into a pond, it tells you of a certain center, it puts you on a certain center—what the Navaho call the pollen path of beauty—but it doesn't give you a definition.

What happens in dogmatic religions, however, is that definitions are contrived to circumscribe the myth and the ritual.

THE NATURE OF GOD

Isn't "God" simply one of the lingering traces of primitive superstition?

Well, the word *superstition* refers actually to something that is "standing over" from the past into a present for which it is not appropriate.[2] I would say that the relationship to divinity of primitive tribal people with what we would call their fetishes is not superstition, because that's the nearest approach in their world to these mysteries.

But for those mysteries to hang on when another mode of experiencing the divine becomes more appropriate to the actual experiences of people, this would be a superstition, something "standing over." And much of what we carry in our popular religious lore is really quite out of date in terms of what our potentialities for experience are.

Experience, not concept, is the way to the divine.

This business of taking your way, your folk idea of the deity, as representing *the* deity, is to miss the point. As the old Gnostics used to say, "The problem with Yahweh is he thinks he's God." He is a reference to a mystery.

The mystic philosopher Meister Eckhart, in the thirteenth and fourteenth centuries, says, "The ultimate leave-taking is leaving God for God"; that is to say, leaving your folk idea, the ethnic idea—the historical notion, with words and pictures to explain—for that which is inexplicable, that which transcends (what the Hindus call "that which no tongue has soiled, no word has reached"), and yet can be experienced as moving within oneself, and also as moving within the field of time round about. That's the pitch that the mythic images are to render.

Then who—or what—is God?

Who is God? The problem is we tend to personify God, you know, as a male. Well, now you're in an ethnological situation. There's our ethnology, the ethnic image: that's the way it is in our history. But you go to India and the God is female. So let's throw out the personification. These are optional.

The word *God* simply applies to a dimension of mystery. What the telescopes in the Mount Wilson Observatory show is certainly far more wondrous than the little picture of the universe that was in existence when the texts of the Bible were written. They've got millions of galaxies now, and clusters of galaxies, and every galaxy as great or greater than our whole Milky Way, with our sun on the outskirts of one of these—my God! The wonder of the divine, the wonder of the universe is more and more apparent and more and more marvelous.

Looking through a microscope and seeing the spinning demons of the atom that you get in the laboratories, this is terrific! So then God is particularly the one who thought of this whole thing. Of course that's not the one in the Bible at all, because all he thought of was a three-layered birthday cake.

The ultimate mystery that we call God is absolutely beyond human conception and beyond human imaging. Even Thomas Aquinas, who wrote the *Summa Theologica* (which was to have been a description, you might say, of God), states in the *Summa contra Gentiles*, "For then only do we know God truly when we know that He surpasses anything that can be said or thought of God."

The God concept moves you toward a realization of this utterly transcendent mystery. The big question is whether you can now bottle that down into a little concept of a personal god. You see, that's what's exploding. And the Orientals don't lean on the personal god at all. In fact, their mythologies are beyond the God concept.

So God as worshipped in Western culture is not God?

Anything that can be said or thought of God is, as it were, a screen between us and *God*. If we take it literally, absolutely, we are in a way short-circuiting our own experience of an ultimately ineffable mystery, something that cannot be talked about.

Half of the people in the world think the reference of a metaphor is a fact. The other half of the world knows that it's a lie. So we have people who believe in God as a fact and people who believe that he's not a fact: theists and atheists.

The real position is to realize that the word *God* is metaphorical of a mystery, and the mystery is absolutely beyond all human comprehension. The first thing to know when you're dealing with these symbolic forms is that the ultimate reference is beyond all categories of human thought.

The whole world of the classical heritage was full of tales of the gods. Each deity is a compound of many deities. And so you have poets, you have seers, you have teachers who know how to compound symbolic forms in eloquent ways. I think all of the great, great myths are put together that way.

I would say a similar thing for Christianity. The myth of Christianity is there was a Fall in the Garden and a Redemption on the Cross. It's made up out of the biblical tradition of a Fall in the Garden; it's made up out of a historical event that happened in Jerusalem, when a young rabbi of adventurous spirituality was crucified for blasphemy; it is made up of St. Paul's Greek education—he wrote Greek—and what knocked Paul off the horse on the road to Damascus, I think, was the realization that the crucifixion of Jesus, whom he had never met, was the death of the Savior as rendered in the Greek mystery religions.

The death of the Savior is then symbolic of the death of the natural man and the resurrection of the spiritual man. The body is given to the cross, which is symbolic of the earth and life, to go to the father, and that tree of the cross then is recognized as the counterpart of the second tree in the Garden, the Tree of Immortal Life. The first tree was the Tree of the Fall, the Knowledge of Good and Evil. It was the second tree from which man was excluded when expelled from the Garden, as it says in the text, "so that he should not eat of the Tree of Life and be like us." Jesus, as it were, went past the cherubim guarding the gate and himself ate of the fruit, and is himself now the fruit on the Tree of Immortal Life. What an image!

This came in the middle of the first century A.D. Paul is the earliest Christian writer we have (his letters are in the fifties and sixties of that century). Now, whether he is the one who really came up with the whole thing or picked it up from the Christians round about and dressed it in a particularly vivid constellation of statements, one doesn't know. There is one symptom that would indicate that the message had already been read this way. That comes in the Epistle to the Philippians—the wonderful passage where Paul writes about how Christ gave up Godhood "to take birth, and die, even the death on the Cross." So he gave up the Godhood and he gave up the manhood in death on the Cross—death to being God, death to being man—and thus was between the pair of opposites, representing the symbol down the middle. Paul had some inkling of that kind, and this is what he teaches—and, as with all great teachings, it's misread, it's debased, it's turned into a historical newspaper report, and the mystical aspect of it is for the large majority lost.

In Christianity, one hangs on to the mythology of the biblical tradition. And this mythology holds a certain line which has to be followed whether you're a Catholic or a Protestant, no matter what sect you are in the Christian religion: that there is one God, the God whose word is in the Bible. *That* is the word of God. There aren't other bibles. There aren't other words of God. Well, that's a theological way of interpreting them—as though the source were outside somewhere.

But in the Orient, there's a whole constellation of texts. And one floats around and changes according to one's own disposition. Since no truth that can be stated is the ultimate truth, it is really short-circuiting the mystery to say, "We've got it here." That kind of concretization of the mystery is the danger that is not to be found in the Oriental texts.

Do you consider yourself an atheist?

I don't think you can call a person an atheist who believes in as many gods as I do.

In your writings you refer to the deities of all mythological traditions as "masks of God."

The masks of God invite us in the direction of the *experience* of God; they are composed, you might say, to fit the mentality and spiritual condition of the people to whom these masks are directed. In the naive relationship of popular religion, people actually think that what I'm calling a mask of God *is* God—but they are intermediates between divorce from God and movement toward the mystery.

It doesn't matter to me whether my guiding angel is for a time named Viṣṇu, Śiva, Jesus, or the Buddha. If you're not distracted by names or the color of hair, the same message is there, variously turned.

You reject monotheism?

There's no such thing as monotheism really.

Members of the dominant faiths in our culture would disagree.

Well, I really didn't complete my discussion of what God is. I did say that the deities are personifications of the energies of the universe. Insofar as you want to personify the totality of the inpouring energies, you could have a high god: Śiva, Viṣṇu, Yahweh—no, let's leave Yahweh out for a minute. There are numerous deities who represent the totality, but the operation of that energy is inflected through various origins and specialized aspects, so you have a polytheism as the normal kind of religion.

But behind them all, and this goes even for the most primitive people, is an undifferentiated energy. This is what in India is called *brahman.* The Bushman of the Kalahari Desert called it *ntum;* they have trance dances where they'll dance all night in a very stiff way while the women clap their hands and then Boom!—the *ntum* takes over and they pass out and go into trance. The Pygmies speak of it, also. This primal energy you have in all religions. But that is not personified; it's antecedent to all personifications. There's a kind of proto-monotheism before you have monotheism.

Now I'm going to tell you what monotheism is. All of the mythologies of the world, with the exception of this one that we've had the great good fortune to inherit, see deities as *personifications* of that energy. The Judeo-Christian tradition sees the deity as the *source* of the energy—total transformation! That's what's called monotheism. And since no one else has a deity of that kind, no one else has a deity. These are all devils.

This is unique.

As soon as God becomes a hard fact, what Hegel called a gaseous vertebrate—a fart—then you are a fact, and you're in relationship to it. But in mythology the deity becomes transparent to transcendence— and you also, at the same time—and then comes that wonderful fun, that wonderful exhilaration of identification with the very energy that is *your* energy, instead of just worship. God would then be the generating energy of the life that is within you and within all things.

The function of symbols is to be transparent to the transcendent, and the whole character of the Judeo-Christian tradition is opaque to the transcendent. Everybody else has got the hang of it except these people going around trying to convert the world to their concretization of the idea of God, who sits there as a kind of roadblock.

What does it mean to be "transparent to the transcendent"?

The simple meaning of the term is that which goes beyond all concepts, that which lies beyond all conceptualization.

You are using *transcendent* as another term for God?

If you want to personify it. *Brahman* is the Sanskrit way of talking about it. *Manitou* is the Algonquin, *Orenda* is the Iroquois, *Wakan Tanka* is the Sioux.

In the Hindu tradition, is there a difference between *brahman* and Brahmā?

Brahman is a neuter noun. *Brahman* comes from a root *brr* that means energy. And *brahman* is the name for the mystery energy of which the whole world is a manifestation.

Brahmā is a personification of the consciousness of *brahman*. Brahmā is a god, a personification. All gods are secondary. The *brahman* is the energy which is personified in Brahmā in his creator aspect. Śiva is another personification of *brahman*. Viṣṇu is another personification. And each one of these personifications represents an inflection.

Śiva is associated with the *liṅgam*, the generating organs, and also with yoga. He is the archetypal yogi. He represents both the energy that creates the world and the illumination that transcends it. Viṣṇu is more the erotic deity. He enters the world in love as an incarnation whenever the world is in trouble. There is no end of incarnations. From the Hindu standpoint, Christ would be an incarnation of Viṣṇu—so when the Christian missionary comes and speaks of incarnation, he says, "What's news?"

Also, Viṣṇu has an aristocratic quality, whereas Śiva does not. Śiva is the yogi out there, meditating, covered with ashes. And he hasn't taken a bath in ten thousand years! Long-haired. Fantastic. But Viṣṇu is an elegant deity and actually is associated with the *kṣatriya*, or aristocratic caste.

Isn't Viṣṇu also called the Preserver?

When these three deities, Brahmā, Viṣṇu, and Śiva, are put together, you have a *trimūrti*, or three-formed god, where Brahmā is the Creator, Viṣṇu the Preserver, and Śiva the Destroyer. But actually Śiva is also a creator. And Viṣṇu is also a destroyer. So that's sort of secondary assignments. This is what happens in mythology. When deities of two different orders and different origins come together in the same systems, they have to be assigned, placed, so you have a secondary departmentalization of the gods. You get this throughout the classical tradition. For example, Poseidon, Zeus: these are both master deities; when the two traditions are brought together—Zeus actually comes from the North, and Poseidon belongs to the Aegean area—they are given assignments.

What about Yahweh?

Yahweh is personified. He is *it*.

But his name isn't to be spoken because he is "beyond."

Well, so Yahweh *ought* to be, but we know all about him—or he's told us all about himself and how we ought to behave.

The basic mythological concept is transcendent of personification. Personification is a concession to human consciousness so that you can talk about these things.

You can reread the symbols again. And they have been reread by mystics and by courageous heretics, and you have a very close play on it. Kabbala and Hassidism come as close as you can to the wonderful rich mystical experience without denying the unique power of Yahweh. But as long as you're hanging on to the unique power of Yahweh and the identity of him as being the only thing of its kind and the actual source of it all, you are still stuck with Yahweh.

So when the infinite reveals itself to us, the human mind responds by saying, "God spoke to me," because it can only grasp what happened in limited terms?

That's right.

And if it speaks to me and says, "I am that I am"?

That's the way you heard it. But as soon as he says "I," he has reduced himself. The Indian word for that is *ahaṃkāra* ("making the noise

Western vs oriental

'I'"). *Aham* is "I" and *kāra* is "to make." The moment you use the word
I, you've slipped.

We stop at the mask in our Western religions?

In the first place, and this is a point that is now becoming a deep concern to our Western theologians, the concept of deity in the Bible is of
a deity who is somewhere else. God creates creation, and God and creation are not the same. God is A. Creation is B. They are not the same.

I would say that the religion that puts God outside and keeps
him out there is not as strong as the one that allows the divine to be
inside—and really inside. This is one of the main problems of our biblical tradition—God is out there, not in my heart. My heart is corrupt
until I am converted, and then it is still corrupt. I can't say *tat tvam asi*
("thou art that" or "I and that are one"). I have to ask instead, Am I in
the proper relationship to that?

Judaism, Christianity, and Islam are religions of relationship. The
way to get into relationship is by participating in the historical cult,
and if you are not participating in that, then you are not in a proper
relationship to God. That I call, to put it bluntly, the way of an inferior sort of religion.

Where the goal of our Western religions is to establish a relationship to the divine, that of the Oriental is to recognize one's identity
with it. Now, that's the key difference. The basic concept in all of the
Oriental religions is that divine mystery, which is the mystery of
the universe, is your mystery as well. You are part of the universe.
And the God idea is the idea rather of a dimension of the natural
world, not of another. So that the high statement in the Chāndogya
Upaniṣad, which is the key to the whole Oriental point of view, is *tat
tvam asi* ("you are it").

That divine mystery which you seek is the very mystery of your
own being. But it's not the "you" that you think you are when you
think of yourself, because there's nothing mysterious about that. You
can name it. You are protecting it. You think of it as a temporal phenomenon that has come into being and will go out of being: you try
to last a long time and all that sort of thing. But that Being which is
the absolute being of your being is timeless, beginning-less, just as that
of the universe.

And so in these religions you have a truly mystical aim—to realize
your own identity with that ultimate mystery and consequently with

all beings in the universe, which in the West is the prime heresy. When one says, "I am God," that is likely to get one burned at the stake.

Now in the Christian tradition, Christ said, "I and the Father are one."[3] From the Hebrew standpoint that was blasphemy, but that is exactly the Oriental mystical insight. However, the characteristic of the Christian religion is that *only* Christ can say that, whereas in the Oriental belief *all* men can say it.

But isn't it a sign of insanity to believe "I am God"? How do we avoid falling down that rabbit hole?

The Orient goes so far as to say you are in your very essence that divine power which you seek to know and which is personified as God. So you can say, and I mean this as a rough translation, "You are God" (they would say, "You are *brahman*," which is a transpersonal form).

So this youth has learned from his guru that he is God and that all beings are God. Inflated and absorbed in this meditation, he goes forth to walk and contemplate upon it. He walks to the village, out into the country. And coming down the road before him is a great elephant, with the elephant driver on his head, the great *howdah* rocking back and forth with some people in it, the net of jingly bells jingling, and so forth. The boy, in his concentration on this miracle of what he is, isn't paying any attention. And the elephant driver says, "Get out of the way, you nut!"

The boy just pays no attention. His meditation is: "I am God. The elephant is God. Should God get out of the way of God?" That's the thought in his inflated mind.

It becomes critical and the moment of truth arrives. The elephant simply wraps his trunk around the boy and tosses him off the road, to the great shock of his poor psyche. He wasn't physically hurt very much, but God, look where he is now! And so he comes back to his guru in this disheveled condition. And the guru says, "Well, what happened to you?"

The boy told him the story. And the boy says, "Now, you told me I was God."

"You are God," says the guru.

"The elephant is God."

"The elephant is God," says the guru.

"Should God get out of the way of God?"

"Well, why didn't you listen to the voice of God shouting from the head of the elephant to get out of the way?"

The point here is that when one moves into these realms of metaphysical realization, one must remember that there is another aspect of one's consciousness, namely, that in the daylight world. And the "I" that you identify yourself with up here is not exactly to be equated with the great principle that supports you. A lot of silly things can happen as a result of mixing things up that way.

For instance, the aims of life and the joys of life melt away when you get to that level, but when you come back you've got to leave that level where it was—know that it's there, but function in terms of time and space and get out of the way of the automobiles!

One's understanding of God, then, can be either a portal to the divine or a barrier.

The psychological way is to recognize that the source is inside, and this psychological way opens into the way of Hinduism and Buddhism, which says that all the gods are within us. We find this same message in certain modes of Christianity.

Particularly in governing our lives, we have to have thoughts that govern us, certain images that we can target to. And these images then become the end. The Christ idea—you put that before you, and it helps you to move to this thing which transcends the Christ idea. The myth is this side of the truth, but it leads you to it.

Jesus is a metaphor?

Christ isn't Jesus. Christ is the eternal Second Person of the Blessed Trinity—yesterday, today, and tomorrow. Jesus is a historical character. He has been identified with Christ, just as each of us ought to be. But so many people who think they're Christians have become fixed on a concrete reference. Even Yahweh is as concrete as can be.

In the Asian systems, even the person who, in his temporal life, is in an extremely subordinate and even miserable condition has the experience of his ultimate identity with this mystery. And this is what's taught through even the most simple, primitive aspects of the Oriental popular religions. They always point toward this identity.

Now, when we see an Oriental bowing before an image we think, "Oh, you know, groveling before an idol." What he's actually doing is bowing before an aspect of himself which he becomes aware of in projection. And the ultimate realization will be, "I am that which I worship as though it were outside."

There's a saying in Zen Buddhism: "If you see the Buddha coming down the road, *kill him!*" As long as you're stuck with the Buddha, haven't killed him on the road, you're in devotion; you haven't got past the pairs of opposites and the cult objects to realize *tat tvam asi* ("that art thou"). If you have concretized the image of the transcendent, *get rid of your image!*

Kill Christ?

One little nun, who said she left the convent because she heard a lecture of mine, came up to me in New York after a seminar and asked, "Do you believe that Jesus was the Son of God?"

I said, "Well, not unless we all are."

"Oh," she said.

So I said, "Go get hold of the Gospel According to Thomas and that will fix you up."

How can you imitate Christ if you're not Christ? The *imitatio Christi*—does that mean go out and get yourself crucified? No. Just realize that you and the Father are One. That's what it's all about. Otherwise it doesn't make sense at all.

The Upaniṣads have a meditation: *neti, neti*. It means "not that." Not *iti*. *Iti iti* means "It is here, it is here, it is here."

Now, there are two orders of meditation. One is not *iti*. That is to say, you are looking for the eternal in yourself, the immortal, and everything that you can name is not *iti*. That's not it. And then, after you have found the immortal, you find that it's everywhere, and you say, "*Iti, iti, iti.*" As the Thomas Gospel says, "The kingdom of the Father is spread over the earth and men do not see it." When you see it, it's here. When you don't see it, it's not *iti*, not *iti*.

And the only way you can make that happen is when you become the Christ or Buddha within yourself?

That's why in Zen they say: "If you see the Buddha coming down the road, kill him." That's because *you think he's out there.* That's the whole point of that one. If you have identified the symbol with what it symbolizes, kill it. And that's the problem with the Christ. See, the *eternal life in in us*

Christians have so concretized the image of the Christ in the character of Jesus of Nazareth that they can't disengage Christ from Jesus. And then how can you have Christ in you if he's out there?

I got into a row in the magazine *Parabola* with some priest who wrote a letter saying nasty things about me. He was saying that the fundamental doctrine of the Church is the *absolute identity of Christ and Jesus*. And so I just asked him in reply, well, how about Paul when he says: "I live now, not I, but Christ in me"? According to the concrete doctrine, Jesus had already ascended to heaven. Did Paul imagine that he'd come down again and taken up residence in himself? The doctrine itself releases you from that concretization. So if you see Jesus coming down the road, kill him, and then you can assimilate the Christ.

It's too bad that we have all this religious lingo for two very simple things: one is my temporal existence, and the other is that eternal life and consciousness which is in *all* temporal existences. It's in me as well. And the big mystical experience is disengaging your identity from complete identification with the physical body and identifying with the consciousness that is aware of the body. Once you do that, the body can go. And once you do that, then all bodies can go. The consciousness is still there. *without a brain ?!*

Meister Eckhart tells us, "The ultimate leave-taking is the leaving of God for God." If we're stuck with Jesus, who physically died on the cross to return in unity to the Father, we haven't taken that passage through the Cross seriously enough.

The enigmatic saying of Jesus that "the Kingdom of Heaven is within you" intended this same sort of idea. When you have that view, you rest, so to say, in yourself—in your deepest part, within the bounds, to use theological terms, of God. And He speaks to you from within yourself. If you throw the God image away, as one does in Buddhism and ultimately in Hinduism, you will immediately recognize that whatever the power is that we speak of as divine operates from within as the source, and you can have faith in your own nature.

So we come back to the idea that God should be "transparent to transcendence."

Not only is the deity to become transparent to the transcendence, but so are *you*.

I take the phrase from Karlfried Graf Dürckheim, a German

philosopher and a great teacher. He was a healer, a psychiatrist, and he said, "Our minds carry us away from our nature—one of the functions of psychiatry and psychotherapy is to bring the Divine back into accord with our nature—and the source of the energies of our nature is transcendent of our knowledge; we don't know where it comes from."

Your life is your experience of transcendent energies. Our first knowledge of them is from within ourselves; you don't know where your life comes from, but you can experience these energies. We're experiencing them right here, just by sitting on them and having them bubble up. And we must make ourselves vehicles of the organization and harmonization of the energies of our bodies. In that way we will become manifestations, you might say, of the luminous, transcendent mysteries of these energies—they will be plain to us—and in that sense we are "transparent to the transcendence."

I recently heard a career vocation counselor, Richard Bolles, who has written several books on counseling; one of his books was for a number of years on the bestseller list.[4] He used almost the same terminology. Bolles said we must become "luminous to the light of the Universe." It's the same thing. That is to say, live—by means of our senses and our mind and rational faculties—in accord with our deep nature, which is divinely grounded, to use a theological term. All that means is that it's grounding, it's beyond our comprehension, and it's beyond the instrumental causal orientation of the sciences.

RELIGION: DIFFERENCES IN PERSPECTIVE

Don't the Greeks come in with the idea that you have a right to assert yourself as an individual, to say "I am"?

You have a right to do anything you feel you have the courage to do, I should think. But then look what you've done: you've eternalized your phenomenality. There's nothing wrong with that, but a phenomenon is not eternal; it's only temporal. And eternity is the mystery source that throws up forms and absorbs them back again.

How can one find any significance in that?

You don't have to. Just enjoy it.

Is the Greek mythos as influential as the Judeo-Christian in shaping the Western world?

Well, I think one of the most interesting contrasts in the field of religious literature is that between Job and Prometheus. God behaved abominably to Job. There's simply no doubt about it. He had this bet with this friend of his, Satan. The thing opens with God saying, "Have you considered my servant Job—what a fine wonderful man and how devoted he is to me?"

Satan says, "Well, why shouldn't he be devoted to you? You've been very, very good to him. Get tough with him and see what happens."

And God says, "I betcha."

And the devil says, "Okay."

So God says, "Go do with him what you can." And the poor man, you know what happens. There he is. His family's been taken away; everything's been taken. And those people who for some reason are called Job's "comforters," they come and say, "You must have been a real bad boy to deserve this."

The Big Man did a real number on him when he finally came. He didn't say, "Job, you've been wonderful" (and he had). Nor did he try by some roundabout way to justify himself. He just says, "Are you big? Could you catch Leviathan on a hook? I did. Try it."

And Job says, "Who am I? Who is man that thou shouldest behold him? I cover my head with ashes. I'm ashamed that I questioned you."

Now that is the proper religious attitude of submission. But it's just the opposite to the Greek attitude.

So, by contrast, Prometheus says, "Why should these gods up there have that fire, that transformative power? I want it for humans."

And then when he got it, the Big Boy Zeus pins him to a rock and sends a little delegation to say to Prometheus, "Apologize, and he'll let you go." And in Aeschylus's version of the play, which is almost exactly contemporary with the Book of Job, Prometheus says, "You tell him I despise him. Let him do as he likes."

This is the affirmation of human values against this monstrous situation.

These are the two religions that we inherit, the Greek and the Hebrew. No wonder we're nuts! Now Monday, Tuesday, Wednesday, Thursday, Friday, and Saturday we're over there with Prometheus,

Sunday for half an hour with Job, and the next Monday we're on the psychiatrist's couch. And what's the matter? The matter is we have two completely conflicting views. One is that of the European respect for the human and the other is the Levantine, the Near Eastern respect for the divine. And not recognizing that the divine *is* in the human, we have them split apart.

Now, you bring this contrast to the Hindu, and he'll say, "What's the problem?" These are two aspects of the one being which is your own life—the elephant *and* the boy.

Deep down isn't every religion the same?

That's the point when I speak of comparative mythology. This one sees it this way, this one sees it that way, but they're all talking about bread. Myth is a universal language that takes on its own local forms from society to society. They have a great deal in common, but they have been translated into a local commitment, so there are also significant differences.

Take, for instance, Judaism and Hinduism. These are religions of birth. Consequently, they are basically ethnic religions—one is born a Jew, one is born a Hindu. Christianity, Buddhism, and Islam, on the other hand, are creedal religions—*credo*, "I believe"—and one's birth has nothing to do with it. It's one's confession or belief that matters, and so they are not race-bound in the same way that ethnic religions are. That's a difference and an important one. It's an important difference psychologically, and it's an important difference historically.

Just as Christianity emerges from Judaism, so did Buddhism from Hinduism, but Christianity and Buddhism are religions of belief. Consequently, Buddhism could go from India to China to Tibet to Korea to Japan—to people who are not Hindu. Similarly, Christianity has gone to people who are not Hebrew. I think of both as taking what might be called the ethical and metaphysical quintessence of the earlier religion. I speak of Christianity as Judaism for export and Buddhism as Hinduism for export; they can go forth with these basic realizations that underlay the mother religions from which they sprang. Just as in Christianity we have the same God as in Judaism—the Old Testament deity is the deity of Christianity as well—so in Buddhism the gods of Hinduism are the gods of Buddhism.

Yet each of these world religions—Buddhism, Christianity, *and* Islam—is exclusive in its own way; there are adherents of the faith, and there are those who are outside. So I would say that in a contemporary world they, too, are a bit outdated.

Buddhism has a peaceful, less aggressive reputation compared to the way Christianity and Islam have spread. What accounts for this difference?

Buddhism, when it went into Japan for instance, did not wipe out Shintō. The two are coordinated. Since all beings are manifestations of Buddha consciousness, the deities of the Shintō are mythological manifestations of Buddha consciousness in relationship to the activities of the local culture. Whereas, when the Christians went into an area, the gods of the aliens were devils. This comes out of a really stunning passage in the Bible, in 2 Kings 5:15. In fact, I would say I haven't found anywhere anything equivalent to "There is no God in all the Earth but in Israel,"[5] except in Christianity, Islam, and Judaism. And that means what are taken for gods elsewhere are not gods—we just can't even think that way with this ferocious monotheism that we carry around; we're the only people who know God and have God. This is what lies behind the ruthlessness of the Christian and Mohammedan conquests.

Which religions best open to the inward way?

Hinduism and Buddhism, I would say. Of the two, I put Buddhism on top because, as I've said, it's a creedal religion, a religion of belief and consciousness, not a religion of birth and caste. So for me, of the traditions that have been inherited from the past, Buddhism—Mahāyāna Buddhism, in particular—is tops. It really is. But I find beautiful echoes in very simple religions like those of the Navaho and Hopi. I think one can receive very important instruction from these tribal religions which recognize the power as within the field of nature and the world, and ourselves. They don't set man apart.

I think one could say there are two main types of mythology. There are mythologies like that of the biblical tradition, which have to do with coordinating the individual into a group. He is a member of that group. He is baptized or circumcised or whatnot into that group. And that is his realm of compassion and sympathy; aggression he projects outside that group.

There's another kind of religion, which grows out of the emotional life of the natural order. We are nature beings, after all, not members of a society primarily. Such religions as the Dionysian religions of ancient Greece, and Hinduism, are full of this, and all the religions that have to do with meditation coming over here from the Orient.

Why is India so prominent in this regard?

Well, because yoga is the source of the Indian reading of the psychology of the unconscious. And the earliest evidences we have are some stamp seals from about 2000 B.C. from the Indus Valley period that show figures seated in yoga posture. So they've had four thousand years of inward exploration.

What is yoga?

The aim of yoga in India is to make the mind stand still. Our minds are spontaneously very active, in constant movement. It's as though a wind were blowing over the surface of a pond and activating all the water; the waves break up images so all you see are broken reflections that come and go. And so it is in our lives. All we see are broken images.

But if you can take the wind away (that's what the word *nirvāṇa* means: "de-spirated, blown out"—the wind is gone), the pond stands perfectly still.

Make the wind withdraw. Let the pond stand still, and you'll see the one image that was broken in all these reflections.

When the mind stands still, you see the one reflection, that Being of Beings of which *you* are a reflection. That is God. Do not identify your historical, physical body with that Being of Beings. Your body is but one of the reflections of that energy that informs the world and informs your life.

Now, in the world and in your life those energies are inflected in many ways: there's the energy that comes through your brain; there's the energy that comes through the breath of the lungs; there's the energy that comes through the sexual organs; and so forth. These have different deities, and so that One breaks up into Many. That's what's known as a pantheon. In this system, the five are regarded as the five elements, which in India are Ether (or space), Air, Fire, Water, and Earth. We are compounded of these.

In *kuṇḍalinī* yoga, the mind is stilled through what's called *prāṇāyāma*, or breath control.

I regard the seven *cakras* or *padmās* of the *kuṇḍalinī* system, centers located up the spine, as being great clues, actually, to help us to coordinate our own Western psychological studies with what the Orient has found. Furthermore, since the second millennium B.C. is middle Bronze Age, and right in the Bronze Age period there are motifs that appear in Europe and in China that suggest relationships to the later yogic traditions, particularly the *kuṇḍalinī* system of India, I think that what yoga has done in India has been to develop, refine, and enrich a psychological orientation that can be already identified in that early time in Europe and Asia.

Did other ancient cultures have this knowledge?

I *know* that the Egyptians knew all about this. There are enough clues in their art. And they had connections, too, with Indian ideas centuries before India had them. For example, I have a picture of that scene of the weighing of the heart against the feather that dates back to about 1400 B.C., in which the upright of the scale has exactly seven little swellings, corresponding to the seven *cakras*. And you know that hippopotamus-like animal that devours anyone whose heart is heavier than a feather? Well, the nose of that monster is sticking right between the third and fourth *cakras*—between the animal-nature *cakras*, the first three, and the fourth, at the level of the heart, of spiritual transformation—and that nose is pointing to a platform on which is sitting the baboon, Thoth, the symbol of Hermes, the guide of souls into immortality.

Another image which we have from India is of the five sheaths that enwrap the *ātman*. The outermost is the sheath of food. Next, the sheath of breath, which activates the food sheath, oxidizing it and bringing life. The next is the sheath of mind, which is attached to these first two sheaths. Then there is a deep break, followed by the sheath of wisdom—this is the wisdom of the body, the wisdom of nature, protoplasm, the body, and the cell, where the transcendent energy that shapes everything comes pouring into the world. And beneath that is the sheath of bliss. And then you look at the sarcophagus of Tutankhamen where there are three rectangular boxes enclosing the great sarcophagus, and the sarcophagus is of two sheaths: an outer

one of wood inlaid with gold and lapis lazuli and an inner one of pure
gold—the sheath of bliss.

How would you describe the resonance between yoga and contemporary psychology?

I think perhaps the opening of my chapter on psychology and yoga in
The Mythic Image states it best. Here, on page 278:

> There are three points of accord that make it possible to speak of
> modern depth psychologies in the same context with yoga. First,
> there is the idea that the fate of the individual is a function of his
> psychological disposition: he brings about those calamities that
> appear to befall him. Next, there is the idea that the figures of
> mythology and religion are not revelations from aloft, but of the
> psyche, projections of its fantasies: the gods and demons are within
> us. And finally, there is the knowledge that an individual's psycho-
> logical disposition can be transformed through controlled attention
> to his dreams and to what appear to be the accidents of his fate.

That really states my position in this matter.

"Controlled attention to his dreams"?

You can actually guide your dreams by consciously paying attention
to them. That means that you are guiding your life and shaping it into
some kind of relationship to the dream force, the force of what's operating right now in the heat of your volcanic insides. In the Hindu tradition, it is said that the forms of waking consciousness are past; they
have already come into being and are experienced as having come. But
the forms of dreams are *now*; they are actually the destiny sign of now.

There's a saying in one of the Upaniṣads: "We go every night to
that *brahman* world where the treasure is." It also says that as one can
walk over a buried treasure day after day and night after night, so do
we walk over that *brahman* world in our sleep without knowing it. We
come that close to illumination every night.

**You've observed that "dreams are personal myths, myths are public
dreams." Does an individual's dream life then mirror the mythology of
the culture-at-large?**

If one reads the accounts of dreams that have been published volu-
minously in psychiatric journals, one does not find that the images

contained in these dreams, images which represent the dynamics of
the human psyche, correspond in many cases to the images that these
people think about on Saturday and Sunday morning during formal
worship. If one's dreams actually corresponded to Christian images, as
they frequently did during the Middle Ages, then that would indicate
that the religion is really operating in one's life.

It is interesting to note that when people crack up entirely and go
into schizoid states of transformation and consciousness, the imagery
that comes up is frequently Hindu. This happens in people who have
never known anything about Hinduism or Buddhism. In the next to
last chapter of *The Politics of Experience*, R. D. Laing tells of a schizoid
crisis in the life of a very mature man. The man comes out by spontaneous remission and then gives an account of what has happened.
The imagery is entirely Hindu. The ultimate image is the Bodhisattva
image.

There then seems to be a disjunction between people's conception
of what the guiding mythology for their lives is and what that guiding
mythology actually is. One of the reasons for that is, of course, that
the imagery of the official, approved religious tradition is archaic. That
imagery comes from pastoral ages which belong to the first millennium B.C. These are hardly the images which are appropriate today.
Thus, while in a deep, idealistic sense the individual may believe that
he is operating on the basis of a religious tradition, that tradition cannot provide him with the life models he needs in a contemporary,
industrial world.

Sleep and dreaming then serve as metaphors for life itself?

One of the classic texts on sleep is the Māṇḍkya Upaniṣad, which
speaks of four stages of consciousness: waking consciousness; dream
consciousness; deep, dreamless sleep; and then the mystery of going
into deep, dreamless sleep *awake*—which is when one breaks through
the plane of darkness into undifferentiated consciousness.

Go into dreamless sleep *awake*?

Yes. That's the function of yoga. In fact, that's one of the monastic
disciplines, where you go to sleep pronouncing a mantra of waking knowledge—kind of a fishing line to carry you from waking to

transcendent consciousness. But the fact that the Buddha means "the one who has waked up" teaches the main lesson here.

The way in which the metaphor of sleep and waking is used relates to exactly that state. The Buddha has awakened to that undifferentiated consciousness. From that point of view, we who have not waked to that are asleep in our rational, normal, and even dreaming lives. That awakening is the great breakthrough.

Another image for this sleep-state that we are in is water. Jesus said to his apostles, "I will make you fishers of men"—pulling the normal fish-men out of the water of their sleep and bringing them to their potential, fully human consciousness. This is a motif from the Orphic tradition where Orpheus is the fisher who lifts us out of our fish-state and brings us to the light at the top of the water.

That's what it's all about. It's the same as the Manichaean idea that the Divine Light is enclosed in Darkness. We live in that double world of Darkness imprisoning the Light, and waking is breaking through and releasing the Light. You find the same idea in the Gospel According to Thomas, where Jesus says: "The Kingdom of Heaven is spread upon the earth and men do not see it." Wake up! It's here in front of your face! (*Bodhi*: "to wake, wake up." The Greek word corresponding to *bodhi* and Buddha is *gnosis*; Gnosticism and Buddhism are the same thing.) "The Kingdom of the Father is spread upon the earth and men do not see it"—*so see it!* That's *bodhi*; that's awakening; that's gnosis.

The role of the Buddha—or the Christ—is to wake up other people?

That's right!

But the Eastern traditions don't take their myths literally, at least not to the extent that happens in the West?

Hinduism and Buddhism recognize the common elements in myths. They understand mythology. But that is not true of the Western religions. There was a very interesting moment when the Dalai Lama came to New York several years ago. A reception for him was held at St. Patrick's Cathedral that was attended by rabbis, priests, the Eastern clergy, Protestant ministers, and so forth. And the Dalai Lama said that all religions represent different ways to achieve the expansion and universalization of consciousness. But then the late Cardinal Cooke got up and said: "We are different." And, indeed, we are.

The reference of the Eastern teaching is always inward psychologically, and not to discredited historical legends.

With respect to Oriental mythologies in general, the reference
has always been psychological. There is an historical echo, which is
not important. For instance, if one were to be told Gautama Buddha
never lived, it wouldn't matter a bit, would it? *It wouldn't matter a bit!*
The question is: what effect did those teachings have on you? Are they
awakening *you* to enlightenment?

But when a Christian is told there's doubt about certain things in
the life attributed to Jesus of Nazareth, he gets disturbed.

Now, the earliest redaction we have of the life of the Buddha is
from 80 B.C. The Buddha is supposed to have died about 483 B.C.
(563 to 483 B.C. are his dates). So there's four hundred years. Nobody
would, I think, really take too seriously the accuracy of any of these
events in the Buddha's life. Some of them are obviously fantastic. Well,
events in the life of Christ are fantastic, too. Jesus walked on water. The
Buddha walked on the water, too, five hundred years earlier (walking
on water and walking on fire are standard mythological motifs). For
one, it's important as a fact; for the other, it's important as an illustra-
tion of the spirit which does not sink in water.

If not the Buddha himself, what then is essential in Buddhism?

Well, there is a strong negative accent in the tradition at first. Take
the four noble truths of the Buddha: (1) All life is sorrowful—and it
is indeed. (2) There is escape from sorrow. What is the escape from
sorrow? (3) The escape from sorrow is *nirvāna*. Now, what is *nirvāna*?
That's what we've got to talk about; and then, how does one achieve
nirvāna? (4) Through following the eight-fold path: right views, right
aspirations, right speech, right conduct, right livelihood, and so forth.

The first trend in Buddhism was the monastic escape from the
world, to disengage oneself from desire and from fear. Those are
the two things that bind you to the world: desire for the goods of the
world and fearing that you will lose them. But the main sense of
the Buddha is that all these pairs of opposites are experienced within
the field of *māyā*. As long as you're seeing a distinction between bondage and freedom, between engagement in the world and disengagement, you are in the pair of opposites.

Around the beginning of the first century A.D., five hundred years
after the time of the Buddha, a new movement appeared known as

the Mahāyāna. About this time they speak of the image of the yonder shore: "We want to go from this shore of pain and sorrow, *saṃsāra*, the vortex of rebirth, to disengagement from it—the shore of *nirvāṇa*," as though that were the holy land, you know, someplace else. And they speak of a ferryboat that carries you to the yonder shore. That's the *yāna*: that word means "vehicle" or "ferry." *Mahāyāna* means "big ferryboat"; *hinayāna* means "little ferryboat." (The earlier Buddhism is called Hinayāna—it's the little ferryboat in which only monks and nuns can ride, those who have given up the world.)

But after you get to the yonder shore, the shore beyond the pairs of opposites, you realize that you were there all the time! And so, the realization of *nirvāṇa* is simply not going somewhere else, not killing your life, but shifting the commitment of consciousness from attachment to things to disengagement—and then the realization *tat tvam asi* ("you are that") and that you're there all the time.

Then there follows the positive statement represented in the figure of the Bodhisattva—the one who has found the eternal within himself and recognizes it in the world—and so they have that beautiful term: "Joyful participation in the sorrows of the world." You accept the sorrows for yourself and for the world, in the realization of what the radiance is that a well-lived life can bring forth out of this. It's *in* the very field of sorrow that the disengagement from life's sorrows, while participating in them voluntarily, is to be achieved.

The idea of Buddha consciousness is that all beings are Buddha beings, and your whole function in meditation and everything else is to find that Buddha consciousness within, and live out of that, instead of the interests of the eyes and ears. These can distract us from our own true, deepest being and purpose. The goal of meditation is to find that inside, and then let that take control.

Translate that into Christianity: that is, finding the Christ in you. It's exactly the same idea: here they call it Christ consciousness; there they call it Buddha consciousness. Well, the figures that represent the two ideas are quite in contrast in that the Buddhist imagery concentrates on the pacific aspect, on having found peace within and serenity, whereas the Christian, with Christ crucified, concentrates on the heroic attitude of living life—tearing you apart and finding the One within you in the midst of the turmoil of the world.

What the figure on a cross represents is the zeal of eternity to partake of the sufferings of time. According to the metaphor, Christ gave up the idea of God. Again, this is in Saint Paul, in Philippians: *And he*

came down and took the form of a servant, even to death on the cross. This
is a zealous yearning for participation in the sorrows of the world. You
have that in Buddhism in the idea of the Bodhisattva: joyful, willing
participation in the inevitable sorrows of life. Wherever there is time,
there is sorrow.

**What do the figures of Christ and the Buddha convey in mythological
terms?**

They are an invitation to life, you might say. They make it possible to
take the blows and know that there's a deeper, larger, more vital aspect
to your being than that of suffering bodies.

SYNTHESIS?

**You observed earlier that the primary focus in the Judeo-Christian tra-
dition has seemed to be more on ethics than spirituality.**

It certainly has—sin and the atonement of sin. That puts a screen
before us, and we can't penetrate through to the metaphysical, beyond
all the pairs of opposites—good and evil, male and female, action and
inaction, man and God. We're stuck with God in his heaven and Satan
in hell—the ultimate pair of opposites! Adam and Eve were thrown
out of the Garden when they ate the fruit of the knowledge of the
pairs of opposites.

I don't want to seem to be advertising the Orient over the Occident, because that's not my position, but in explaining this particular
difference I have made this stress: when you think of the Western attitude of worship, it's one of prayer and address outward—the hands are
clasped and one is addressing. But when you think of the Oriental, it's
the repose of the meditative yogi or sage. And that's the whole key. The
Oriental religions are essentially metaphysically oriented. They turn
inward to the ultimate mystery. But the Western religions, because of
this relationship situation, stress ethics more. They stress the temporal
and spatial relationship of person to person more. This is what underlies what we think of as progress—and there *has* been ethical progress.

Now, I must say, though, that throughout Western history there
has been this other line. It has simply been unorthodox, but it is

present. And there is no reason in the world why the very symbols of the Christian tradition cannot be read this way.

The Western line is based on the biblical tradition. Now, in the Bible, you have a Fall in the Garden of Eden. Adam and Eve gain the knowledge of good and evil and are then exiled from the Garden, and now there comes the problem of atonement with an offended Father. And we are not in Eden because of a sin for which we are *all* experiencing the punishment. That's the original sin idea.

No "Fall in the Garden" in Eastern traditions means no original sin?

In the East there has been no sin committed. There is, rather, the effect of our senses, which tend to attach us to the distracting separate entities of the world and remove our thoughts from our own inward unity with the divine will (or, you might say, with the dynamism of nature), so we become distracted. Also, we become careful about our personal existence; we are afraid of death, and we are desirous of life.

It's that very fear and desire that separate us from the innocence of childhood, where there isn't that fear and desire. And the notion there, is that by dispelling within ourselves this concentration on our own ego existence, we can put ourselves back in touch with that great source out of which we come and back to which we must go. This removal is the result, then, of our own psychological attitude. By a psychological transformation we can return, as it were, to the knowledge of the tree, whereas in the Western tradition it has to be through an atonement with an angry Father. They're two totally different attitudes, but the symbols are remarkably the same.

So, while Adam and Eve are booted out of the Garden, the Eastern position is essentially "Welcome to this Eden. Welcome to nature and knowledge."

Now, you have two problems when you are welcome. One is, are you going to let the world drop off? Are you going to give up the ways of the world? Are you going to stop defending yourself, defending what you love? Are you going to stop striving for achievement? If so, you become a monk and the world goes.

But if you're not going to become a monk, then you have to assert this other thing also. And this is a problem that our young people have not yet worked out. They're like that kid who heard that he was God and he's gonna let the elephant walk all over him, because he thinks that it won't hurt. Well, it will.

And the only decision to make is which road you're going to take: retreat from the world or engage in it. You can't take both of them.

In Judaism, Christianity, and Islam, the creator is apart and distinct from creation. Does this mean nature, the world of matter, does not partake in the divine?

I recall the amusing opening of a lecture that Daisetz T. Suzuki delivered at Eranos some years ago.[6] He stood there before the audience, with his hands on his hips leaning forward, and announced very slowly, and as though solemnly: "God against man. Man against God. God against Nature. Nature against God. Man against Nature. Nature against man. Very funny religion." He summed it up just like that. Where you have absolute final duality, you don't have the ultimate message.

This division begins with...?

The mistake of historicizing the mythic content in the Bible in the Judeo-Christian tradition.

The Bible talked about the childhood of the Hebrew race; all of its mythology was grounded in the pseudo-historical events of Israel. The main thing about the Jewish myth was that it had no trust in nature. Look at the Jewish festivals. They were the same festivals everybody else celebrates, but they were made to refer to pseudo-events in Jewish history. Passover was the resurrection of Adonis. Hanukkah was the birth of the Sun. When the Jews historicized these myths, they lost contact with the world of nature. The Bible is anti-nature; according to the Book of Genesis, nature is "fallen."

In Christianity and Judaism every spontaneous natural act is sinful unless it is either circumcised or baptized. That is quite in contrast to the Shintō idea that the processes of nature cannot be evil; they are good! Here you have religions in the Far East, and in China, and in India, that see nature as good, and the goal of the ritual is to put you in accord with nature.

But when you have a religion like that of the Near East, whether it's Zoroastrianism, Judaism, Christianity, or Islam, that sees nature as fallen, then your problem is to correct nature. *It is not!* Nature, the natural world, is a mixture of good and evil. This is why that Chinese image of the *Tao*, you know, the black and white in action, is exactly contrary to that of the position of the Judeo-Christian notion of nature. We identify ourselves with the light against the dark, and we are always correcting nature. *Nature religion* is a derogatory term for us.

The psychic counterpart of the world of nature is the collective unconscious. Let me translate: we share the same gods—we are informed by the same archetypes. The natural forces that animate us are common and divine.

This was the feeling in Europe before Christianity came in from the Eastern Mediterranean. The Greeks, the Germans, the Celts, the Romans, all these people—their shrines were in groves so that you could always be there with nature, whereas in the Old Testament, it's the grove that's being attacked. And when the kings of Judah and Israel would turn again to the shrines in the grove, they were disciplined.

This is the beginning of this split, this cutoff. It's a very technical and difficult question as to why these people in the Near East cut themselves off with what I call mythic dissociation, where the divine is outside and not in the very core of nature. This is a troublesome thing because most of us now don't have that feeling. And yet the religion is teaching us that feeling.

You have identified the Hero's Journey as perhaps the most common motif recurring across mythologies of all cultures. Who is the central hero in the Jewish mythological tradition?

What you have in Exodus is a constructed mythology that was built very late, post-Ezra, around the fifth century B.C. It indicates the Jewish idea of what's important about their society. In Genesis, you have Joseph and the patriarchs going into Egypt—a family. And what then comes out of Egypt? What comes out of Egypt is the people.

The chosen people—a collective hero?

The people turn out to be the big jewel found in the abyss of Egypt. Always in a myth if you see where we went down and where we start up, and seek what went down and what came up, you will see what the jewel is that was found in the abyss. The great jewel in this case is the people. That is the hero of the biblical tradition—the Jewish people.

Moses is simply the agent who brings about the release of the people. He did not get to the Holy Land himself. So you have the emergence: Joseph goes down through a well, through water, into Egypt; the people come up, through water (the Red Sea), out of Egypt. They pass through water again at the Jordan when they go into Canaan. This passage through water is a standard birth motif, and it certainly is associated with the birth crisis, the amniotic fluid, and all that.

But here it is used to tell a story, that a very important thing occurred for the history of humanity: namely that the Jewish people took shape in Egypt and were released from what was bondage but also from the place of generation.

After the diaspora, Jewish history loses its focus. It becomes a scatter. The attitude that I have learned from rabbis and other Jewish people I know is that Judaism is really a religion of exile—we are in exile, this is the exile outside the Garden (*fallen nature*). And there's a kind of melancholy associated with that.

The problem becomes, then, to hold the people together. The idea of the messiah in Judaism is that wonderful leader who will restore Israel. This *is* the messianic age for the Jews. It really is, in terms of their own tradition. And they *have* been restored, by the United States mostly, to their place among the nations.

Why didn't the Jews embrace Jesus as the messiah?

I don't know. I guess one reason was that he was really preaching Gnosticism. This comes out in the Thomas Gospel. The last thing that happens in it is that they ask him for signs and wonders, and Jesus says, "The kingdom of the father is spread upon the earth and men do not see it." That's sheer Gnosticism.

Do you believe that statement?

Yes.

If the chosen people are the primary hero in Judaism, who is the hero in India's mythological traditions?

I had a very interesting experience right along that line. When I was in India, I became associated for a while with a little avant-garde theater company in Bombay that called itself the Theater Unit. This was a company made up largely of non-Hindu Indians. The chap that was running it was of Arabian background, and his closest associate was an Indian Jew (there's an old-time Jewish community in India). Many of the people participating were Parsees—Zoroastrians whose ancestors fled from Persia to India. And what were they doing? They were performing *Oedipus the King*. They had their own clientele who were used to what they were doing. I saw them present this in front of their own audience in Bombay, and then a couple of months later I was in New Delhi, and they had just arrived and were going to perform *Oedipus Rex* for a totally Indian audience.

God, you couldn't believe it! There I sat—I had been in India long enough to participate in the audience's point of view—and the horror! Those people were utterly appalled. I've never seen such a wallop come across from the stage. They had never seen a Greek tragedy; they had never read a Greek tragedy; they knew nothing about the Greek tradition.

The emphasis in India is all for wiping out the person: he isn't there. In Sanskrit, there isn't even a word for "individual." The Indians aren't individuals: they're members of a caste; they're members of the family; they are in certain age groups; they are in certain moods—all of these general things. But here was this personal thing of the most violent and taboo-breaking sort! The audience was just knocked out.

You could see that it was an absolute violation of everything they ever thought should be put on the stage on every level, because there's no such thing as a tragedy in the Orient. How can you have a tragedy when you believe in reincarnation? The traditional Asian theater is a kind of fairy-tale theater: lovely nuances and playful situations, but nothing really serious. That which suffers in the Oriental tragedy is what ought to suffer anyhow, just this impersonable body. Let it get thrown away—who cares?

I remember years and years ago, when I was writing *The Hero with a Thousand Faces*, whenever I wanted an example of a failure, I looked to the Greeks. For the Greek heroes were the ones who suffered. The Oriental heroes are the ones who go cruising right through the myth.

The hero, the theme of emphasis in the Indian mythology, is not the person; it is the reincarnating Śiva, which puts on personas and puts them off. And the Greeks shift it to the person. (The Greeks were the first to realize that the human being is an entity.) In the Orient, the person who fails in the adventure is a clown, a fool. In the West, it is the human being.

So the hero in the contemporary Western world is the individual?

I would state again and again that, in the Orient, the individual as an individual does not have the importance to the culture as in the West. It seems to me the obvious concern in the Western world of the Hebrew and of the Christian for his fellow man, in a perfectly matter-of-fact way, stands out in radical contrast to the really appalling indifference in the Orient.

In the Orient, the path of salvation is to follow a way that already has been marked out by the guru. You go to a guru with perfect faith and no questions. He didn't question his guru, and so on. So, theoretically at least, the pure light of antique wisdom comes down unmodified by the creative impulses of the individual. Personality must be erased in order for truth to emerge. The goal of Oriental mysticism is to wipe out the ego. When you get rid of desire and yearning, what remains is nothing—*nirvāṇa*. And that is the goal of the East, not yearning and personality.

For instance, in the East you don't even have individual salvation; in the West you do. When Odysseus goes to the Underworld, he recognizes everybody there. When Dante goes to Hell, Purgatory, and Heaven, he recognizes everybody there.

But if you were to go into an Oriental hell, heaven, or purgatory, you wouldn't recognize anybody there because a soul throws off individuality. The Bhagavad Gītā, this great sacred book, says one puts on the body and puts it off as a man puts on and puts off clothing, whereas our whole emphasis is on that personality (which in the East is that to which one is indifferent). It's by putting off that individuality accent that one goes back to the Garden.

Nature is indifferent about individuals. I remember hearing a Buddhist monk swat a fly and say, "Come back in a more acceptable form."

And the person who dies and is coming back...well, if you've got only one life, it's a much more precious thing.

Is the Western approach then the best?

Well, on the other hand, when one does identify with the Self, one's life is invigorated. One acquires a new strength, a new courage in life. The phenomenality of one's life yields to the eternal power which is within one. It is a powerful, strengthening realization. One doesn't lose one's self by identifying with the All, at all.

In the West, we just have another accent, and I think it's one that must be cherished.

Though this accent on individual experience is part of the pagan European heritage—"Greeks, Germans, Celts, and Romans"—the prevailing religion today in the West is a graft from the Near East. What happens when that original individualist strain encounters Christianity?

Pelagius in the fourth century was either a Welshman or an Irishman, I think. He was a contemporary of Augustine who held the individualistic Western tradition against what I would call the tribalism of the East. The pope was in Rome, but he had very little to do with it. The councils were held in the East, and the poor pope played a small role there. It was the councils that decided on all the doctrines of the Christian church.

Such as...?

Well, one of the big questions was did Mary give birth to Jesus or to God? Did Jesus become a vehicle at the moment of baptism, or was he born as the Son of God? The decision was made at Ephesus, in A.D. 431, that Mary was the Mother of God. And then what was the relationship of the Father to the Son and the Son to the Holy Ghost, and all that kind of thing? That was all in the councils—the Council of Ephesus, the Council of Jerusalem, and so on.

There are records of these councils?

Yes—everything. Everything. This is all very tidily recorded. Go to the library and look up Migne.[7] You'll find about two hundred volumes of the Greek fathers, the Latin fathers, and the whole darned thing. It's fantastic! Migne was the man responsible for that enormous publication in Paris during the nineteenth century.

But Pelagius was a heretic, and he stated the main points against the doctrines of which Saint Augustine, his contemporary, was champion. One was the doctrine of original sin. Pelagius said you cannot inherit another's sin; therefore, Adam's sin is not inherited by anybody. Another thing Pelagius said is that you cannot be saved by another's act. That takes care of Jesus on the Cross and knocks the whole thing out. Of course, that was rejected.

Pelagius was defending a doctrine of individual responsibility. I don't know where it comes from, but certainly it was typical of European, as opposed to Eastern, points of view. You were an individual, not merely the member of a group.

How does one arrive, East and West, at these two different approaches to the transcendent?

There's an enormous difference between the training of an Oriental in childhood and the training of a Western person. The Western kid is asked, "What kind of ice cream do you want, chocolate or vanilla? Whom do you want to marry, this one or that one?"

The Oriental doesn't have any of this permissiveness with respect to the development of ego decisions. His ego is devaluated and wiped out from the start. He isn't—I mean, I'm speaking of a traditional Oriental—he's not asked what he wants to do. He is not asked to find his vocation. He's told what his vocation is and what he must do, when he must marry. He's never even seen the girl he marries. She's never seen him before. When the veil is removed, that's it. And there's no fighting against it. It's really a total system for canceling ego, whereas ours is for developing ego.

What happens when East comes West, as is happening today?

When these mythological images (which are in our tradition glued into historical events that never occurred) are presented again by the Oriental teacher as referring to the psyche, one finds there the connection with something that was built in when you were young—namely the symbol—and the flow of communication between conscious and unconscious domains is reestablished.

I've been interested in all these things for a long, long time. My first encounters were about 1923; I was in it myself for a while, then out of it, and then back in, and so forth. And I have many, many friends who have been involved in this.

When the Westerner puts himself through an Oriental meditation system, which is designed finally to smash an ego that's hardly there at all, and he brings his developed, enriched ego consciousness and world up against that, he keeps wondering what's the matter with him because his ego doesn't disappear. It's as though you were trying to break a boulder with a tack hammer, which will do very nicely for a glass jar. And so, a certain frustration comes along—only one is then alienated from one's own culture tradition and trying to be an Oriental, which one cannot be.

The way that's more congenial to us is one of bringing, little by little, the unconscious orders into play in our conscious world; that is to say, a slow integration through the course of life. And it can happen. I think you get a kind of illumination there that is typical of the Western mind, which is a different order from the Oriental.

I'm not saying one is better or worse, but they certainly are different. And you can't make dogs learn how to say "Meow," you know. It's another order. But I would define the great value of the Oriental instruction for us as this: the translation of mythological symbols into psychological references, restoring the symbolic content that the disintegration of our religious traditions has taken away from us.

We have read our own mythological symbols as historical references. Moses *did* go up the mountain and get the tablets of the Law from God, came down, broke them, went up, got a second edition, came back again. This is taken to be literally true. The Jews *did* go through the waters of the Red Sea, and after that they *did* go through the waters of the Jordan. Jesus *was* born of a virgin, *did* rise from the dead, *did* ascend to heaven. So here are these symbols, important symbols of revelation, of spiritual birth, of exaltation, all read as historical facts.

The same symbols come to us from the Orient, read however as having psychological reference, representing powers within the human spirit—within your spirit, my spirit—which are to be developed, and which can be evoked by contemplation and meditation on appropriate symbolic forms. The symbols then point to things that are in ourselves. This is what the Orient is telling us.

I feel that the symbols of the East are more flexible than those that we have inherited through our tradition and that consequently they can adapt themselves and be adapted to experiences in the present. What's most remarkable is the influence that these Oriental imageries and thoughts are having on contemporary Western minds.

This came as a stunning realization just at the end of the eighteenth and the beginning of the nineteenth centuries, when translations from Sanskrit began to come in. The whole Romantic movement in Europe was actually electrified by it, and the Transcendentalist movement in New England—Emerson, Thoreau, and those men—this struck them

as the word they had been seeking. And it's coming right strongly
through again.

**You're talking about Eastern philosophies and religions making inroads
today?**

The success of all the *rinpoches* and gurus and *roshis* that are over here
now speaks for this. And I think the influence is not only touching
young people who are searching for something that will have meaning
for themselves, but from my talks and visits with the clergy of various religions—and I do a lot of that now, since they're all interested
in these materials—I am aware of influences from the Orient in our
own orthodox traditions. I was invited to lecture a couple of months
ago at a seminary that trains people for the priesthood. The priest who
invited me to come said he was eager to have me come because my
books had introduced him to the inner life. And when I got there—I
remember Catholicism from, what was it, sixty years before when
I was a Catholic—these priests were something else again, studying
Zen techniques of meditation and so forth. So this impact is hitting
even dominant schools.

But then you go and take over also all their old archaic sociological problems. Doesn't fit. You dress like a Japanese or like a Hindu.
So you are deracinating yourself, uprooting yourself—you are not
reading the message in terms of your own condition, but are trying
to change your condition, and it just doesn't work. Or rather very,
very seldom does it work, and it works only in the most sophisticated
people—those who have absorbed the Oriental material thoroughly
and know where it meets them, where it doesn't meet them, and how
to move into it. If they want to continue practices in Buddhist mon-
asteries and that sort of thing; they know precisely its value to them.
But this is extremely rare.

Where would we look for this approach in our own world?

You can find it in mysticism and get in touch with mystics who read
these symbolic forms symbolically. Mystics are people who are not
theologians; theologians are people who interpret the vocabulary of
scripture as if it were referring to supernatural facts.

There are plenty of mystics in the Christian tradition, only we
don't hear much about them. But now and again you run into it.

Meister Eckhart is such a person. (Thomas Merton) had it. Dante had it. Dionysus the Areopagite had it. John of the Cross breaks through every now and again and then comes slopping back. He flashes back and forth.

I think Joyce is full of that symbolic marriage of the mystical and the phenomenal, the everyday. And Thomas Mann had it in his writing, though it isn't as far out as Joyce. It's strange how after Mann's death it disappears, and you don't get it anymore.

Schopenhauer brings this out beautifully. It's in Schopenhauer and Nietzsche and Goethe and that whole German romantic tradition that the coordination of the Occidental and the Oriental positions has been best achieved.

CHAPTER FOUR

"Yes All the Way!"

The Metaphysics of Myth

You are often identified as a Jungian.

I am not a Jungian. I am a Schopenhauerian.

Schopenhauerian?

Schopenhauer and Nietzsche are my people.

How so?

Well, it was Oswald Spengler who broke the ice for me and let me really get the excitement of history.[1] Spengler's *Decline of the West* wasn't about the downfall of Germany after the Great War.[2] It was a book of positive character. In terms of the Spenglerian cycle, we are in the period of the Carthaginian Wars and the rise of Rome. We have the whole Roman thing out in front of us. The Age of Caesars hasn't begun yet; it's coming.

Then he says everything he knows he learned from Nietzsche and Goethe. So you go to Nietzsche and you find you can't read Nietzsche until you read Schopenhauer. You go to Schopenhauer and find you can't read Schopenhauer until you've read Kant. Now you've got the whole German thing—and you've got the whole mythological thing.

The beginning of the situation, as I see it, is with Immanuel Kant's *Critique of Pure Reason*, where he points out that all experience is conditioned by the organs of experience. In his transcendental aesthetic, everything we experience is experienced in terms of time and space—and then, on *thinking* about it, is conditioned by the categories of thought. These involve *being* and *not-being, here* and *there, I* and *Thou*, and so forth. We are bound in this field.

The English position is basically the old one of the tabula rasa: there may be some sort of differentiation that comes in as a result of imperfect vision or something like that, but basically those things are out there, and just a step out there beyond them is God, who is considered a fact. One reason that Anglo-Saxons have more difficulty than Germans with mythology is that they never really got the message that Kant delivered: *all* of our experience is conditioned by the aesthetic forms of time and space. The mind is not a tabula rasa.

Around 1800, the first translations were coming in from India. Schopenhauer read the only translation thus far of the Upaniṣads (which was Duperron's Latin translation from a Persian translation from the Sanskrit—Duperron was a young Frenchman who joined the French army in order to go to India and fight the British; while there, he researched and brought out of India the first material we have of Zoroastrianism, and the early Upaniṣads).[3]

Schopenhauer was the first to recognize that the Indian idea of *māyā* is exactly the Kantian conditions. Time and space and causality are *māyā*, and it's in Schopenhauer's *World as Will and Idea* that the first coordination of the two principles takes place. Nietzsche builds right on that, takes a strongly affirmative aspect of the possibilities, and develops those in his thinking. It is right out of that that this coordination can take place in perfectly valid Western terms, but in Eastern terms as well.

What is it that aligns these Western philosophers with Eastern thought?

The realization of *tat tvam asi* ("you are that"). And you're there all the time! This is represented in the Bodhisattva ideal again epitomized in that beautiful phrase "Joyful participation in the sorrows of the world." It's in the very field of sorrows that the disengagement from them, while participating in them voluntarily, is achieved. This is truly positive, and this is Nietzsche.

Schopenhauer is more on the negative side of the disengagement, but he says himself that once you have canceled the commitment and engagement, then the whole world comes to life in a new way. This is the very end of his *World as Will and Idea*. It's a beautiful passage.

Nietzsche then picks up the Bodhisattva aspect and states it in a tremendously exciting way.

What does Schopenhauer mean by "the will"?

The dynamic of life. Energy. The energy of life.

Not the way it's popularly used today?

Oh, no. That's the eighteenth-century idea of will—intellectually determined. You make up your mind and you have "will power," the will power to do what you want. But then you find there's another will that overtips it. Now, this shift in the interpretation of the will took place just about Schopenhauer's time.

So interpreting the will as "willpower" is unnatural?

Well, it's secondary. It starts with the individual as a separate entity that has this head here that does all of this thinking. And the head says, "Well, it's important not to do some sin or other"—say, follow the girls—so he's got will power, and he's not going to commit that sin. But *the* Will, the other will, says, "Oh yes, that *is* the way you're going." So then he finds he hasn't any "will" left to do anything.

A number of people tend to say you shouldn't read Schopenhauer or Nietzsche or Spengler because the Nazis read them.

If you don't want to read things that people you don't like tend to read, and you know enough people you don't like, you don't read anything. That doesn't make any sense to me at all. It's like saying, "I shouldn't eat spaghetti because Mussolini ate spaghetti."

How does the German tradition address the divide between ethical religions and the Perennial Philosophy?

Well, in Nietzsche's *Thus Spake Zarathustra*—that's his great, great book—he says Zarathustra (Zoroaster) is the one who first formulated the idea of an absolute ethic: Good and Evil as absolutes, not as relative. He said that we've learned a lot from this ethical accent, but if Zoroaster were to come back today, he would say, "Okay, you've learned that lesson, now let's take the next one. *Beyond* good and evil is the mystical principle."

Morality is the local and contemporary, and the metaphysical vision is transcendent of that—the "elementary idea," rather than the "folk idea." This is the basic problem in religion: relating the ethical notion of good and evil, which is local, to the metaphysical view, which is beyond that, which is eternal. There is no such thing as absolute good and absolute evil. This is locally transformed in time and space, and then these two, good and evil, come together in our life.

We have to make decisions about good and evil in life, but in our metaphysical knowledge we must go past, to wisdom.

Now, Nietzsche says the idea of the good man is an inorganic idea. What you have done has been to cut man in half. *Every* act has both good and evil results. What's good for the tiger is bad for the antelope. But the antelope acquiesces in it. This is the idea of the old primitive hunters: this is the nature of life, and there is a covenant between the animal world and the human world. The animal gives itself as a willing victim with the understanding that a ritual will be proposed by which the life will be given back to its source; the animal will come back. With that you have a disregard of the finality of the physical. The physical is *not* final; it's the garment of something that lives past it, and the recognition and gratitude for that which transcends.

This is a theme that Wolfram von Eschenbach brings up in his Grail legend, *Parzival*. He starts out by saying every deed involves light and dark; all that can be done is to intend the light. But the dark will come out. And I think we have learned that: two world wars that were for one thing have yielded another, haven't they? We've been working for virtue and have achieved something else.

The acts of God are like acts of nature, indifferent to good and evil. Heraclitus is the one who said, "For God all things are good and right and just; but for man some are right and some are evil."[4] And so Nietzsche in his *Zarathustra* puts us back on the "beyond good and evil" stretch.

But if one's goal isn't triumphing over evil, what's the point? What does it mean to be "good"?

Nietzsche, in his *Genealogy of Morals*, speaks of the two ways of reading the word *virtue*. There is the earlier way of *virtù*: a virtuous lion is a lion who fulfills all the potentialities of lion-hood, such as tear a lamb in half. That's a virtuous lion. A good knife is a knife that cuts. This is analogous to the Indian idea of *dharma*—fulfilling one's destiny, one's duty. But with the ethical way of reading the word, we get simply a synonym for "good"; good versus evil is the way it's thought about, not "good versus no good."

One of the characteristics of Western thinking again, in contrast to the primitive and the Oriental (which I'm beginning to be more and more respectful of), is the notion that nature is to be corrected. It comes from the old biblical idea that nature is corrupt and man has been given dominance over the animals and nature and everything else, and there's going to be a reformation when we restore the good Day of Yahweh, and all will be grace and perfection again. This is sheer nonsense, but it's what's moving people.

The virtue manager is the real curse of the modern world, I think—the one who's got righteousness on his side and knows that everyone else is to be corrected.

What is the alternative?

The great health-giving and spiritually supporting attitude is that of yielding to nature, even in its ferocity and its terror. We think the ferocity and terror is evil. It isn't. It's part of the operation of what is natural. But there's a faith in nature that's involved here which we do not have in our biblical tradition, a faith that all things manifesting themselves in their perfection coordinate to a perfect manifestation in the world. There's a saying: the processes of nature cannot be evil. That's a dreadful thought, but realize what the processes of nature involve.

I saw a picture several years ago in an issue of *National Geographic* of three cheetahs eating a gazelle. The gazelle was still alive. They were at his belly, and the gazelle's head was lifted. And I said to myself, "Do we say yes to that?" We do.

The way you are talking about "saying yes" to it all—doesn't that risk condoning immorality?

Sure. That's what's tough about it; it's the essence of the problem. How long can you look at it? How deeply can you see? What can you take? Or are you going to play a little game: "Listen to the birds, aren't they just sweet? Don't look at the gazelle being eaten by three cheetahs."

You make your choice. If you want to be a moralist, go ahead. If you want to go love life, do—but know that life is nasty. And it *will* involve death. Sorrow is part of the world. That's not what you're to worry about; what is to be worried about is perfection, is fulfillment. The idea of Nietzsche's "superman" is the one who fulfills the potentialities of man. Not the one who is "the good man."

So we participate in life's violence?

No, you don't participate in it, but you can't condemn it; this is part of life.

It takes an awful lot of guts really to say "yes!" all the way. Do you have the energy and strength to face life? Life can ask more of you than you're willing to give. And then you say, "Life is something that should not have been. I'm not going to play the game. I'm going to meditate. I'm going to pull out."

Through life and lust one comes to know something. And then there are two ways of knowing it: one, simply in its sensational aspect, and the other in the way of the mystery that is speaking to you through these. It's the same mystery, birth and death, and this is the way life works.

Then there are two ways of participating. One is compulsively. The other, after you've got something of the experience, is to gain control of your dealing with life and death. It's a delicate walking on the edge. If you do too much to control life, you kill it. The other option is to let life move.

During the Middle Ages, the power of life was symbolized in the horse, and the power of the mind in the rider. So, in Wolfram von Eschenbach's *Parzival*, when Parzival seeks the Grail Castle, he lets the reins lie on the neck of the horse. He could not have guided the horse to the castle; the horse knew where it was and automatically led the way. You have to be guided by nature, not by this head up at the top.

There's something rather exhilarating about putting yourself on the side of life, instead of on the side of protective ideas. When all of these protective ideas about life that you've been holding break down, you realize what a horrific thing it is—and that *you* are it! This is the rapture of the Greek tragedy, what Aristotle calls catharsis. *Catharsis* is a ritual term. It is elimination of the ego perspective. Wiping out the ego system. Wiping out rational structuring. Smashing it and letting the life—*boom!*—come through. The Dionysian thing smashes the whole business. And so you are purged of your ego judgment system by which you're living all the time.

Is this what Nietzsche is addressing when he speaks of the interplay between the Apollonian and Dionysian traditions in Greek culture?

Apollo is the lord of the individuated forms in the light world: the charm and delight in the individuated form. Dionysus is the lord of the passage of time, which shatters forms while bringing forth new ones: the explosion! And the two operate in life. What Nietzsche says is you must recognize the Dionysian in life. You don't have any dynamic, you don't have any energy, unless the Dionysian is there, along with the Apollonian recognition of the individual, and this kind of double optic of seeing the two, recognizing the two, and affirming the ambiguity.

And that's the point, *not* saying "no" to it.

Nietzsche is celebrating the ability to bring the two together.

And to have the balance. He opposes that to some of the Oriental ideas where the Apollonian principle does not dominate and you have too much accent on the Dionysian, on the joy and rapture simply in shattering and destruction—what might be called the revolutionary principle: pleasure in destruction without any idea of what it's going to lead to, just destruction.

What is your key takeaway from Schopenhauer and Nietzsche?

You are not the phenomenal historical character; that is simply the vehicle of what you truly are. You are that consciousness that informs all things.

There are two orders of truth. There's the phenomenal order of the facts, and relating to those is the problem of prudence and fortunate living. But what you experience in the way of interpreting these in relationship to yourself and who you are and what am I, this is the aim and intention and accent of the discipline. The prime question is, "Who am I? Am I this phenomenal body which is the vehicle of consciousness, or am I consciousness?"

And when you realize "I am consciousness," then you are one with the consciousness that's in everybody else.

Nietzsche, then, helps unlock symbolic thought?

"Everything transient is but a reference," wrote Goethe, to which Nietzsche added, "Everything eternal is but a reference also."

MYTHIC MOTIFS IN LITERATURE

Where do these ideas go from there?

I think Nietzsche's most important influence in literature is in Thomas Mann. In *The Magic Mountain*—the key novel of Thomas Mann—there is a scene of the hero, Hans Castorp, trying to solve this problem of good and evil in the world. He goes out skiing, becomes very tired, falls asleep out there in the snow, and has a dream—a dream of the world of the Greeks and how noble and beautiful it was. Then he senses someone looking over his own shoulder, and he turns and sees a hag tearing apart a child. The Apollonian light and the Dionysian shadow. And Castorp says it is the knowledge of this abyssal aspect of life that makes necessary the decorum and beauty and decency of civilization. You have to affirm both sides but put your accent over on the side of the light.

I was teaching Mann in school, and it occurred to me I had read that before somewhere. So I turned to Nietzsche's *Birth of Tragedy*, and there it is, the very last paragraph, exactly the same image.

Now, I had a friend who knew Thomas Mann very well, and I spoke to her about this. I asked, "Did Mann realize what he did there? That he was simply quoting Nietzsche years and years after his own realized experience of Nietzsche in his youth?"

And she said, "Well, I'll ask Tommy next time I see him."

I have a letter that she wrote to me; she said, "I brought it up, and it was as though I had hit him in the solar plexus." He had *not* realized that. This is how important this image has been in the work of Thomas Mann.

Could that have been coincidence? Or perhaps, in Jungian terms, parallelism—a spontaneous separate upwelling of material from the unconscious psyche?

No, it's not parallelism. This is what's known as cryptomnesia. This occurs in literature occasionally, but this is the most dramatic example I know of—the culminating realizations in Mann's book, which he thought he had come to himself, he had already learned from Nietzsche when he was a young man. Of course, they were both soaked in German romantic philosophy, but Mann has an enormous literature of essays in which he writes about himself and what's moving his works, what brings them about; Nietzsche plays an enormous role—and here it was, in this novel.

James Joyce's *Ulysses* came out two years earlier—these two books, *Ulysses* and *The Magic Mountain*, were written during the First World War. These were the first books where a mythological underground is supporting what is apparently a naturalistic novel. The name Magic Mountain indicates a mythic base (the magic mountain is the *mons Veneris*, the Venus mountain, the mountain into which one goes beyond the realm of time). And the name Ulysses also indicates a mythic base; there's nothing about Ulysses in the book at all.

I found great personal guidance in Joyce and Mann, particularly those two books, *Ulysses* and *The Magic Mountain*; in their sheer mythological ground they showed how these mythic images actually function in a young man's life today.

Was Mann aware of what Joyce was doing?

When I completed *A Skeleton Key to Finnegans Wake*, I gave a copy to Mrs. Eugene Meyer, and she sent a copy to Thomas Mann. Thomas Mann then wrote her a letter, and that letter is published in the collected letters of Thomas Mann, of which I have a copy. Of course, when I see a thing like that, I look up my own name in the index, and I find that there is a letter about me.

So I'm reading this letter to Mrs. Eugene (Agnes) Meyer that says, "Thank you for sending me Joseph Campbell's book. I appreciate having it very much because I could not possibly, myself, read *Finnegans Wake*. But, reading this book, I am confirmed in the suspicion that I have had for some years, namely that James Joyce was the greatest novelist of the twentieth century."

This is from Thomas Mann. It's there in print. And that's big on his part. That's really big.

You might say this great work, *Finnegans Wake*, is for me a modern Bible. Would you like to hear an epiphany I had about Joyce's theme?

Of course!

There's a number that runs all the way through *Finnegans Wake*: 1132. It appears as a patent number; it appears as an address—32 West 11th

Street; it appears as the number of people in a room; it appears as a date, and so forth and so on, all over the place.

Years ago, when I was working on *A Skeleton Key to Finnegans Wake*, I tried to interpret this. In *Ulysses*, Leopold Bloom is wandering around the street and frequently he thinks, "The law of falling bodies"—you know that one, "32 feet per second per second."[5] So 32 would be the number of the Fall. Well, that seems fair enough. Eleven, then, appears in *Ulysses* in the terms of Leopold's little boy, who died when he was eleven days old, and Stephen Daedalus is twenty-two (11 plus 11 is 22, and so Stephen signifies for Leopold the return of the boy). Also, the decade runs out—1 2 3 4 5 6 7 8 9 10; 11 then renews the decade. Eleven, then, is the number of the Redemption. So it just seemed to me that Fall and Redemption was what that meant.

Well, some years later I'm preparing a lesson for my students at Sarah Lawrence in comparative mythology, a class on early Christianity—the rise of Christianity and the Christian myth—and I'm freshening up by reading the epistles of Paul, when I came across a sentence in the Epistle to the Romans that just hit me in the eye: "For God has consigned all men to disobedience that he may show his mercy to all."

This seemed to me to catch the whole sense of the irony of *Finnegans Wake*: God has committed us all to disobedience so that he can show mercy—and, as Joyce would put it, be as disobedient as you possibly can and let him unload the whole load of his mercy! There is no reach beyond the reach of God's mercy.

In *Finnegans Wake*, you can't think of a crime, of a nastiness, of a sordidness that isn't there in his hero—but Joyce is always merciful toward him. The reach of your mercy is the reach of your life, and the reach of your art. As soon as an artist starts criticizing life, he puts himself above what is, and is giving us a didactic work.

Anyhow, "For God has consigned all men to disobedience so that he may show his mercy to all"—*Romans 11:32*! I don't think anyone else bumped into it; I think this is my little revelation. I then looked back—when I was working on *Finnegans Wake* I had made a kind of concordance of things—and in my concordance for 1132, within three lines of one of the very important 1132s I find the syllable ROM. This was absolutely intentional; there's no doubt about it.

Imagine the experience I had when I copied that scripture, and then wrote chapter 11 verse 32! Chapter and verse!

So we are to embrace life in all its agony and cut out all analysis?

No, I'm not cutting it out. Mann isn't cutting it out. He says you must analyze; it's the function of the artist to do that. To select the mot juste, the correct word, that takes analysis. But with it goes affirmation of that which is negated by that word. And that is Mann's plastic irony.

What do you mean by "plastic"?

Plastic means it's not flat. There's light and shade and play between the two. That's plastic—it's not flat. There are two eyes operating. Strindberg said, "All politicians are one-eyed cats"—they see it this way, or they see it that way—but the artist takes a "double optic" approach, where he sees things in perspective.

That's the best I can do on that. Art is ironic, in the sense Mann is talking about it.

Was Thomas Mann as "plastic" in person as in his writing?

This comes out in *Death in Venice*, which is about himself, really. It's about an author, named Aschenbach; people said, "He was always like this, never like this." Mann had a lot of that in him.

I had the pleasure of meeting him three times and being with him rather a long period at one of those meetings. He was a man in form, and he was very formal in his manner. But it was with ease. It's like writing sonnets, or the Japanese tea ceremony: you have to know the form and so master the form that you can be at ease in it. This is an important point in art; you don't have an artist who doesn't have a technique.

Mann knew what he was doing—his work is a perfect translation of the hero quest into a modern context. Aschenbach was one who just followed the first step of the Hero's Journey. There are three steps. One is leaving the flat land; the next is experiencing initiation, which may involve an encounter with death. The third is coming back and addressing the life of the flat land with new insight.

Now with Aschenbach, he's simply bringing him into death. In Mann's early stories, it was all about leaving and going. And *Death in Venice* is the culmination of that. The leaving and the going. Then, with *The Magic Mountain*, you have Hans Castorp coming back after he has undergone the whole psychological transformation of the relationship to life and lust, ready to affirm life at its worst—but he comes back into the war, which is the field of death still, as life is death. The book ends with him in the trenches voluntarily. Then Mann carries that over into the Joseph novels to see how, through mythology, that works out.

I remember reading Mann as he was writing these books. It was fascinating to see how his whole dimension of consciousness would change from one to the other. The next book came out and, gosh, that would be something entirely fresh.

Mann's four Joseph novels aren't just a dressing-up of old Bible stories?[6]

They are conditioned to a culture so far from ours, but the great advantage of the biblical story is that these are the images that have been put into us even in infancy. To read them now, not as something that happened out there but as something that's going to happen to you, and *is* happening to you, that's translating this material into spiritual food—something that really carries you along. That's why I think it's so exciting what Mann has done, to take our tradition and then read it in this way. Jacob and Esau and all come to life in a new way inside us, as aspects of our own energy systems.

I think his climax is in the second volume of the Joseph novels: *Young Joseph*—that's a terrific book.

The second volume? Why not the last?

That's another phase of Thomas Mann. It's a total transformation. That's after Hitler and his own self-exile from Germany—total disillusionment and grief and a political awakening.

How did that manifest?

Mann's work on the Joseph novels starts in the early 1930s—that's when Hitler came in—and they weren't finished until the mid-1940s. It's a long season, and those were pretty bad years. Mann had left Germany and was in Switzerland giving lectures when his son and daughter, Klaus and Erika, advised him very strongly not to go back to Germany. That's when he began his political writing.

Now, he'd never done anything like that before; when an artist or literary man begins to move into the political sphere, he's in danger (just think what happened to Ezra Pound). His property in Germany was confiscated by Hitler, so Thomas Mann came to America, and he starts flinging bombs across the lines into Germany. He gave one talk over the radio in which he excoriated Hitler and the Nazis.

This was a very interesting and strange thing to happen to him. That was the time I knew him. He had become completely political, and he was writing papers about "The Coming Victory of Democracy" and so forth, urging the United States into the war.

Are you saying it wasn't proper for Mann to take a political stance?

Oh, no—it was proper for him. I'm not saying it was improper; as a man it was proper, but as a novelist it was dangerous stuff to lose your balance that way. After all that time he was spending writing propaganda, when he came out of this, he found that he could not get back to the Joseph novels; he couldn't do the fourth volume. In the interval he wrote two other books—*The Beloved Returns* and *The Transposed Heads*—and then he went back to the final volume of the Joseph novels.

By that time, everything was gone. He had lost all the strings—all the mythological strings. The wonderful things that were in movement had just vanished, and I found it the dullest, heaviest reading. It was simply the story of a young man who had gone into Egypt and made his way to become psychoanalyst to the pharaoh, and who was in a position of prestige as a result of his skills, and then his family comes down to Egypt for welfare and gets it from him.

I don't think he ever recovered; the negative feelings that he had for the Germany that had come out and shown itself under Hitler destroyed that delightful plastic irony and the compassion motif which was so important in his earlier works. So when he got to the later big novel that meant so much to him, *Doktor Faustus*, I couldn't finish it. I read about two-thirds of it and then I thought, "Why am I putting myself through this?"

Everything that was in those early and middle works, all the irony and play, had gone. Now there was judgment, there was condemnation, there was despising, and so what?

That was my feeling.

Didn't you find anything of value in that final volume, *Joseph the Provider*?

Oh, yes, sure. There was a playful interpersonal dynamic between Joseph and the pharaoh. Mann could handle it, but it was terribly low-key after what we had in *Young Joseph* and in *Joseph in Egypt*. Even the style had lost its tension.

Are Mann and Joyce unique in their introduction of mythic themes?

It's at that time in literature that myth begins to come in, just as it begins to come into visual art in the 1930s out of the surrealist movement. There was a wonderful magazine published in Switzerland by Skira called *Minotaure*.[7] Skira invited Picasso, Matisse, Dalí, and several others to paint pictures for the cover of the magazine in its different issues. And just at that time, they all began to work on the mythological that underlies the psychological; first you had the psychological interest in surrealism, and then the opening to myth. And this opening in the 1930s took place thirty years after it had opened to Jung.

When we're talking about artists like Mann and Joyce and Picasso, you're in a field of deep problems. Why should these men have given their whole lives to working on problems like this if they weren't of life-shattering depth? This is the problem of the relationship of life to art. Is it a killer of life, or is it a fosterer of life? It's a fosterer.

THE PSYCHOLOGY OF MYTH

Why does so much of your work focus on the significance of mythological symbols to an individual's psychology?

When I was teaching at Sarah Lawrence, it was precisely this aspect of mythology that the women in my classes made me think about. I believe that women have a far more intuitive grasp of what operates as life, in life, than men. When men arrived at Sarah Lawrence, I noticed that they were interested in the same historical concerns that had occupied me for so many years. It was the women who forced me to stay on the psychological beam. *The Hero with a Thousand Faces* came right out of my experience with them.

I certainly know that the reason my books are read has something to do with the fact that they are concerned with the matter of the psychological import of mythological symbols. That message can be seen as something to be regarded, to be responded to, to be open to, and to accept as a guide to enlarged spiritual horizons.

Psychology as a gateway to spirituality?

Spiritual is a kind of fuzzy word; it can get to be even silly—but I would say what gives it its majesty is the recognition of really potent powers within us, which speak through the signs and symbols of our dreams, our visions, and, if we are in a fortunate mythological context, through the myths of our people, to our functioning ego system.

How would you define spirituality, as opposed to religion?

I would say spirituality is the recognition of the commonality of humanity in the various inflections of our lives throughout history and the sense of participation and, above all, compassion for one's fellows. This fellowship may extend to the world of the birds, and bees, and nature itself. One is then to know oneself as functioning in this field, in a way of self-interest, this self-interest itself comprising the interest of the whole community.

The psychologists' problem is to ask, Why do we keep having the same emergent archetypal elementary ideas? Their base is below the level of conscious intention and interpretation.

Are these elementary ideas a manifestation of the structure of the unconscious existing outside the field of time, or do they develop in a dialectic with the culture and historical events?

That's a beautiful question. The elementary ideas are grounded in the psyche. My approach to these has been from the point of view of psychology in studying them. The most helpful psychology in relation to this problem is that of Carl Jung. He picks up Bastian's *Elementargedanken* ("elementary ideas") and calls them the "archetypes of the unconscious." So your initial characterization is the correct one in my view.

Now, the dialectic with society is what shows in the folk idea (*Völkergedanke*). In relationship to the environment, in relationship to the specific industrial or technical character of the culture, in relationship to its concepts of the cosmos—all of this is the mirror that then reflects the projected archetypes. The archetypes are, as it were, included and encompassed by the elementary ideas so that an individual participating in the rituals of his culture, which engage him in that culture, is at the same time being introduced to and engaging the archetypes.

theme of everlasting life as being part of you, —inside of you

Eventually, there comes a time when the culture disengages him, and then the shell of the idea drops off and the elementary core guides him back to his own psyche. That's the story: the first half of life moving into the historical field by way of the folk mask and relating to it in your way; and the second half, led by the archetypes, of moving back into your own realization of the life-that-is-everlasting actually being *your* life, and *your* identification with eternity (which is what you are a little particle of).

When a society is in transition, is it the elementary ideas or the folk ideas that have to change?

The elementary ideas do not change. The problem is not to lose touch with them. When the folk ideas, which relate to a certain social order and structure, are no longer functioning because another structure has come along, we are in psychological disarray.

This is one of the problems today. And these days the social system and social ideals and even the physical environment are changing so fast that there is no opportunity for the crystallization into a tradition to develop. Just in my own lifetime I can't believe the transformation—not only physically, but also transformations in terms of ethics and how people are expected to behave—it's prodigious.

Where do the ideas that supply a culture's myths originate?

Where does the imagination come from that creates the myths? It comes from the depths of the psyche. And so in India these same two aspects of the mythological forms are recognized. The folk aspect, the simple popular aspect, is called the *deśī*. This means provincial, local, popular. And the word then for the elementary idea is a very interesting one—*mārga*. *Mārga* means path. It comes from the root *mṛg*, which has to do with hunting—following the trail of an animal—and so in following the elementary ideas and recognizing in their mythic forms messages of the psyche, one is following the path of the animal that left those tracks, and the animal that left those tracks is the human psyche—what Jung calls the collective unconscious.[8]

Which brings us back to the Jungian approach as your point of departure.

Well, it wasn't my point of departure. It was a point of discovery along the way.

When I was a student in Germany in the late twenties, I discovered the great world of psychological scholarship in this subject, and this helped me to appreciate the psychological grounding of myths. Freud, Jung, Dilthey, and many others connected with the psychological interpretation of cultural and mythological materials. For a while I was equally committed to Freud and Jung as the principal explicators of myth in psychological terms, but during the years the Jungian position has seemed to me to be more and more important.

Why not Freud?

Freud was important for me for a while. But I don't think he is a good guide to mythology. He shows the way mythology becomes pathological. For instance, when a person is hysterical or neurotic, he reads mythological symbols only in terms of his limited personal fix. Freud's basic mistake was in trying to extend the situation of the infantile crisis and family romance to provide an interpretation of the totality of culture. The basic myths that have supported historical cultures do not represent a regression of the race to childhood patterns; they are an aid in opening the human spirit to infinite domains of possibility and fulfillment.

Freud made the same mistake of historicizing myth that was made in the Bible in the Judeo-Christian tradition. The Bible talked about the childhood of the Hebrew race; all of its mythology was grounded in the pseudo-historical events of Israel. In the same way, Freud found the formative principles of personality in the pseudo-events of childhood—in the Oedipal drama—and later in his theory of the primal horde. He projected this pattern onto society as a whole.

Freud's suspicion of the instinctual forces of the id, and his assumption that they must be shaped and controlled by the ego, was a reflection of the animosity between Yahweh and the goddesses of nature. Everyone in the Freudian tradition—and this includes existentialists like Sartre—is afraid of nature. To them, nature is absurd. It causes nausea.

How would you distinguish between Freud's and Jung's psychology?

The Freudian approach sees the phenomena of the unconscious mainly as residual of early infant experiences and early life experiences. That is to say, they are biographically based, whereas for Jung they are

biologically based. He sees two levels of dream: one on what he calls
the personal level, where the personal concerns and personal experiences predominate as the motivating factors; and another where one
breaks through to transpersonal systems—here mythological forms
emerge that cannot be interpreted in the biographical way.

Furthermore, Freud sees mythology really as symptomatic of neurosis, while Jung sees it as complementary to the psychology of the
individual, opening to larger areas and depth of experience than those
of one's ego-oriented consciousness. His work, consequently, included
Freud, but did not stay with him.

**So the student surpassed the master, at least as far as psychology's
relationship to myth is concerned.**

No. There's been a radical misrepresentation of Jung's relationship to
Freud in that he was never Freud's student. Never! He was already
a recognized practicing psychiatrist at the Burghölzli sanitarium in
Zurich when Freud's first book, *The Interpretation of Dreams*, was published in 1900.

**Could you help untangle the complex relationship between Freud and
Jung?**

Jung was a younger man than Freud. He was the first psychologist of
any repute. Jung's first paper on occult phenomena, "The Psychology
of So-Called Occult Phenomena," dealt with all the work that had
been done up to that time on such mysteries as automatic writing,
somnambulism, and trance states and so forth. He started this as a
result of his own interest in a case of trance table tapping and séances
that he had studied for some two or three years.

After Jung had started his psychology of word association (it was
he who realized the importance of the timing of the word association
tests—delays in association and so forth), it was in working on all that
that he read Freud's *The Interpretation of Dreams*.

Jung's main teacher was Bleuler, the man who invented the word
schizophrenia. In that sanitarium there were schizophrenics with
whom Bleuler and Jung were working. Freud's principal concern was
neurotics. Now, there's a difference. The psychotic is way down there
in that realm of the collective unconscious (biology). The neurotic is
in the realm of the personal unconscious (biography).

In one of Jung's papers, he did something that nobody else dared do at that time. Freud was persona non grata and one could lose one's reputation even by mentioning his name—and Jung came out in Freud's defense. He was the first to write favorably of Freud.

Did Jung become a disciple of Freud?

Jung made a statement right in that first paper of what he regarded as Freud's great contribution and also what he could not accept. He could not accept Freud's pansexual theory as though that were the beginning and end of the story.

What he thought was great was Freud's theory of repression, the mechanism of repression. Jung had already discovered the repression problem, but he gave praise to the mechanism of repression which Freud brought forth. And then Freud invites him to Vienna, and those two men talked for thirteen hours without stopping. Now, who told whom what? We know that the word *complex* is from Jung; the words *introversion* and *extroversion* are from Jung; and so forth and so on.

Freud immediately saw that here was someone with whom he wanted to work. He required the gentlemen of his International Psychoanalytic Society, which had just been founded, to make Jung their permanent president, and Jung was establishing centers in France and Germany and so forth. Now, that's *not* your student! Anyone who has read that marvelous book of the letters of Freud and Jung that was brought out by Princeton University Press can see these two men were joined together, and Jung was the leader, by Freud's choice, of Freud's society.

The roots of their eventual split existed from the beginning?

Freud was an older man than Jung, I guess about sixteen or seventeen years older; he said to the younger man, "You are my anointed power." And it was then that Jung asked him, "Well, what do you think about the problems of the occult?"

And Freud said, "Baloney!"

You know this story? The fantastic thing is that Jung, respecting Freud, did not want to say what he wanted to say. He felt heat building up in his diaphragm, and there was an explosion in the bookshelf. And Jung says, "You have just been witness to a projected catatonic, catalytic phenomenon."

Freud says, "Bosh!"

And Jung says, "It's going to happen again." And it did. And there's a letter from Freud to Jung trying to explain that thing in purely mechanical terms.

Well, then the breaks began to come. They came to America together in the same stateroom, reading each other's dreams, to collect their honorary degrees in 1909. And after that, Freud fainted twice in Jung's presence, whenever it looked as though Jung was psychologically going to supplant him some way or other (he had his Oedipus complex in mind). Oh, they are fantastic stories!

The real break came, however, when Jung wrote his *Wandlungen und Symbole der Libido*, this book on transformations of consciousness which has been translated as *Symbols of Transformation*. That big work was the thing that opened the world to me when I read it years and years ago in German. There he points out that the dream life of the individual is the counterpart of the symbol and myth life of the culture. *The myth is the public dream, and the dream is the individual myth.* And Jung showed how you can amplify your dreams to open out the personal into transpersonal fields of reference and so put yourself in touch through your own life with the great norms of human experience and ride on them instead of be tortured by them.

When that work came out, Freud read it and found it was not Freudian, and he no longer would have anything to do with Jung. It was Freud who broke off; he broke off with everybody—Otto Rank, Adler, anybody who had a different idea was out as far as Freud was concerned. But the rancor with respect to Jung was particularly sharp because he had put such faith, such hope in Jung as the one who would be the carrier of *his* ideas. And so they split socially and in terms of the organization.

Then what happened was an obscenity, really. The whole Freudian crowd, of whom Jung had been the president, turns against him, calls him a neurotic, says that he is a danger, and all these things. They even went on into the Second World War period calling him a Nazi when he was *not* a Nazi.

Jung did have contact with the Nazis.

Jung's correspondence with the Germans, at that time, was in order to keep the German section of the psychoanalytical society going so that the Jewish psychoanalysts in Germany could have an international backing behind them. To do that he had to write to Göring's cousin, who was the head of that department.⁹ Jung was not a Nazi; he was not a lunatic or anything. I know a little bit about this experience of this total isolation from your colleagues who then turn against you with nasty remarks; it's not an easy thing to handle. This is what is called his psychological crack-up. This was thrown at him. He swallowed that and was able to survive. Any injury, any brutality that you are able to survive makes you bigger than you were, and this is what Jung went through. This was a magnificent man; I met him. It really is a dirty story, and people just don't want to write about it.

So when Jung speaks of the racial unconscious, he's not making a case for Aryan superiority?

That has nothing to do with what we normally think of as race. I think Jung suffered considerably from a misinterpretation of that word and was regarded as a racist, which he simply is not. The race that he's talking about is the *human race*, the collective unconscious or the general unconscious which we share. You can recognize a human being anywhere; the psyche that goes along with that physique is what is the ground for the collective unconscious.

Given your understanding of the split between the two men, Jung is the one who was correct?

No, this doesn't say that Freud's wrong, doesn't say that Jung's right. These are two totally different ways of reading these thrusts of the psyche. In my thinking, I see Freud as tremendously important for letting us know how a psychologically disturbed person understands mythological symbols, reading them down into personal references. And I see Jung as the one who tells us how to open out these personal references to the transpersonal sphere, which from my point of view is proper to the study of myth.

Now, my own field that I've worked on all my life has been mythology, not psychology. When I look for the psychologist to interpret myths, I don't find the Freudians interpret them the way they look to me to function in their cultural context. To reduce all of the glory of art and the philosophy of the ages to sublimations of a child's fear of his father and desire for his mother seems to me absurd to such a degree that no one would accept it if he didn't think, "Well, this man Freud would not have proposed it if it weren't true."

After I wrote *The Hero with a Thousand Faces*, which is a time when I was balancing between the two, I spent time working on a Freud paper, and then a Jung paper, and then a Freud paper, and then a Jung paper, trying to get the real point of the break-off and difference. At the time of doing *The Hero*, I was giving Freud more than I would give him now and Jung less than I would give him now. But the book appealed to both schools. So I have many Freudian associations and many Jungian associations.

What finally made me tired of the Freudians was they would always send me their offprints, papers based on something they had done in connection with mythology. Well, they'd take a myth or a folktale way up here, and I'd read the tale and say to myself, "Now I wonder how he's going to get that back to the Oedipus complex?" And after a long, devious to-do, he'd show that here was the little boy wanting his mother and afraid of being castrated by his father, one time after another.

Not everything can be reduced to Freud's sexual theory?

When you go out in our foyer, you'll see a Tibetan *tanka* hanging.[10] It is of one of the great Bodhisattvas of the Bardo Thödol, the so-called Tibetan Book of the Dead, embracing his consort in one of these horrendous dance postures. Well, since everything refers to sexual intercourse according to Freud, what does sexual intercourse refer to in a picture?

There's a wonderful story that I love of a man who was troubled by a dream. He comes and gets in touch with a psychiatrist and says, "Now, I've got a lot of money and very little time. I want to tell you my dream. You tell me what it means. And that's that. I just want to be quit of this recurrent dream."

And the doctor says, "Well, I don't do that kind of thing that way, but I have a friend who does. So you go to him, and he'll do it."

Here's the dream: "I'm in a boat on a lake, a rowboat. And I begin to feel that a storm is coming. I look around to see where I can go for refuge. There's a nice little wooded cove on the shore, so I start going for that. The closer I get to it, the stronger the storm. The storm becomes more and more tempestuous. Finally, it breaks my oars and I'm unable to reach the cove."

"Well," says the second doctor, "now that's a very simple story. You have, of course, a mother complex. You want to have intercourse with your mother. And the cove is the mother that you want to reach. And you're afraid of your father's wrath. So the father is the storm. And finally, you're castrated. You're impotent when you lose your oars."

"All right," says the man. "Here's my money."

A couple of months later he meets the first doctor. And the doctor says, "Did you see Doctor So-and-So? And was it all fine?"

"Yes."

"You're not troubled by that dream anymore?"

"No," says the man. "Now I have a totally different dream. I dream that my mother's in the kitchen. I want to rape my mother. I go in, and down the stairs comes my father roaring, picks up a carving knife and castrates me."

"Well," says the doctor, "that's a rather disturbing dream. I should think you'd have a bad time."

"No," the man says, "I know what it means. It means I'm in a rowboat in the middle of a lake. And I want to get to shore."

This is the problem: you can read the symbols in only one direction. That's what I'm afraid the Freudians do.

JUNG ON MYTH

How does Jung's psychology relate to your understanding of myth?

Well, I discovered Jung's writing when I was a student in Germany in 1927.

Jung himself was at that time exploring the scholarship of mythology. This had begun for him around 1909, when he was at work on the volume *Wandlungen und Symbole der Libido*, where he first dealt with the relationship of dream to myth and the primacy of myth.[11] From that time on, he was devoted to the psychological understanding of myth. I think that he has gone further along that line than anyone in the field.

Jung would himself not have said that he had completely explained mythology, or that his point of view is the only one from which myths can be interpreted, nor even that he had fully interpreted any single myth. From his point of view, each myth must be interpreted in its own right, as saying something different from any other, though using the same language.

For my part, Jung has taught me more about the psychology of myth than anyone else, chiefly by opening individual psychology to mythic psychology. He speaks of "little" and "big dreams"; the dreams of one's own personal, local problems, and then those that open from the great human realizations of the problem of Being, truly visionary dreams. But he never claimed to have circumscribed the subject. He was exploring.

And how does myth relate to your understanding of psychology?

That is what interests me in Jung's method of therapy, which was designed to amplify rather than reduce the fault in the patient. Dreams reveal the repressed side of personality with all its strengths and weaknesses. Balance comes as a result of leaning on your faults. This is also a common theme in the folklore of *The Thousand and One Nights*—where you stumble and fall, there you find the gold.

This is the point that I made in my *Hero with a Thousand Faces* back in 1949. You go into the abyss, and you come out. One can go crazy—or one can go through craziness and come out the other side. That's another point: the Freudian psychoanalysts generally try to abort the psychosis, knock it out, which can prevent one from going through the whole path, the whole trip, and coming out the other side.

A good thing to remember is that what looks like devils from an angelic point of view are actually angels that have not been properly regarded. If you have seen the play *Equus*, you'll remember the problem of the psychologist. He realized that what he was doing was removing his patient's worship, and he asked himself, "What is a man without his worship?" Nietzsche makes the same point when he warns us to be careful lest in casting out our devils, we cast out the best that's in us. A person can be filleted, gutted by a psychoanalytic cure, you might say.

That was Jung's idea also—that psychosis and neurosis had a direction. It is not something to be aborted, shut off, but something to be fostered and furthered so that the person can go through.

Didn't Jung descend into that abyss himself?

Yes. When he had finished and published *Symbols of Transformation*, Jung said, "I realized then what it meant to live with a myth, and what it means to live without one. And I asked myself by what myth I was living, and I found I didn't know." And so he said, "I made it my task of tasks to find by what myth I was living."

How did he accomplish that?

Jung asked himself what play he did when he was a little boy that so distracted him and engaged him that time was nothing. He remembered a little game he had of building little cities and towns out of stone; hours would elapse, and he thought they were minutes—with that you pass from time to the eternal dimension. So he goes off to the other end of the lake at Bollingen and buys himself a piece of property and builds a miniature lake housing development, and eventually graduates to big stones and the famous tower he built with his own hands.

What did this do?

It activated his imagination. This was an enormous inward experience for Jung; he had to work it out in himself. And what we have to do is find out about what our myth is, just as Carl Jung did. Listen to your dreams. Your conscious mind, your ego thinks it's running the show—you're doing things for this reason, and they mean that for you, and your dream tells you, "No, sir! This isn't what's running your life. You're making a mess out of it because I'm pushing you." Find out what that is.

If you find your own chosen deity, what it is that is really cooking in your life, your life will be functioning in terms of that cooking whether you know what it is or not. But it helps to know who your god is and live with it. This is the great thing of finding your own dynamic.

A personal god?

In Buddhism, there is a type of deity called in Tibetan the *yidam*, and in Sanskrit *iṣṭadevatā*—the chosen deity. There are many types of *yidams*. Kālacakra would be one. Cakrasaṃvara is another: your chosen deity over the face of the Buddha, so the Buddha speaks to you through your chosen deity.

Is this common across mythologies?

The normal situation was that the major deities were the cosmic deities, and the secondary deity was the local tribal deity. For example, in India, Varuṇa was the Lord of the Cycling Heavens, Agni the Lord of Fire, but Indra was the patron of that particular society. And each individual would also have a patron. That's the *iṣṭadevatā*, the chosen deity. It doesn't refute the others. But it gives you support in the field of the others, your guiding support.

When I was a little Catholic, I had a guardian angel. The guardian angel is your *iṣṭadevatā*, the one who's taking care of you and to whom you address yourself in your personal trouble. You address yourself to the high gods in your reverence for the universe and your attempt to put yourself in accord with it. But "How and what do I do now?"— you don't ask Zeus for that. You turn to your guiding power. That's what I'm talking about.

This is a major idea, this one of *iṣṭadevatā*. How this great lesson of the world touches your life, your *iṣṭadevatā* will tell you. How does it affect me, in relation to the state of mind, the state of life, the state of human relationships that I'm in now? You can't ask Zeus for this. And this goes also in Egypt. When you look at the tomb art and there is the Ba and the Ka, which are aspects of the individual who is being buried, the Ka is the guiding aspect.

Did Jung discover his?

He found his guide in the image of a wise old man with a long white beard appearing in his dreams and visions, whom he called Philemon.

Jung's Philemon is the image of the human being of the soil, of nature, who is being overrun by civilization. Civilization is a whole system arising from the conscious mind. Philemon can be thought of as the voice of his nature. Your mind is taught how to build computers and handle those things. Your body is making another statement. How are you going to bring these together?

This is what Jung is interested in, and this is what Philemon represents. So he found that which was his guide. Philemon is his god; Philemon is his *daemon*. And what is your *daemon*? You may think you're living by the mythology of whatever religion or classic tradition or whatnot you are devoted to. But what is the real dynamic of your life?

These gods are real?

I'm not saying there are gods. I'm saying there aren't. These deities don't exist. They are just forms to contemplate and project your own psychology onto. They're metaphors. And they're metaphors to help you link yourself to this vast thing that is being alive. So your chosen deity, over whatever instructor or instruction comes to you, you see it through that—and then it will either work upon you or not, according to whether it actually is in accord with the chosen deity.

Man is the animal without a fixed character. Nietzsche calls man the sick animal—*das kranke Tier*. He doesn't know what his job is. He's such a virtuosic creature he can be ninety-eight different things. And your friends can lead you off your track.

You have a track. Find it, in relation to this particular environment—what the world offers in the way of possibility. Find that which hooks you, grabs you. If you don't find yourself there, there is nothing there. If you do find yourself there, grab it! This is your chosen deity; this is your guide. Jung found Philemon as his chosen deity. And when you have a chosen deity, then all lessons that you get from the world must come through that to you. And they will.

If ego represents our rational, conscious mind but is an unnatural entity that doesn't come out of our nature, then what is its source?

Did I say it was unnatural?

You seemed to—

No, I said its mode of thinking was not necessarily in accord with the order of nature. Just look at this building that we're in. The mind built this and it's rectangular. Rational thinking doesn't necessarily create forms in the shape of trees and plants and all of that. Gaudi does!

The problem with our rational mind is that it's the child, really; it comes out of our animal and human nature, and it must not put itself in the ruling position. It is the agent of life, not the dictator to life. When it gets into the dictator position, you have a splitting apart. This is what has happened in our whole biblical tradition. It's the doctrine of the Fall we discussed that brings this in: the world is not to be affirmed as is; it is to be corrected.

Does "ego" in the Upaniṣads or Buddhist texts have the same signifi-cance as it does here today—the "I" or self"?

The Sanskrit word is *ahaṁ*. *Ego* is simply a Latin word for "I." What this represents in our psychological lingo is the consciousness of one's self and the thing that stems from consciousness, which is ego con-sciousness. And that's exactly the Sanskrit *ahaṁ*.

Now, "the Self," as Jung uses it, refers to the dynamic of this biological energy within the confines of your body. That's not what "the Self" is in Sanskrit. That's much more what is called *jīva*, the liv-ing monad, the entity that puts our bodies on and off. The ultimate Self, *ātman*, if you are going to translate it, is undifferentiated con-sciousness.

The ego, as a center of consciousness, doesn't know anything beyond what it is conscious of—but in Jungian psychology doesn't the self include more than just consciousness?

What Jung is interested in is consciousness embodied in *you*. Not consciousness undifferentiated; that's the Hindu interest. But Jung is talking about consciousness in the human body—and not only in the human body, but in a specific human body: yours. And it is limited and committed by the character of this body.

Now, there are new notions of consciousness that are beginning to come in now, in this holographic paradigm idea: we are all, in our consciousness, One, and we're One with the totality—and potentially, actually, omniscient. But the brain brings us to focus *here*, so that we can live in this particular time and space. So the brain is a constrictor; it's a contractor of our knowledge. We know all these facts that help us, *here*. We've got to live in terms of the here, now, in affirmation of this particular focus, but with the knowledge of other foci, other pos-sibilities, and the whole range of totality. The vehicle has a limited and focused consciousness, but the true being, that which you absolutely are, is a manifestation of consciousness. Best I can do on that.

But there is some overlap with the Hindu concept of consciousness?

In Hinduism there are four aspects of consciousness that are symbol-ized in the syllable *AUM*: A, U, M, and the silence out of which *AUM* comes and back into which it goes.

These are four orders of consciousness. *A* is associated with waking consciousness, the consciousness that we're all functioning in, in relationship to each other now. In this, I am not you, you are not me. We are separate from each other. We are gross, heavy bodies, illuminated from without. We're not self-luminous. We change form quite slowly. And the logic that is proper to this level of consciousness is Aristotelian logic: *a* is not not-*a*. I am not you. This is not that. That's one order of consciousness, and that's the one from up in the head.

Then you go to sleep. You have a dream. This is the *U*, another order of consciousness. Dream consciousness. You are experiencing your dream. As subject, you are surprised by the dream. You don't even know what it's saying. But the dream is an expression of yourself; subject and object are the same, only they don't know it. The bodies in the dream are self-luminous. They're radiant. They change forms quite rapidly. They have many, many meanings.

Aristotelian logic has fallen to pieces here. *This is the realm of myth.* Dream, vision, God. Your god is what you are capable of experiencing and realizing and thinking about as God. So *your* god is a function of yourself, just as your dream is—you and your god are one.

This eliminates the whole claim of monotheism. There can't be one God for everyone because you can't even have the same god for three people in the same chapel! Each is having his own experience and his own notion of God. This is the second level of consciousness. This is the level of myth. These are the radiant images, self-radiant, what in Buddhism is called the *saṃbhogakāya*, the bliss body. There's bliss here, the bliss of dream.

Then we have the next level of consciousness, represented by the *M*: deep, dreamless sleep. Now, your body is still conscious. It gets cold, you pull the covers up; if it gets hot, you push them down; you roll over, you're comfortable, you're uncomfortable, the heart is beating, the nerves are functioning, but your "up here" consciousness is not in touch with the "down there" consciousness. This is the consciousness of deep, dreamless sleep. This is your plant body—what I call the wisdom body. This is where the energies come from that are informing the dream.

The goal of yoga is to go into that realm awake, to bring this consciousness down to that, and what is experienced, then, is undifferentiated consciousness. Not consciousness of anything, not consciousness of relationships, but just sheer undifferentiated consciousness.

This is something Western philosophy does not deal with. It is the fundamental concern of all Oriental philosophies. And that was what

Schopenhauer was talking about when he spoke of the consciousness with which you are identical, and which is you.

You knew Jung?

I met Jung in 1953. And by then I had worked twelve years editing the *posthumata* of Heinrich Zimmer, a friend of Jung's who was a great friend of mine, too. So that along with Zimmer and India and my own interest in Jung's writing, when my wife and I had the great privilege of being invited to have tea with Dr. and Mrs. Jung in their place at Bollingen on Zurich Lake, it was a grand hour we had. But it was just an hour, you know. That was it.

Where do you differ from Jung's followers?

I deviate from the point of view of the Jungians in that I'm interested equally in the historical aspect of mythology, how the myths are diffused. And since in Jungian circles diffusion is a naughty word, I guess I can't be reckoned as an altogether devoted Jungian disciple.

On the other hand, when I do turn to the psychological aspects of the subject, I don't see anyone who's gone further than he. I find him just marvelous. And the way he connects inward the Oriental materials is beautiful. For instance, in his introduction to *The Tibetan Book of the Dead*, he points out his own limitations and indicates that he has learned greatly from the Orient.

I don't know how you can possibly talk about psychology today without talking about Jung. I don't see how you can do it. You can't bring behaviorism into the questions, into the interpretation of symbols. You can't. It falls to another range of human experience.

Is this because behaviorism ignores emotion?

Not emotion at all, but experience! You may have the emotion after the experience, but the experience of space that a cathedral gives you is not a feeling; your feeling comes as a result of the experience. What the hell are these people talking about? They don't even know the difference between a stimulus and a response!

Jung is far more sophisticated in his approach to symbols. What he tells me is that these symbols are talking, and what they are talking about.

Jung as a guide

There has to be something to help the individual make modern sense of these traditions for his modern, individual search. And there, I think, the writings of C. G. Jung on individuation are about as sound and helpful as anything we've got. They don't represent a tradition, but they do represent the insights of a very, very deeply grounded psyche.

I think there's no better guidance—and I can now say this with confidence—than Jung for young people. He lets you know what your task is.

And what is that task?

Your task is to relate yourself to your world; not to some world that ought to be, not to some world that's somewhere else, but to *your* world. Find a position in it. And then, around the middle part of life you'll begin to find new dimensions of the spirit coming to you through the world in which you're living. And finally comes the drop-off, when you have to drop off, and you have then this rich second half of life thing that Jung talks about so well and that I know now because I'm well into it. It's something that comes along all by itself.

You live your way honestly, with respect to yourself with integrity. And don't make more concessions to life than you have to; I mean to the life of the world as it's asking you to be.

I don't know of anybody else whom I could give that much credit to as a guide.

CHAPTER FIVE

"An Inward Turn"

When Foundations Crumble

In an age where the old myths are no longer effective, what's a person to do?

There's always an inward reference when mythology is alive: when contemplating iconographic structures, one is really, by way of a mirror reflection, contemplating one's own spirit, one's own inward truth. But when those pictures fall away, when they're no longer speaking because they have become archaic and we are no longer in the field of experience out of which those pictures came, there then comes a need for an inward search directly on the part of the individual.

Has this happened before, a society losing its myth?

I have an analogy to the contemporary situation that I think is a rather good one. The Plains Indians of America were buffalo hunters for the most part, and their whole social order was based on the buffalo as the central symbol. It's a normal thing among hunting peoples that the animal on whom their living depends should become their spiritual messenger.

Here the problem is that you live on the death of others. And the myth of the hunting people in general was that the animal gives himself as a willing victim, with the understanding that certain rituals will be performed that return his blood to the soil, to the mother womb for his rebirth, and he comes back again the next year. He leaves his body, but his life is transcendent of that death. The whole society is organized around that ritual context; the buffalo is enormously

symbolic. You get a wonderful example of this in the Black Elk books
that have come out of Joseph Epes Brown and Neihardt.[1]

Then in the 1870s and 1880s, they were wiped out by the buffalo
killers, who went out there to get rid of the buffalo—first so that the
railroad could go along without interference and the wheat-planting
white people could go out into those plains, but also so the Indians
wouldn't have their normal food supply and would have to go onto
the reservations, which is what happened.

But the second thing about this was that they lost their cult. The
symbol was no longer there. You can't just go on about buffalos when
there are no buffalo around and that's not what you're eating anyhow.
The social cult disintegrated entirely. And what happened next? The
peyote cult comes up from Mexico and sweeps the plains. What does
peyote do? It gives you visions from inside. So the outside social structure is no longer sanctified through rites. The rite has been taken away;
the object of the ritual no longer exists, nor does the manner of life
that made it relevant.

That's a way of getting down into your own interior and finding
there the forms out of which all symbols come. They will not come
forth in the form of buffalo anymore. They'll come forth in new ways
peculiar to each individual in terms of his own context of trouble.

Any other examples of a culture untethered from its myths?

Yes, another parallel is what happened in the period of the Hellenistic
mystery cults. The mythology of the *polis*, the earlier city, had broken
up, and people were living in a *cosmopolis*, a world city—not in the
vast dimensions of today's world city, yet very much the same, relatively, for those times. And there again, as today, there was this inward
turning. There was also a coming on of Caesarism: the regulation by
a Caesar of a mob, instead of a folk—for there is a great difference. A
mob is a conglomeration of people of quite heterogeneous origins and
heterogeneous beliefs, all thrown together with no common ethos.
They have to be held together by force—otherwise the society goes to
pieces. And it was at the time of the rise of the Caesars that the inward
turning of the individuals, to find within the structuring forms that
were lacking in the world without, came along.

An inward turn, then, is the only resort for the individual—he
finds his religion inside—and that's what's happening to ourselves
right now. Whenever the social structuring of the unconscious is

dissolved, the individual has to take a heroic journey and go within to
find new forms.

What precipitates this?

The historicization of our mythologies, where all the symbols are
interpreted as having had a historical factual origin, so the authority
of the inherited religions is now in question. The biblical tradition,
which provided the structuring myth for Western culture, is largely
ineffective. Its pretensions to revelation are refuted. Moses crossing the
Red Sea, on the mountain getting the tables of the law, Jesus's virgin
birth / death / resurrection and all that, nobody can take that seriously
anymore. It's finished. Christianity and Judaism are on the rocks, at
least for many of the young people in our culture.

These symbols—the main motifs of these myths, whether it's biblical or American Indian—are universal to mankind. "All the basic symbols are universal" implies that a historical event cannot have been the
main reference. It was through that historic mythologization of a historical event that the history of the society was given a special psychological
value that invoked the participation not only of consciousness, but of
the unconscious, and you have a viable living world. We don't have that
anymore. Our society is based on technological, rational principles.

So there must be a new quest. Along comes the peyote and LSD
fad of the sixties—inward turning. And today it's no longer LSD so
much, but meditation. The symbols that were caught in that historical
continuity are lost. They're released. One goes down into one's interior, and here are the same basic forms coming up from the inside, not
with historical references but with psychological references.

The sixties, then, turned out to be a pivotal period.

That was the era of inward discovery in its LSD phase.

**LSD in the sixties, peyote on the American plains, mushrooms in Mex-
ico, ayahuasca throughout Latin America, and now scholars are making
a case that ergot in a barley-based beverage was central to the Eleusin-
ian mystery cult in ancient Greece—are psychedelics our savior?**

I think drugs have uncovered the unconscious depths in a society that
is lopsidedly rational and evaluative. They have shown many people

that the archetypes *are* in the unconscious. In the sixties, people were finding that these powers symbolized in the myths or represented in myths are actual in themselves. They are as real as tables and chairs.

However, the drug culture had been caught in the fuzzy end of things—astrology, Kabbala, tarot, witchcraft, divination, and the like—as well as in a more serious encounter with the religious myths and practices of the East—Zen, meditation, yoga, etc. But there has been too much violence and frenzy in all of this. The young seemed bewildered by the world of the psyche. They came into it too fast. It is like the situation in Greek mythology in which a person says to a god, "Show me yourself in your full power." And the god does, and the person is blown to bits.

Suddenly, *The Hero with a Thousand Faces* became a kind of itinerary for the inward journey, and people were finding something in that book that could help them interpret their own experience. The book is a presentation of the one great mythic theme—that of the inward journey of the quest, and the finding and the return. Anybody going on a journey, inward or outward, to find values, will be on a journey that has been described many times in the myths of mankind, and I simply put them all together in that book. The archetypology of the heroic quest is what I have put forward there; that is the quest that people are embarking on now and for which society no longer gives us instructions.

THE HERO'S JOURNEY

In our pluralistic culture, then, each must create one's own personal mythology?

That is the essential meaning of the journey of the hero, which I consider the pivotal myth that unites the spiritual adventure of ancient heroes with the modern search for meaning.

The Hero with a Thousand Faces, originally published in 1949 and in print ever since, covers in detail the motif of the Hero's Journey as it threads its way throughout the world's mythologies. You have written and lectured extensively on this subject in the ensuing decades. Can you offer a concise, succinct description of this recurring pattern for those unfamiliar with your work?

As always, the hero must venture forth from the world of common-sense consciousness into a region of supernatural wonder. There he encounters fabulous forces—demons and angels, dragons and helping spirits. After a fierce battle, he wins a decisive victory over the powers of darkness. Then he returns from his mysterious adventure with the gift of knowledge or fire, which he bestows on his fellow man.

How did you isolate this schema?

Well, the thesis that I started with came after a good many years of studying mythologies of various peoples. It was based on the idea that there is a fundamental sort of morphology of myth, a basic form principle that shows itself in myth and is illustrated in all myths everywhere. Now, this was just a general idea in my head that came from the men I had been working on.

A basic myth motif is suggested by Leo Frobenius in a work of his called the *Zeitalter des Sonnengottes* (*The Age of the Sun God*).[2] And it's based on the idea of the descent into the underworld—going into the belly of the whale—and coming out again. And he gives no end of material of that myth. Reading Jung, I found that Jung actually used Frobenius as the model for this descent and return. And then I was working on Joyce and on Thomas Mann, and I found in their novels that this was the mythic image also.

Then I decided I was going to study Ovid's *Metamorphoses* very, very carefully, because here is a whole compendium of mythic themes from the classical tradition. I thought I'd see if they would fit on that cycle. And by God, the whole darn thing fell out in that cycle! So then I thought, "Well, this is it!" That was when I started teaching my course at Sarah Lawrence College in Comparative Mythology, using this as my core structuring theme, and studying and always looking for some refutation of this, some way to blow it up. I found I couldn't blow it up.

After I had worked on *Finnegans Wake* and brought out *A Skeleton Key to Finnegans Wake* with my friend Henry Morton Robinson, Robinson was writing a book for Simon & Schuster.[3] He called me to say, "Simon & Schuster want to have a luncheon with you"—my *first* author's luncheon!—"and they want you to do a book on mythology. Now, if you get up on your high horse and reject this, I won't talk to you again!"

I had a talk with one of their editors, and I asked, "Well, what kind of book do you want?"

"We'd like a modern *Bulfinch*."

I said, "I wouldn't touch it with a ten-foot pole."

"What kind of book do you want to do?"

I said, "How to read a myth. What myths are saying."

He described it as a self-help book but said, "Okay, write a presentation."

I do and get a contract: $750! Two hundred and fifty dollars advance on signing, $250 halfway through, $250 when it's done.

I started writing simply what I used to say in my course at Sarah Lawrence. But it got longer and longer—this was the introduction—and my wife said, "Joe, isn't that a long introduction?" So I chopped it up and had the first half of *The Hero with a Thousand Faces*. But when I finished it, they wouldn't accept the book. I finished it and sent it to the publisher, and then there was total silence. When I asked about it, they said they were no longer interested. Later Kurt Wolff at Pantheon looked at it and said, "Who'll read it?"

So I sent it to the Bollingen Foundation. I got a telegram from them—"The Hero is a Honey." Bollingen published it then, and it has been a big seller for them. That was the beginning of my writings. It was a funny sort of falling into it.

Did you start with the title?

No, I called it *How to Read a Myth* or something like that. *The Hero with a Thousand Faces* came about two pages before the end of the book.

Why do you think it has consistently sold so well over the decades?

Because it's a damned good book. Also, it opens things that people knew but didn't know that they knew—that this whole world breaks through to the realm of what we call the Muses, those spirits that are the inspirations of the imagination and also the impulses to life.

How many steps are there in the Hero's Journey?

There are three steps. One is leaving the Waste Land and going to the place of initiation. The next is experiencing the initiation, which may be an experience of death. The third is coming back with an amplified consciousness and addressing life, the life of the Waste Land, which is no longer the Waste Land, in those terms.

What do you mean by "the Waste Land"?

The Waste Land is the land of people not living their own authentic lives, but doing what people expect them to do. One goes and gets a job because you've got to live, and so you're doing the daily grind.

How does the Hero's Journey play out in the life of someone taking that inward journey today?

One is born into a society. The society impresses on one certain ideals, certain aims, certain possibilities of life. These may not accord with one's own personal potentials. Or one may also, through one's intellect, see their defects and deficiencies. This is what happens with the dropout; it's a typical youthful experience: that those motifs that are being impressed on me for life do not correspond with those that are asking to come through.

Then comes the business of questing. And you're going into a dark forest where no one has been before because you're looking for your own spiritual life, not that of somebody else. This leads you into realms of terrific danger. And there are typical crises. That first one, of moving away, is the one I term the Call to Adventure.

If you are living in the Waste Land, the Call presents a positive alternative?

It can be in the form of a negative or a positive call: "I'm in this place, I can't stand it, I've got to get out" or "Oh, gee, there's something wonderful over there!" It can come either in the way of following a lure that your family doesn't want you to follow or having to do something that you feel is beyond your powers or even immoral. One way or another, you're pulled out of the context of life as usual.

What does that lead to?

The Departure.

What if you hear the call but decide not to answer?

There can be the Call and then the Refusal of the Call. A refusal of a call that has been heard is very bad, because everything in you knows that a required adventure has been refused. That creates a situation of stagnation.

Do all heroes in myths refuse the call at first?

No. Sometimes a hero is out hunting and follows an animal. The animal is a very seductive one and leads him into his adventure—for example, leading him into a hill that is the abode of the fairy queen, a realm outside time.

So you hear the call, or refuse the call but get past that—what comes next?

Then one moves toward the threshold of experience, a realm transcendent of your knowledge. Psychologically it's a gateway into the unconscious; otherwise it's into a field of action of which you know nothing, where anything can happen, which might be favorable, might be unfavorable.

The Call. The Departure. The Threshold. There's always trouble there: dismemberment, crucifixion, or being swallowed by a whale… it's not pretty.

Then, if it's really your life that is moving you (and not because everybody else is doing it these days, but if it's really *your* call), aids will come to you. There will come accidents of life that help you along which you could not have anticipated. I call this the Magical Aid: some guru, some little helper, some Spider Woman or something to give you the clues to how to get through this thing.

It's a wonderful thing. I know it. It comes. I've seen it in young people in teaching: "What am I gonna do? Well, my father wants me to be a lawyer, but I want to be an anthropologist. But gee, there's no money in anthropology. And besides, the anthropology I want to do isn't that which is taught in schools."

So, what *are* you going to do? Be a lawyer? That's a guy who refused the call. He's going to have trouble a little later.

The one who accepts it and goes, he finds all kinds of things— after struggle, after a long time perhaps, but things do come along that were not anticipated. And he leads *his* life.

So with the help of this unexpected guidance, the adventure continues...

And with that comes increasing tension in the tests that one has to experience on the adventure. That's the pathway: Call, Possible Refusal, Departure, Threshold, Magical Aid, Tests.

There is the allure then of the charm of life—the seductress motifs and all. There are monsters. These are standard motifs in these stories. One trial after another. You may crack up. (I'm not saying this is a happy story. It can be a disaster—and there are plenty of them around about.)

But there comes a time, after you've left, when you come to the crunch and you meet with the real threat, because what you have called up is that aspect of yourself in your own psyche which is not controlled by culture forms, by rational principles, by moral orders, or anything. And you don't know how to handle it.

You come then to the final experience (it may be thought of as "way up there," "way down there," or "way out there") of discovering and making your own what was lacking in the place you departed from—the thing that was missing. It may have been stolen from there, like the golden ball in the tale of the Frog Princess, or it may be something that you just intuit and know must be somewhere, that would make life what it ought to be.

That's the big battle with the monster—what Jung calls the Confrontation with the Shadow.

How do we experience that?

The culminating adventure is represented in four typical ways in the myths. One is the marriage with the perfect bride or with the perfect husband where the earthly lover meets the goddess and is worthy to become her spouse. Or vice versa, the young nymph is approached by the god and is not blown to bits just by the very presence of this divine being but is able to absorb the experience.

That's one—the *hieros gamos*, or sacred marriage. The whole sense of all of these tests is bringing together pairs of opposites: consciousness and the unconscious; the male and the female; the son and the father. So the first and normal one is this erotic image of the divine marriage. That's one that goes back the whole length of mythological history. This motif of the sacred marriage predominates in fairy tales.

The second one—this is the one you get in an essentially patriarchal-oriented tradition like that of the biblical line—is the atonement of the son with the father: coming to the father and being recognized by him. There's an estrangement from the father, who represents the natural order; you have been removed from that and are trying to find your character, which you inherit from your father.

The son and the father is a motif that is dominant in our biblically based tradition; it occurs in many other traditions also, in a secondary way, but here it is primary. In the Judeo-Christian tradition, it's called atonement, which means "at-one-ment" with the father; you've been separated and now you come to atonement, to "one-ment," with him. Very often in those traditions the last temptation, the last threat, is a sexual temptation, and one must reject that and go through. What the son represents is the temporal consciousness; the father is the divine eternal principle to be recognized. And they come together.

This is from a masculine perspective. Do women have the same experience?

I don't know what the counterpart would be in the woman's case.

Is that because there is none—women don't experience the Hero's Journey?

All of the great mythologies and much of the myth storytelling of the world is from the man's point of view. When I was writing *The Hero with a Thousand Faces* and wanted to bring in female heroes, I had to go to the fairy tales. These are told by women to children, you know, and you get a sense of the woman's journey.

There is a feminine counterpart to the trials and the difficulties, but it certainly is in a different mode. I don't know the counterpart— the real counterpart, not the woman pretending to be male, but the normal feminine archetypology of this experience. I wouldn't know what that would be.

Who *would* know?

Women will have to tell us the way a woman experiences the journey, if it is the same journey.

What is the third way the climax of the journey is represented?

The third form is the one you get in the Buddhist tradition, where the one finds that the divine being is himself: apotheosis. That is to say, we are the vessels of Buddha consciousness and what we must do is identify our consciousness with that Buddha consciousness, and then we become a manifestation of that in our own life and being.

You're not allowed that in Christianity, except in Gnostic Christianity—you can't say, "Christhood is in me." I was giving a lecture many years ago where I spoke of bringing the Christ-in-you into operation; only a couple of weeks ago I met a woman who said, "I was at that lecture where you spoke about the Christ-in-you. There was a priest sitting beside me, and he said, 'This is blasphemy!'" So you mustn't talk about Christ; you talk about Buddha consciousness.

Those are the three main lines.

The fourth is the one that is quite popular in exciting myths of the hero who is resisted by all the powers and yet thrusts through and steals the boon (Prometheus stealing the fire, or the bride-theft motif where you go and capture your bride and escape with her). And then comes the problem of all the threatening aspects of those powers which have not been reconciled to your act—what happens when, let's say, you take LSD and go down and get the wisdom too fast. You haven't worked it all out.

There we have the motif of the Flight Back to the World.

Those are the four ways of experiencing fulfillment: one in the way of the male-female relationship, another in the way of child-parent relationships, another in the way of realizing it's all yours, and the fourth way of the fire theft. Or bride theft. Or LSD trip—a situation where you go like a thunderbolt with violence to get down there and draw this out, without having prepared yourself. You have the high experience and then, boy, you gotta take it.

Do you have all four of these experiences in one adventure?

There's a saying in the Catholic Church—when you've committed one mortal sin, you've committed them all. There are four doors by which you can come into the room and find fulfillment. And when you are fulfilled, all the doors are yours.

It doesn't matter which one?

One finds different orders of story. For example, in the fairy tales, it's usually the finding of the bride—or sometimes stealing the bride—and the sacred marriage motif. In the Roman Catholic tradition, it's the atonement with the father motif—and there the woman becomes either the guide to the father in the form of Mary, or seductress in the form of Eve and her children. In the Christian tradition, one is not to experience the apotheosis. You are not to think of yourself as the Christ, whereas in the Buddhist tradition that's the way.

You undertake the adventure, experience a realization. Then what?

Then comes the real problem of return to the world you had left with what you have found—and the introduction of that to the world you've left, so that there's a harmonious environment in accord with the requirements of your own nature.

You don't have a complete adventure unless you do get back. There's a time to go out in the woods, and there's a time to come back. And you *know* which it is, you really do. That's a bit dicey, a major problem not only in the spiritual life, but in any kind of questing and finding. Do you have the courage? It takes a hell of a lot of courage to come back after you've been in the woods.

It's not an easy thing to know how to handle that return threshold; it's even more difficult than the departure threshold. *But it is the same threshold.* It's the threshold where that which has been missing is reintroduced to that which missed it, but didn't know it missed it.

Do you come back to a different world?

The world you come back to is the one you left—otherwise, the journey isn't complete. The main problem is changing the location of your mind.

So you come home.

Yes. It may not be exactly the same locus, the same village, the same town, but you might say it's the same career. You are coming back to your life.

The greatest satisfaction of course is that of finding that what you have to say is something that ought to give us something that really feeds us and is wanted. But not everyone has the luck to meet the generation that is ready for that. Take a person like William Blake, for example, who just sang a song to the wind; it was only half a century or so later that he began to be recognized as a real teacher.

When society isn't ready to receive the boon, what then?

When one then comes back to the world, there's this experience (every artist who has really worked on his art has this experience):

You've left your home. You've gone to Greenwich Village. And with the aid of certain nymphs and other helpful beings you have finally found your life, your art. You bring it up to 57th Street or wherever it is now to sell it, and you get this cold, hard look of the art dealer who says, "So what? We can't use this."

The problem of coming back and bringing your jewel to the society again is a very, very difficult one. It's even more difficult than going away. I think of it as presenting four possibilities.

One, you can say, "Oh to hell with it!" and go back to your studio. And if you have some kind of financial resources, you can just work away yourself, alone, with the thought that two thousand years from now the world will find this work and know it was the best that was done in this century.

Or you can say, "Well, what do they want?" and then use your acquired skill to give what is wanted. That's the commercial artist who gives what is wanted and gets his money, but then always has a feeling inside of something unfulfilled.

Another attitude is, "I don't like them. I'll blow them up." That's the juvenile bomber motif, you might say.

The fourth—the only one I think that really yields the gratification if you finally are able to do it—is to try to see what group in the culture corresponds in its need to what you have to give. Because there will be people who had the same kind of difficulties you've had to whom you can give some kind of help. This is the pedagogical operation of bringing your work to those who require it. There's no use giving it to those who don't; they won't know what it is. Introduce what you have gained to people who are studying with you; find some language that they can more or less speak, and introduce it to them in small doses. That provides a hook that presently will allow you to deliver your message to the larger society.

If nothing else, you can get a job teaching.

Doesn't that pull you off track? How does that work?

An artist comes back and takes a job teaching art. That's not exactly giving all that he has, but it's giving something that he has that's in line with what he has to give. He's receiving an adequate income to sustain him, while he goes on with his painting here, and gradually builds up a gallery public. It's the difficult way. It's the discouraging way. But there it is.

I know what *I* did. I was out in the woods in the middle of the Depression with nothing to do but read, and I read for five years without a job. I was willing to get back, but in my day, during the Depression, people who were what might be called "counterculture" had been kicked out. The culture itself had collapsed, so you're out.

I was following a star, and I really found what I'm now telling you during those five years. And, finally, the little message comes, would you like a job? At Sarah Lawrence College, at a salary of $2,200 for the year.

So that's the cycle in general. It's a cycle of departure, tests and ordeals, with a realization of some kind. It may be great. It may be little. But it gives you the sense of realization. And then the return with your realization to the society that you left, and somehow contributing to it what you've gained (bringing back the elixir, the boon). All the stories of founders of cities, founders of civilizations, founders of religions, founders of great art traditions, and so forth—that's the story. You'll find it one way or another. Those are the stages. And that came right out of Ovid and these myths. But I can say this from my own life.

GRAIL QUEST

Where does this motif appear in the Western tradition?

This comes up in the Grail romances, which form my notion of the key mythology for the European world.

King Arthur would never allow the Knights of the Round Table to begin a meal until an adventure had occurred, and of course, in those wonderful days an adventure would *always* occur. In one particular incident, the Grail, covered by a satin cloth, appeared in midair in the hall and then disappeared. Sir Gawain, Arthur's nephew, stood up and proposed that all should go forth upon a quest to discover the unveiled Grail.

Gawain is the leading knight, really. He was known as "the ladies' knight." In the later stories, Lancelot, Percival even, Yvain, and other knights take the adventure, but Gawain is always with them somehow.

Now, being a lady's knight, he's a perfect example of the beginning of the adventure that I've talked about: a hero out hunting follows an animal, which leads him into the hill of the fairy queen. She is in trouble because a fairy king has sent his army of little fairies to conquer her fairy hill so he can marry her. The hero who has entered her hill then becomes her champion and wins the day for her.

Gawain is the nephew of Arthur. He is the original knight. Now, what Gawain does—adventure after adventure after adventure—is to come to a castle where there's some chatelaine who is in trouble; he becomes her knight, does the job for her, then rides off and comes to another.

The Arthurian stories don't refer to historical episodes?

The Arthurian romances are really based on Celtic myths. This has been completely demonstrated. The Celtic myths go back to a pagan warrior age which ended in the fifth century A.D. when Christianity was introduced. There was a latent period of about seven hundred years, and then, in the twelfth century, these stories come up again, associated with Arthur and the Knights of the Round Table.

Now, the story of King Arthur—drawing the sword from the stone, marrying Guinevere, going to fight the emperor, and then coming back to find Guinevere having betrayed him and all of that—this is fostered particularly in England. Our principal example of it in the English language is rendered by Malory in *Le Morte d'Arthur*. But when the stories appear on the continent, particularly in France and Germany, the people are not interested in Arthur; they are interested in the knights. And these different knightly stories go back to the Celtic courts.

How did these Celtic myths make it into the twelfth-century French tradition?

William the Conqueror was a Norman Frenchman who conquered England in 1066 A.D. The English had conquered the Celts. So you have a three-layer cake here: the Celts (the Celtic people), the British (from the Angles, Saxons, and other Germanic tribes), and the French Normans.

The Celts became the principal entertainers of the French courts. The Celtic bardic songs were rendered in the Norman courts in

French, and the old Celtic heroes were transformed into Christian knights. So you have a real makeover. One of the major cycles in the Irish tradition involves Cúchulainn, who is the nephew of King Conchobar. Another cycle is that of Diarmuid, who is the nephew of Finn MacCool. They are the great heroes involved in all kinds of adventures, each in the service of his uncle, who is a king. Gawain, nephew of King Arthur, is the knightly counterpart of those two chaps.

And it is Gawain who proposes the quest for the Grail.

Yes. After Mass they were to depart. And here is the line that inspired me: "They thought it would be a disgrace to go forth in a group. Then each entered the forest at the point that he had chosen, where it was darkest and there was no way or path," because—and now I'm interpreting—where there is a path, it is someone else's path.

How then do they expect to find their way?

By questing. And that's what we all do in life. Otherwise, you'd follow someone else's path, follow the well-tried ways. Whenever a knight of the Grail tried to follow a path made by someone else, he went altogether astray. Where there is a way or path, it is someone else's footsteps.

Each of us has to find his own way. Nobody can give you a mythology. The images that mean something to you, you'll find in your dreams, in your visions, in your actions—and you'll find out what they are after you've passed them. No one in the world was ever you before, with your particular gifts and abilities and possibilities. It's a shame to waste those by doing what someone else has done.

This epitomizes for me a quality of Western man that is gorgeous. Every individual is a unique phenomenon. The task of life is to bring this uniqueness to fruition. This accounts for the strange quality of yearning in the Occident. What does Western man yearn for? We yearn for something that never was on land or sea—namely, the fulfillment of that intelligible character that only the unique individual can bring forth. This is what Schopenhauer called "earned character." You bring forth what is potential within you and no one else.

This is what gives our Occidental world its initiative and creative quality. In terms of the sociology, there are two aspects of the Orient. One is your engagement in society as you fulfill the duty that is put upon you by the society. And then in later life comes the finding of the Self within. First is the *Dharma* (or virtue) of the Village, and then there's the Yoga of the Forest. In the West, the two are brought together. This is the great mystical power of the West, which can get lost very easily.

This symbolic content can be coordinated, and has been coordinated, with the idea that each is All, and All is what we are. The experience of compassion, a fundamental theme in the Grail legend, is the experience of one's identity with the other (in German, *Mitleid*: "suffering with").

If "each is All," what then is the drawback to going forth as a group? Isn't it possible that a dozen or a hundred people could reach the same conclusion—in essence, arrive at the same place in the forest and join in a common search for the Grail?

Yes. But the group is the agent for actions that have been decided by individuals. The individual is to the group as the quest for the Grail is to the organized church. In the Arthurian legends, the Grail appears only to the person who is ready for it, who is spiritually eligible for the vision.

In the church, there are leaders who tell the followers what to think and how to worship. The priests hear confessions, celebrate the Mass, and assure the faithful that salvation is theirs. But the adventurer must always quest for the Grail alone. By definition, you can't bring the crowd along. After the adventure, the hero can teach the crowd if he chooses.

In the myths of Christ and the Buddha, there is a very interesting point. In the Buddha legends, Ānanda is the Buddha's favorite body servant and a person of charming character. Saint Peter plays the same role in the Christ legend. Ānanda never got things quite right. Neither did Peter. Christ says at one time, "Peter, you do not understand spiritual things. I will make you head of my church." The Buddha says to Ānanda, "Why can't you get things straight? I will make you the head of my church." The leaders of the crowd are necessary people. But they don't get things quite right.

That is precisely the problem of modern man. In traditional societies, the symbols and myths that were the vehicles of social values were presented in socially maintained rites that the individual was required to experience. All the meaning was in the group, none in the self-expressive individual. Today the situation is reversed.

MYTHOLOGIZING LIFE

Rather than rely on an institution, we are on our own?

The individual must go in quest of his own mythology. His own sanctification, his own justification, his own vivification of his life. It's an individual quest.

The institution can help by giving you a few clues, but you've got to do the journey yourself. And you've got to find your own way and what these things mean to you in terms of your life beginning and your present situation. This is the Hero's Journey, what I wrote about in *The Hero with a Thousand Faces*. The individual has to go on this quest himself. This is not ruthless individualism; you're not hurting anybody by finding out who the hell you are, you know. And then coming back as a living being, you become an instructor and something that can give things to people.

That is essentially what the shaman did. The shaman had a spontaneous experience in the way of a schizophrenic crack-up, of going down into the source of the poetic images—namely his own psyche—and coming out again. That's what we all have to do. That shamanic imagery is why the Castañeda books really had an enormous effect out of all proportion to what one could have anticipated, particularly among young people in quest for a meaning to their lives.[4] The older generation wasn't giving it to them, at least not the generation that was doing the talking.

So one has to find it for oneself. That's my notion of the present moment. You've got to go on your own trip. You don't hurt anybody by doing that; that is not a hurtful act. And when you are told, "Well, this is individualism, this is solipsism," and all that, by this bunch that wants you to associate with some picket line somewhere, this is all distracting. If you haven't gone on that trip and found your own way, you're somebody else's cat's paw. You're doing things for somebody else.

Looking at life in terms of the Hero's Journey, how do you know if something is leading you onto another part of the path, another part of the journey, as opposed to leading you astray?

That's the big trick. You get it time after time in the myths—of the deceptive guide, the one who leads you into the abyss. So you have to be careful; we have plenty of deceptive gurus now—I see them all over the place, and they have very big followings. Just think of that awful, absurd thing that happened in South America there.[5] So you have to have the head going a bit.

You have written about many authors who have used myth to provide a framework (James Joyce, T. S. Eliot, Thomas Mann), but your own writings have served, in a way, as a handbook for contemporary writers.

They are, not only to writers, but to other artists as well. Just recently I was at a party in New York for me, for my eightieth year. At first, I hated to have that party. I thought, "Goodbye, Joe! Adiós, muchacho!" But it was so lovely. And I got a word from Martha Graham saying how much I helped her, and from Richard Adams, who wrote *Shardik* and *Watership Down*, saying how my books had made a writer out of him. And then *2001: A Space Odyssey* was based on my books, too—definitely *Primitive Mythology*, chapter 1 (when I saw it, I thought, "Oh my God, that's right out of my book!"). Arthur C. Clarke said so after it was made.

Many of the mythological themes and patterns you describe in *The Hero with a Thousand Faces* appear in the *Star Wars* films.

George Lucas says they're based on my books.

My *Star Wars* experience is really a special story. It's quite lovely. I hadn't seen a movie for thirty years. As a kid I had my heroes; my ambition was to be a synthesis of Douglas Fairbanks and Leonardo da Vinci. Then I went to Europe as a student, and when I returned, the movies had become talkies, and presently they were in color. I expected them pretty soon to be walking in the room with you. But the fun of it was gone for me, where life was just projected on a plane of silence and mind. A Charlie Chaplin movie, you don't have anything like that now. It gave you a pitch into another dimension. And furthermore, by then I was deep into my scholarship.

And then George Lucas came out to Hawaii, where I'm living now, and let me know he was interested in my work and educational television. He invited my wife and me to his place in San Rafael, California, and we saw *Star Wars* in the morning, *The Empire Strikes Back* in the afternoon, and *Return of the Jedi* in the evening. And the next day we saw that delicious thing, which everybody seems to know but I knew nothing about, *American Graffiti*. Isn't that great? All those kids getting themselves into deeper water than they knew they were in. Then he showed us his first film, *THX 1138*. I was really, really impressed! This is a major career. Those giant strides from one to the next.

Did you experience the same "aha!" moment as when you saw *2001: A Space Odyssey*?

I can tell you I could easily recognize my own material. I thought it was marvelous. I was really excited. It seems to me in the history of Western art, this is a major work. It speaks to the multitude—it's talking to young people and old people—those to whom the mythic imagery must be addressed. The elite can sit home and read and soak themselves in these great things, but it's the general public that must be informed of these images and ideas.

And my gosh, some of those scenes [in *Star Wars*]: the one in the bar where he finds his astronaut in the first film, and then at the end those marvelous people going through the forest on those motor rockets. It's a grand thing! And at the end of *The Return of the Jedi* comes the father/son atonement, where the son saves the father. I'm very proud that my books have initiated something like this; I was delighted!

But I also recognized a wonderful imagination that's up to the possibilities of seeing the modern world in a mythic mode. It's the job of the artist to create these new myths. Myths come from the artists.

I *knew* when I hit this that I found something that could activate artists. I'm just writing for artists and for my students.

What form does that mythic mode take today?

Modern myth has to do with machines, air shots, the size of the universe—it's got to deal with what we're living with. It's one thing to get the old structure of the hero myth, but now they are pitching it out into the void, into space, where it's possible to let the imagination go. You're not bound to historical fact. You get bound to history, and then you lose the spirit. That's the problem with the Bible; everything gets to be historical instead of spiritually activated.

But the other thing about Lucas is that he identified the contemporary problem: machine or humanity.

Now, when I saw that, I'll just tell you what struck me was that this was a continuation into a totally new medium, addressed to an immense audience, of the theme that Goethe is addressing at the end of *Faust, Part II.* You remember the contract Faust made with the devil? Goethe's point is that Western man, or what Spengler calls Faustian man now, is *one who is always in quest for something beyond anything he has.* He's not going to rest satisfied with the given. He's going to strive past that.

Mephistopheles is the machine maker. He can furnish Faust with anything that is necessary to achieve the aim that Faust wants. Mephistopheles cannot, on the other hand, determine what Faust is going to want, or be. *Star Wars* deals with that same essential problem: is the machine going to control humanity, or is the machine going to serve humanity?

Those who are dominated by the machine are those monster robot figures who have lost their humanity and become themselves simply victims of the machine. Darth Vader is a man taken over by a machine, he becomes a machine, and the state itself is a machine. There is no humanity in the state. What runs the world is economics and politics, and they have nothing to do with the spiritual life. So we are left with this void.

The Jedi represent the principle of humanity which the machine must serve. And the Ewoks, those wonderful earth people that come up at the end of *Return of the Jedi,* the Ewoks represent nature and the vitality of life asserting itself.

Now, I don't know whether I'm supposed to communicate this, but Lucas told me his inspiration for that last affair in the Jedi, where the little earth people undo the big machine thing, was the Vietnam War, where the people of the earth, the simple people, broke up the program of a computerized machine civilization.

When I read *The Hero with a Thousand Faces*, I was thinking mainly of hero myths—but you've also spoken of this motif as an alchemical process.

That's quite correct. The alchemical imagery is one way of telling this same story in terms of getting the gold out of the base matter. The gold is captured in base matter. *Prima materia.* And through the alchemical cooking and whatever else they're doing, pouring things in and so forth, the gold is brought out.

The gold is your own spiritual life that is clouded *in* the base matter (the life of your physical interests), and the operation of the mythic meditation is to bring out—to elicit—the gold of your spiritual character.

This is a lengthy process?

Yes, but it can also happen in a minute of your life. Sometimes, when you're not quite ready and are experiencing things in the gold sense, you're rendered impotent. I mean you're just knocked out. You can't move; you're getting it too quickly. You have to move into this slowly, and that's what these ordeals on the journey mean. The ordeal is a gradual clarification and purification of your life. The main thing is to get it out there and to operate and live in terms of the gold, rather than of the dross, of your life combination.

You can never become your own master until you find your own truth.

Does this inward turn have the power to transform our culture?

It is my belief that there is a very strong movement in the United States today to find—or at least for the *individual* to find in himself—that center, that centered and centering Eye. And perhaps if enough people discover it in themselves, it may be put to work in the government as well. But unless there are people who have come to the realization in themselves of the point at the center, beyond pairs of opposites, and the way of thinking in such terms, the principle of evenhandedness is not going to operate in public life. It has to be found first in private life. I would say that whatever is about to occur in the way of transformation of consciousness will have had to have occurred, first, in the hearts of individual human beings, who will then have had—as a result of their very presence—an influence in the larger community.

How do we come to that realization in our own lives?

How do you find the divine power in yourself? The word *enthusiasm* means "filled with a god." So what makes you enthusiastic? Follow it.

That's been my advice to young people who ask me, "What shall

I do?" I taught once in a boys' prep school. That's the moment for young boys (or it used to be; I don't know what's going on now) when they had to decide their life courses. You know, where are they going? And they're caught with excitement. This one wants to study art, this one poetry, this one anthropology. But Dad says study law; that's where the money is. Okay, that's the decision. And you know what my answer would be—where your enthusiasm is.

So, I have a little word: "Follow your bliss." The bliss is the mes- ⌐ sage of God to yourself. That's where your life is.

Even if that goes against society's ideals?

With that system of ideals put down on you, you are then evaluating yourself, whether you want to live in terms of those values. You really haven't escaped them until you say, "These are the values. The hell with that. They're not hurting me at all." That's the crisis, if they are still a nag. If they don't nag anymore, well then, don't worry, but if those things are still giving you a bit of an agony, you have to get rid of them. Just think that those are local. They were made up by somebody else a long time ago for some people living somewhere else. There's a whole new world. What are *those* values?

This is what I mean by following the bliss and saying that *that* is what counts in my life. And anything that takes that away, you can have it.

I remember when I was a student in Paris, at the University of Paris. I was studying philology—how Latin and vulgate Latin become transformed into French and Spanish and Italian. I was sitting in the little garden at the Musée de Cluny on Boulevard Saint Germain, and I thought to myself, "What use is all this knowledge to me, when I don't even know how to order a decent meal?" So I looked for the place where my bliss was, where I felt my life was, and that academic thing dropped off.

You certainly seem to have illustrated the truth of that adage in the way you've lived your life.

Well, I tell you I have. And in the middle of the Depression, without a job for five years, I was still following bliss.

To find your own way is to follow your own bliss. This involves analysis, watching yourself and seeing where the real deep bliss is—not

the quick little excitement, but the real, deep, life-filling bliss. My way
has been the way of bliss in reading. I will not finish a book that bores
me, no matter how important it is. This has been my discipline. As
a result, I have left unread a lot of things I ought to have read, and I
have read many things I ought not to have read. (It is not respectable
to admit it, but I have read everything Frobenius ever wrote.)

How did you arrive at this concept?

Well, in the Sanskrit, there are three terms that bring you to the very
brink of the transcendent: *sat, cit,* and *ānanda.*

Sat—"being": In your living you can't possibly know what the
experience of being is. You're having an experience, but is it being?

Cit—"consciousness": But is my consciousness of myself, or my
consciousness of consciousness actually the ultimate of consciousness?

But *ānanda*—"bliss"—you can know. And I say your bliss, your
rapture, is your guide to transcendence. Follow your bliss, and all
the archetypes will come flocking to you. So my word, one way or
another, to youngsters is to "follow your bliss"—that thing in which
you're interested. A kid has got to get to be interested in something or
he's a dolt! Get to be interested in something and then that will lead
you to a life, whatever it is, and your bliss is in that.

**Wonderful advice for those who are young. But for the many of us
who have come to these realizations late in life, after we've taken on
commitments and obligations, are we then to throw those over—forget meeting the mortgage, ditch our spouse, miss those Little League
games, and traipse off on a bliss quest?**

I remember a chap came to me once who was deeply troubled. He
insisted that I should see him. I said I'm no psychiatrist or anything of
the kind. But he came and when he started talking, he said, "Do you
think I should go to India?"

I asked, "Well, do you have any responsibilities here? Are you
married?"

"Yes."

"Do you have any children?"

"Yes."

"Then you can't go to India. You've got to make India come to you."

"Well, how do I do that?"

"Do just what you're doing now, only after you've had one of these experiences, write it down, associate with it, bring it into your consciousness, and India will come right up in your own life."

And it worked. Well, there were a couple years when I thought the guy was going to go crazy, but it really worked on him.

What about someone working the assembly line who might feel they're living in hell right now, trapped in an unfulfilling life?

Hell is being stuck where you are. And the quest for heaven is going past that. I think two men on the assembly line, well, one might be in hell and the other might be in heaven.

I don't know anyone on an assembly line who is in heaven.

I do.

Seriously?

It actually depends on the spirit, or the attitude that the man brings to what he's doing. What is difficult is when a job becomes tedious. I can tell you that writing can become as tedious as any assembly line. And teaching can become as tedious as any assembly line. For a person to think that there's never going to be a tedium in life, he's just got it wrong. You've got to have enough life commitment to that thing so that it's always an act.

One of the principal religious disciplines in all the religions of the world is the monotonous repetition of a single syllable. This is called *Japa*—saying your beads.[6] I've heard it in Buddhist temples. This goes on and on and on. That's like being on the assembly line.

But the purpose is different. The assembly line worker and the Buddhist reciting a mantra are of two different orders.

Well, you can make them work together. It depends on whether you know how to make a *Japa* job out of putting a nut on a bolt. What that does is to release your consciousness from its cogitations and just release the experience of being alive.

Of course, for most people that wouldn't be quite enough.

You're not recommending people just settle wherever they are?

No. I'm not willing to be a missionary for the assembly line.

But every job has its tedium—every job has a dishwashing aspect. Correcting student papers, I tell you, is a fine example of washing dishes. That's part of what you're doing. But even while you're washing the dishes, that can be a meditation. It's not a chore—it's an act of life. Make a *Japa* job out of it.

How would you suggest in our culture today we pursue a revivification of mythology?

My field was literature. I would say study poetry. Learn how to read a poem. You don't have to have the experience to get the message or to get an indication toward the message.

There are a lot of ways of coming to the transcendental experience. One is the way of ritual. A ritual is an enactment of a myth. By participating in the ritual, you prepare something in yourself to roll with the image, and the message comes through. This is the story we know.

Are there warnings to go with that?

My first word would be: don't overinterpret your present position. This is a basic principle in the mystical life. You walked into the sea and your ankles are wet and you think you're drowning. You also think you've reached the abyss. This kind of thing happens very, very fast because even the shallows are exciting. It's a wonderful world of experience.

I find in young people (I taught for thirty-eight years) that they can get just pulled off into a ditch by these invitations from the unconscious. That I think is too bad because those are exactly the years when one should be moving into them with consciousness and know what you're doing. And there's plenty of guidance around now. You don't have to drown.

And mythology can serve as a guide?

The use of this mythological material that is of most interest to me is for the individual finding his way in the free fall of contemporary life, where society does not give you the guidance—all it gives you, I might say, is misguidance, one way or another. How do you get back into the area of truth and honesty speaking about the thing that is mysterious in terms that keep you in touch with the mystery and, at the same time, link the mystery to the course of your life? How do you do that in a world with such conflicting calls upon you?

The aim has been to recognize that, in what have been the concrete activities and experiences of our lives, there is a metaphoric implication which is that of the archetypology of myth.

Myths teach us how to bring actual life into accord with nature. If you live with the myths in your mind, you will find yourself always in mythological situations. They cover everything that can happen to you. You'll recognize a metaphoric implication in the concrete activities and experiences of your life, you'll recognize a metaphoric implication that is of the archetypology of myth. And that enables you to interpret the myth in relation to life, as well as life in relation to myth.

See your own life through the lens of myth.

That's the marvelous thing about this stuff. Everyone gets it in terms of a space of his own.

So, from a mythological perspective, even in bad situations you can see the thread?

Absolutely! The bad situation is one of the disintegrating moments in myth out of which integration comes. What is it that's collapsing? And why? Because something was missing. It's collapsing because it was off-balance. Well, let that go and find the opposite.

I have been at growth centers like Esalen, the Mann Ranch, the Oasis in Chicago, and I have seen that when adults are really in trouble, and they can come into a protected environment and make fools out of themselves, something really gets going. I know now a considerable number of people who were involved in those seminars and meetings, and I have seen what it's done for them. Basically what one sees operating in these cases is this: when a person experiences a blockage of some kind, nine times out of ten that blockage will be one with a counterpart in mythological traditions. Pointing out to such a person just what the mythological parallel is to his own blockage can produce the most spectacular results. I have seen this work.

Can we be held captive to mythological beliefs?

I had a very interesting experience at Esalen a long time ago when I was doing a thing with Sam Keen.[7] I don't know whether I ought to talk about it or not.

Sam was damn good at analyzing people and finding just where things pinched. It's been for many years my thought that a psycho-analysis is the last thing anybody needs. Most people are in trouble because there's something blocking them and it's all up here, some-thing in the head that's in the way of the flow of their energy. And I had a theory that if Sam could find where the person was stuck, I would find a mythological counterpart, so the person would know something about their mythological journey, where he or she was. And you know, this thing worked one time after another.

There was one experience that was one of the most moving—a woman who came in on crutches and was terribly lame. Let's call her Ruth. She had in her young girlhood suffered some kind of sexual vio-lence; as a strongly believing Catholic, she accepted that as her guilt. So she thought this terrible thing that had happened to her, a bone disease of some kind, was God's punishment.

Sam was marvelous. He managed to get her to realize she really didn't believe that, but that was a way of screening something from herself. This was one of the most admirable performances I've seen. I don't know how Sam got the idea so fast. He took a chair and put it in front of her and said, "Okay, Ruth, sit down then." Sam turned and asked two of the strong men who were there to then pick Ruth up and stand her on a different chair on the stage.

There was a big piece of driftwood in the room, so he placed the piece of driftwood on the chair where she had been sitting, turned back to Ruth, and said, "Now, you're God and this is Ruth. You tell her why you did this to her." So Ruth tries to talk like God and is going on and Sam's looking at her. He then says, "Okay," and has the boys come, take her down again, put her in the chair, and put the driftwood as God up there. "Now you tell God what you think of him for doing that to you." And she's talking. Finally, Sam interrupts and says, "Ruth, I have never heard you be this honest before, but you don't believe a bit of this."

Then, I thought, well, it's my turn now. Now I, who have never suffered anything greater than a toothache, I was talking to a woman who was in real pain. And I said, "So that God that you thought did this to you didn't do it."

Ruth said, "Yes. That God is gone."

I said, "Where does a god go when he goes?"

Well, she knew enough to say, "In here," and she pointed to herself.

So I asked, "Who did that to you?"

She said, "I have."

Now—and this is a hard thing to say—I said, "You've got to think of your life as a function of *your* will. And it was your will that did this to you in some mysterious way. This has been your life. Your pain has been your guru. Something in you has asked for this and that's why you've got it, and there's no point in blaming anybody else. Bring it into yourself."

Now, this has nothing to do with whether I was right or wrong. I'm talking about what happened to that woman. I know what happened to her. She lost her fear. She lost her guilt. She gained joy in her life and her condition. I said, "If you say no to your condition, you're saying no to your life because it is your pain, it is your suffering that has turned you into the beautiful person you are. And without that guru, your pain as your guru—you've chosen that guru somehow." And she found later that before her mother gave birth to her, she dreamed that she was giving birth to a monster. So this thing is in her whole life.

This, I tell you, this is a big one for me. But the orientation of your mind and saying "Yes!" to your life as it goes is the affirmation Nietzsche is talking about. And that woman phones me every now and then saying, "Thank you, thank you, thank you. My life is beautiful,"…and it is.

There is no pain that life can't absorb if you're with it. But I must say, as I was telling her that, I was thinking, "Who the hell are you to say a thing like this?" It was like some violent act. But it worked. And it was right. The only reason I knew it was right was that I had read Nietzsche and learned the value of affirming everything you have.

ART AND THE MYTHIC IMAGE

If you can't afford a workshop or attend a growth center, or don't have a Sam Keen or Joseph Campbell near to guide you through this process, what can be done to activate that level of the imagination?

The rescue for an individual today is in art activity of some kind or another—and it doesn't matter what it is—some creative action that becomes significant as one becomes more and more inured to the difficulties of the new art. And it becomes then a vehicle of throwing that libido into creative and functioning expression.

You may be interested in the arts in a kind of discursive, art historical way, and then suddenly one day one of the works of art really grabs you and you become literally transformed by that. Or think of how it is with music. At a certain age a certain kind of music interests you and captures everything you've got and you're participating with that, and then that drops off and another order of music comes in. I can remember the first time I ever heard Rimsky-Korsakov's *Sheherazade*—I was about eighteen years old, and my God! I thought it was terrific! I can't hear it now.

The art is talking to what is possible within you of an experience. And you can develop the experience. Stay with music and you presently will be listening to Scarlatti and Bach instead. Then just think of the Hindu music with the *rāgas* and another whole world of messages.

You're speaking of personal experience within reach of everyone, but you also specifically address artists. In your book *The Inner Reaches of Outer Space*, you compare art to mysticism.

The last chapter of the book has to do with aesthetics. My wife, who is a dancer, said one day, "The way of the artist and the way of the mystic are very much alike, except that the mystic does not have a craft." I took this as a lead. The mystic goes into the inner life and its relationship to the universe to find identity with the soul and its god. That is like aesthetic arrest, except that the mystic can be called out of the world by his inward quest, whereas the artist is held to the world by the materials he uses and by his intention to make an object through which this mystical realization will be reflected. I discuss art in the West and art in the East, particularly as represented in the art of India, where the relationship of art to the religious experience is very clear.

You believe the artist fills the role of a seer today.

I do indeed. All mythic images are rendered by what are called seers or prophets; today we would call them artists. The artist is one who's opened the eye of vision and sees past the phenomenal forms to the morphological principles that animate them, and then renders them to us.

I consider the artist the one who has to reintroduce us to the Promised Land *in our own land*, here and now. It's his vision, I think, that brings to us a vision of the knowledge of the spiritual radiance that shines through the world, which many of us do not see. Remember, in the Gospel According to Thomas, Jesus says, "The kingdom of the father is spread upon the earth, and men do not see it." I think the artist sees it, and he can show it to us.

The real message of art is the glory of what we have with us here and now. Not that nature and the world have to be changed, but that nature and the world are already and forever radiant of the divine spirit.

Art can pitch one into another dimension?

Yes—a state of being that confirms you in your own deep nature. You cannot appreciate what Robinson Jeffers called "divinely superfluous beauty" if you're looking for kinetic results all the time.[8] Art suffers greatly from this attitude.

Could you expand on what you mean by "kinetic results"? Does this relate to your understanding of what is proper and improper art?

The term "proper art" (from James Joyce's discussion of aesthetics) refers to art that serves a function that is peculiar to art, a function that nothing else can serve. "Improper art" serves some other function that is not specifically aesthetic—for instance, art as advertising or as social theorizing or social propaganda.

Aesthetic?

The word *aesthetic* means having to do with the senses. An art object, then, is fulfilled in its address to the senses and not in some message of sociology or advertising. Joyce uses the terms *static* and *kinetic* in this context. Proper art, he says, is static. Beholding it, you are held in what is called "aesthetic arrest."

On the other hand, art that is in the service of some other function will either draw you toward the object with desire—what Joyce calls "pornography"—or repel you from the object, as in sociological propaganda. Static art simply holds you in rapture to the picture or to the glory of the music. "Pornographic" or "didactic" art is kinetic, in that it sends you out to do something. Anyone who has never had an aesthetic experience can't possibly know what we're talking about, but anyone who has will know immediately.

Pornographic art presents the object as something to be possessed or made use of, rather than opening your heart to the object with compassion. It fills you with passion rather than compassion; to use the terms of Martin Buber, you are looking at the object as an "it," not as a "Thou."

And you consider that improper?

I want to make clear what is meant by "proper" and "improper" art. It has nothing to do with ethics. The word *proper* means "that which is appropriate to art." Art has to do with aesthetic experience—the visual experience. The aesthetic means having to do with the senses. Now, when it is not the aesthetic experience but the erotic experience that is evoked, you've got improper art; it's serving a purpose that is not proper to art.

And to qualify as pornography, at least from James Joyce's perspective, art needn't be sexual?

In terms of Joyce's definition, all advertising art is pornography. It's making you want to want, and own, and purchase, and have, and make use of the object presented. I remember there used to be a kind of apple called the Skookum apple, and it used to be advertised with just pictures of Skookum apples that would make you want to go up and pick the thing off the wall and eat the painting.

But no one would want to pick up Cézanne's apples and eat them. He was interested in the form, not in the advertisement of this as something to buy. The fact that you want to buy the picture—that has nothing to do with it. It's that you want to make use of the object in the picture, in some way or other, that is the pornography.

Art serving in a kinetic way is moving you toward an object or away from an object in outer space. But when art functions as proper art, it opens you to a realization of the form and nature of your own being, and hence you are held to it. It speaks to inner space, whereas pornography and didactic art speak to your relationship to outer space. When you experience aesthetic arrest, you are not moving in outer space, you are absorbed in an inner space experience. And so it is in a sense a metaphor. A metaphor, you might say, is an art object that opens to you the dimensions of the inward life.

Commercial art is a thriving field today—pornography, by Joyce's definition, visual images trying to sell things. It can pay the bills and then some. Do you feel an artist can successfully participate in both kinds of art: proper and pornographic?

I don't mean that an artist is incapable of doing a pornographic work. In fact, in the secret archives of every artist we've got plenty of pornography. That's a good way to get it out of your system. But that's not the final work.

Also, you have to have this in mind; that what may seem to you to be pornographic may not have seemed pornographic to the artist. He may have taken certain things for granted that, for you, are surprising. For instance, Hieronymus Bosch's *The Garden of Earthly Delights*, that big triptych—that's a purely mythological image. He's using what for us could seem to be, perhaps, pornographic matter, but that's not the intention and that's not the effect it would have had in his period.

But proper art has the power to move us within.

There are, one might say, two orders of art. There are the arts addressed primarily to the intellect, representing moral purposes, judgments, and so on. And then there is the art of Tragedy, which Aristotle writes in his *Poetics*, "erases the birth of practical man" and opens the mind to the *mysterium tremendum et fascinans*. That is what is meant by his term *katharsis*. The Aristotelian *katharsis* is a "cleansing" of the mind of its practical fears and desires by an opening of the heart, through simultaneous experiences of humanistic pity and metaphysical terror, to the transpersonal sentiment of compassion.

James Joyce has discussed this question magnificently in *A Portrait of the Artist as a Young Man*, where he declares that the "kinetic" emotions, which move one either to desire things or to loathe and to fear them, are erased and transcended in Tragedy, where the emotions evoked are those which he calls "static"—namely *pity* (identification with and participation in the suffering of another) and *terror* (recognition of what he calls the "secret cause" of another's irreducible sorrow).

Pity and terror are static inasmuch as they "arrest the mind" in a realization of the nature of all temporal being. One is not moved to do anything about it: there is nothing to be done. All practical action based on fear and desire is annulled, in this realization, as fruitless.

I have found it highly significant that in Buddhist thinking, desire and fear are *exactly* the two life-governing emotions that were transcended by the Buddha, when he sat in meditation on the so-called Immovable Spot at the foot of the Tree of Illumination. There he was tempted by the god who inspires in man, first, desire (*kāma*) for possession of the goods of this world, and then fear, the fear of losing them in death (*māra*). This is the god by whom all living beings are motivated. But the Buddha, the "Awakened One," was unmoved.

In Joyce's view, it is only by the artist similarly unmoved by compelling desires and fears that the objects beheld in this world can be seen as they truly are.

Cézanne said, "Art is a harmony parallel to nature." It shows something of the essential organization of powers and relationships in the field of nature itself. And nature is both in you and out there. Art is like an X-ray photograph showing you the inner grain and structure of nature, and your inward nature responds to the object with fascination and aesthetic arrest.

When I was a student in Paris I met and came to know as a teacher and friend the great sculptor Antoine Bourdelle; I remember him saying to his students: *"L'art fait ressortir les grandes lignes de la nature"* ("Art brings out the grand lines of nature"). And these grand lines are irreducibly informed by death, suffering, and sorrow. The artist's eye views, affirms, and participates in all this—beyond fear and desire. And mythology moves us from that aesthetic level to the realization of transcendence.

Art is a message to you of your own being.

Cézanne and Bourdelle are saying art should imitate nature?

The imitation of nature that they are talking about is the imitation of nature in its manner of operation. Not the surface of nature, but the dynamics of nature. That brings us past the merely naturalistic approach to nature. Naturalism belongs to Marxism, as representing an intellectual approach to everything. Art opens the inner eye to the mystery dimension of nature and goes past the immediate surface.

"Just look what happened!"—that is journalism, is it not? But art is of the everlasting realm of the Muses and of myth. What is the impulse and the consciousness behind all this? What is the dynamism? What is the process that we are experiencing here, with which we must put ourselves in accord?

One man shoots another man. You are viewing this. The mystery is not what caused Mr. A to shoot Mr. B, but what is it about the destiny of Mr. B that is rendered intelligible through this shooting? Or what is it about the character of Mr. A that is made visible in this shooting?

Art that speaks to our common humanity?

Oh my God, does art engender humanity? It awakens your humanity. But humanity has nothing to do with political theory. Political theory is in the interests of one group of humanity or one ideal for humanity. But humanity—my heavens, that's what proper art renders.

The inner harmonization, the opening of the heart to humanity, is the main thing—and it must open to all humanity. This is no retreat, but a rejection of the partial judgment on humanity that is characteristic of social theories. The artist goes past that. This is the transformation of the Waste Land.

What is the Waste Land here?

The Waste Land is the field of contending political parties.

I understand the broad concept of proper and improper art but am still having trouble wrapping my head around how that might apply to specific works. Tolstoy's novels, for example—is *Anna Karenina* pornographic, by that definition?

No, I can't see anything pornographic in *Karenina*. Not at all. Well, if you looked at it in a certain way the artist may not have intended. You could say this about Joyce's definition of pornography: if all you want is a picture of Susie because you love Susie, then the picture is a reference to something else. It's not the picture for and in itself that you're buying.

But in *Anna Karenina* it feels like Tolstoy is inspiring me to emulate some characters and not emulate others—guiding me to take action.

Oh. That's a very good question. That's very close on the line, there. That's very good. That is to say, when you're reading, and find in a work a character whom you would like to emulate, he becomes a role model?

Quite right.

That would not be what Joyce would mean by pornography. The idea of that person would be there to evoke from you that quality in yourself, which would make it possible for you to emulate him. That is the function of religious art. It's to provide what are called role models. That's different.

What about the opposite, where a character provokes revulsion, and you see something in yourself you want to avoid?

If the artist presented it with the intention of revulsion, then you'd have a didactic piece. I remember when I was a student, and I was living with artists and we were talking about these things. There was always that edge—the pure, proper art. But then suppose you're doing a nude. Can you put a little salt on there and make it just a little bit appetizing?

There's a magnificent nude by Velázquez of a woman lying with her back to you, looking in a mirror. Well, it depends on you whether that's pornography or not. But it's interesting that the female nude has played such an important role in Western easel painting art and also in sculpture. I think that piece of Velázquez's comes as close as you can come, just to the edge, but it is not a pornographic piece at all.

Then there's the other thing, which you've now brought in—the didactic aspect, as a lesson taught. If the artist's intention was to teach a lesson, then it's deliberately didactic. But lessons are pouring out at you all the time from myths, which are neither didactic nor pornographic. So, you see, it really is a thin line here—where you keep your mind as an artist, and whatever you're experiencing when you look at something. Are you seeing *that* thing, or are you seeing it in relation to me?

What about, say, Dada?

Oh, Dada isn't pornographic.

But Marcel Duchamp talked a lot about the idea of putting art in the service of the mind instead of the eye. Isn't that didactic, which would make Dadaism improper art?

No, I don't think there's anything improper about Dada. Dada was a didactic piece, though. It was an intentional violation of the rational system. Then what happened, as a result of these strange arrangements that appeared, was that one had a *feeling* reaction. That was the beginning, then, of surrealism. And just at that time, Freud's *Interpretation of Dreams*, which was published in the year 1900, was beginning to soak into the intellectual community.

See, Dada and surrealism were literary as well as visual art movements. They went together, and there was a literary accent there. But then it really became visual, I think, with Dalí and the idea of the crisis of the object. He moved it into another level. He really did, although his style was about the same as Maxfield Parrish—you know, that kind of illusory style—and, from a purely aesthetic point of view, was not highly respectable. But what he was showing was a dream landscape. Well, de Chirico also had that kind of dream landscape.[9] It was a wonderful period in art.

There are a lot of lessons constantly being taught in the rituals of primal cultures. From a Joycean perspective, why could that not be classed "improper"?

You're really pushing right around the edge, here, of the problem. A living mythology is rendered in terms of ritual. When you participate in a rite, you are participating in a myth. You are, as it were, acting as though you were a deity.

The function of the ritual is to organize the life of the society. Early societies are based on rituals, and every aspect of life is ritualized. So, you can think of all rituals as originally life-structuring. That's its function, and that's not exactly didactic. It's pedagogic. There's a difference between pedagogy and the didactic. It's a very nice difference, but it's there.

This has been, for me, a very instructive theme, how close all these basic pedagogical aims of mythology are to the didactic.

What do you mean by "pedagogical"?

I mean inducting people into certain knowledge and ways of teaching. It's there for teaching. "Didactic" is not really teaching; it's putting forward a cause: I have a certain cause, a certain moral instruction to deliver, and I'm writing to put this forward.

Perhaps I asked an unfair question, since many cultures didn't think of the things they were doing as something separate, didn't think of it as "art."

Yes, but it was associated with ritual. All the early art is religious art, and it's linking you through personifications to these life-structuring archetypes.

And art today?

Well, I think our society is more or less assimilating art. But one of the problems is that so much of art is really studio art. It's for people who understand elegant, aesthetic problems, and it's not speaking to the spiritual hunger that is a spiritual hunger in this country, and in certain parts of Europe now, that is prodigious. The churches aren't serving it. The churches are talking about sociology, and the metaphysical dimension is not being talked about. The United States is full of these human potential movement centers like Esalen. I've been lecturing at many of them, and you just can't believe it—the force and importance of this in people's lives. This is what religion should have been serving, but it's not. It's sociological now. And this doesn't say that sociology is bad, but sociology doesn't serve this function of awakening your own, inner, spiritual life. That is the function of the artist—the rendering of "scripture." In India they're called the *ṛsis*, "the ones whose ears have opened to the song of the world." That's what an artist is.

It's not a nice thing to say, but I think a good deal of the integration of art has been snobbism and, also, the investment. When it dawned on them that money was possible here, that this artist's work might be worth I can't tell you how much more in thirty years, then you begin buying art, and it begins to influence the community that way.

But an artist, when he cleanses the portals—cuts himself out, with his particular preferences and desires and programs for the world, and just looks at something—there takes place aesthetic arrest. That is the identification of your identity with that other object, or with what that object is.

So I see in the world today the actual disciplines of art as the highest disciplines being presented. I think they're not giving you this in the churches. But I think in the art studio, when you have to work it out and look at a thing without personal, pornographic, or didactic intentions, you're opening up to the spirit. Then your artwork will open other people to the spirit, and that's the message.

What we're taught today mainly has to do with economics and politics. We are not nurturing our spiritual side. So we are left with this void. It's the job of the artist to create these new myths. Myths come from the artists.

Jung

merv is evil!

→ "To Complicate the Plot"

The Indifference of Nature

Just as psychology seems to have taken the place of religion in explaining our inner world, so today science and religion are at odds in explaining the world around us. Could we consider science itself a mythology presenting its discoveries as truths?

What was given us by the ancestors is "the Truth."

How does that answer the question?

Just consider the total contrast between the traditional and the scientific way of thinking about truths. In the traditional way, the older a tradition, the truer and more respectable; in ours, a scientific book of ten years ago is already out of date. It doesn't know the laws that are operating now in the very field that it was addressing.

There's no such thing as a scientific truth. There are scientific working hypotheses. It's only the person who has not been trained in science who thinks that scientists are trying to present truths—but scientists are willing to drop it and change it on the proper evidence at a moment's notice. And they're doing it all the time.

You wouldn't describe evolution as a myth?

Well, it is the current working hypothesis to interpret the phenomenology of nature, and it seems to be pretty well documented. I don't think we can say that it's likely to be a discarded theory very soon. Also, the findings that are coming through now about the antiquity of the early hominid type, putting the date back nearly four million years—this gives a different notion about the place of man in nature from the one that would have us all created together with the world in 4004 B.C. It makes the problem of deity, which most people think they like to relate to, a very different one from the problem of the deity who created a small world six thousand years ago.

Now look at these galaxies beyond counting that the scientists are showing us—literally millions of galaxies, and every galaxy a Milky Way of stars, and every star with a possible solar system around it, and some of these solar systems probably inhabited. And the more one knows about it, the more miraculous it is! What does that do to the whole history of Creation and the Fall that we have in our inherited tradition? It just breaks it up.

Is there then—or should there be—a relationship between science and myth?

Well, evolution is a scientific finding to which the mythology must adjust itself. If it isn't adjusted to, there is a stress between the mythological (or religious) and the actual experience of the world.

I would say that all of our sciences are the material that has to be mythologized. A mythology gives the spiritual import—what one might call rather the psychological, inward import—of the world of nature round about, as understood today. There's no real conflict between science and religion. Religion is the recognition of the deeper dimensions that the science reveals to us. You find all kinds of suggestions in the world of modern physics. And boy, you can translate them into Sanskrit without any trouble. The Hindus have the whole thing already!

Science deals with what in logic are called instrumental causes. But then there's another order of causation, known as the formal cause, and that is very mysterious. Scientists are right at this moment running into the mystery zone. They've pushed right to the edge of what can be known, analyzed, and interpreted simply in terms of instrumental causalities and are themselves recognizing this.

Erwin Schrödinger, this great physicist, turns to Hindu imagery in his book: "*tat tvam asi*" and all is *brahman*![1] That's what he ends up saying. Here is an intuitive insight that goes past the fields of time, space, and observations and realizes that the sphere of time and space is secondary to another.

What is in conflict is the science of 2000 B.C., which is what you have in the Bible, and the science of today. The mythic image does not fit the contemporary mind. So the message can't get into the contemporary body. You've got to translate these things into contemporary life and experience. Mythology is a validation of experience, giving it its spiritual or psychological dimension. And if you have a lot of things that you can't correlate with contemporary nature, you can't handle it.

The main problem, as I see it, is to find a way to put ourselves in accord with the way of nature, which is quite indifferent to the programs of our consciousness. When your consciousness distracts you from those positions which are of the law of nature, you become uneasy, ill, and everything else. By putting yourself in accord with the world of the natural powers, which are your own powers, you are restored.

Myth has a restorative function.

What about the idea of a return to nature—forsaking modern society for a simpler life?

For me, that's just silly. People who have that idea and at the same time want their tape recorder and television set—it's ridiculous! You can't have an industrial society to make your television and support the science that makes such things possible and at the same time have a little, uncomplicated society. You just can't have that!

I would say that, at least in respect to New York City, that advice can't be followed. If you found Minetta Creek, which ran where Minetta Lane is now, so what? It would be a sewer. I don't think you can go back. This is not the land it was. I remember, when I was a boy in New York City, there were goats grazing in what are now skyscraper lots. It's gone. You have to move on somehow and find the organic character of the structured city. Because it *is* organic in a bizarre way. It's life that builds these things.

Could those who do step away from civilization to embrace a simpler, self-sufficient, semi-indigenous lifestyle inspire our modern society to reexamine its values?

I don't think so. I think the ones who can speak best to help us straighten out our lives in the world—that is, this one that we're living in—are the people who have stayed in the world and faced it. I don't mean the ones who in staying in the world have become trapped in it, but those who have lived in the world and lived their own rich lives as well.

Psychologically it's good to restore your connection with nature, but if it involves an unfriendliness to the world as it is, it's an unfriendliness to an aspect of your own mind, your own life. It's one thing to go back to nature. It's another thing to be of nature in the first place. It's like saying, "Let's be virgins again." You can't do it.

What is the relationship of mythology to nature?

Myths come out of the same basis as the trees of the woods do. They come out of the *vijñanamayakośa*, the wisdom body of the universe that's in us.

Is nature then looking out for us?

Nature is absolutely indifferent to individuals—and myth is an order of nature. We take the moral position of the phenomenon and say that the phenomenon has certain rights. But the phenomenon is simply a puzzle thrown up by this great tide of being. And the myths are more interested in the tide of being than in the phenomenon.

The universe doesn't care?

It doesn't! You know, there was that Lisbon earthquake in the eighteenth century, and Voltaire thought it was a case against God that a civilized community had been wiped out that way by an act of nature. Nature doesn't give a damn about this. The whole function of surviving in nature is like surviving in a storm on the ocean: you've got to know how to navigate. And it's not nature's fault if you don't navigate.

Myth, then, like nature, is irrational—outside reason?

Yes, but nature is not so chaotic. Energy comes to us already inflected, specified, and organized. You can't call nature absurd simply because it does not fit into the Cartesian coordinates, because it can't be reduced to a system of clear and distinct ideas. Its order is marvelous, although it frequently escapes the narrow categories of our reason.

archetypes

An ideology is not a mythology. Ideology comes from the head and imposes on nature the intentions of a rational mind. These intentions are economic, political, and practical in their nature. Nature, however, is not in this sense practical. Beauty is not practical. The will in man is not practical. It is spontaneous, moved from within, and myth comes from that spontaneous level.

I think Carl Jung's term, "archetypes of the collective unconscious," is fundamental and appropriate here. The archetypes of myth are manifestations of the nature of man in accord with the nature of the universe. Interpose, before these, ideas derived from man's limited knowledge of the world, and we have then a system of rational thought. In dream, the rational mind becomes aware of the impulses of the larger nature, of which it is itself but one organ. Impose the will of that one organ upon the whole, and the imposition has to be by violence. It has to be enforced by police-state methods.

But when you touch nature, the center of force is shifted. Nature speaks for and of itself, and this is the main point. Against this we have the violence of a society based on the idea that nature is evil, or that nature is stupid, or that nature is not good enough, and we are going to correct it. We are going to change nature.

The full force of this point of view first struck me when I read of what in Russia had been done to Vavilov, one of the most advanced and important botanists of the present century.[2] His emphasis on genetic inheritance as establishing the characteristics of biological specimens was repugnant to the point of view of D. T. Lysenko, representative and spokesman of the idea, favored by Stalin, of the environment as a determinant of biological inheritance. At a series of meetings of the Russian Academy of Sciences, Vavilov was denounced by Lysenko as a purveyor of reactionary Mendelist-Morganist genetics and in 1940 exiled to Siberia, where he died—we do not even know when. One of the major scientists of the century, destroyed because his findings represented nature against the wishes of a local social establishment!

The Bible, too, is anti-nature. According to the Book of Genesis, nature is "fallen." So that what we have here is a desacralization of the natural world and natural man, already announced in the Bible, continued through historic Christianity, and now carried on "progressively" in Marxism: a season of some three thousand years of institutionalized violence against nature. Yet it has never totally triumphed. Nature comes breaking through, creatively, all the time.

Are you suggesting a resonance between communism and biblical traditions?

Political ideologies lack a metaphysical dimension. They lack what I regard as the first function of mythology—to open up a view of the mystical dimension, the mystery dimension. Communism has all the signs except one of a functioning mythology: it is absolutely devoid of a mystical sense. Communism is impudent with respect to mystery. It is a sterilized variety, I would say, of biblical mythology. It foresees only one society and the triumph of that society over the whole face of the earth. People outside aren't even considered to be people—they're liquidated with perfect impunity, and nobody feels any guilt for it.

Another interesting thing is that they have a book that is venerated as a kind of revealed bible.[3] The big ideological quarrel between Russia and Red China, for example, was over who is interpreting this scripture correctly. It is a kind of scholastic quibble with reference to an unassailable book. Then you have those saints of the tradition who are embalmed and are its true interpreters. Instead of icons of Jesus in his mother's arms, you had images of Mao and Stalin everywhere, so that the individual is related to the society by way of mythologized human figures.

Next, there's the notion of the good guys and the bad guys. We're the good ones, the others are the bad ones, and that's it. There's a conflict between the forces of good and evil which is in the process of being resolved and will culminate in the day of the revolution—or in the Day of Yahweh, or in the day of the Second Coming, when evil will be eliminated and there will be nothing but the good world. That's when the struggle ends; history will cease.

This is a perfectly mythological structure—and it is a completely dogmatic one. There's no room for deviation. The way in which those purging trials were conducted in Russia—people were brutalized very much as Galileo had been when up before the inquisitor. Here again are inquisitors, and there is torture applied. Also, there is campaigning against all other religions: a kind of holy war. It is an anti-God campaign being waged absolutely against Buddhism, Christianity, and even shamanism in Siberia. So it has everything except the mystery dimension—it tells you what to do and what to believe in every detail. I see it as a completely reactionary system totally eliminating the individual experience. Consider what went on and *is* going on in Tibet *right now*! It is one of the most appalling stories, including genocide and everything else, but do you read about that in our papers?

Communism is more in sync with the Judeo-Christian mythos than with Buddhism?

Communism isn't Buddhism. It can't be Buddhism. But Buddhism can coalesce with anything.

What Buddhism shows is the Buddha consciousness in all the phenomenology of life and the world. When it has gone into an alien field, Buddhism has never knocked down the gods; rather, it has said, "These, too, are Buddha things."

In Japan, for instance, when people get married, it is a Shintō priest who marries them. When they are cremated, it is Buddhist monks who are in charge of the ceremony. These are two aspects—the ethnic and the elementary. One leads you into life; the other conducts you out. They recognize this. And there's been no problem in Buddhism in India. When we get to the fifth and sixth centuries A.D., about a thousand years after the beginning of Buddhism (563–483 B.C. are Buddha's dates), Buddhism and Hinduism begin to look alike. And so, I should think that the Buddhist would have no problem living his life in a Communist world. But would the Communists allow it to happen? That's the problem there.

I wish I could show you a couple of pictures I have. One shows the Potala, the great palace in which the Dalai Lama lived: beautiful architecture, symbolic of the world mountain where sky and earth come together, where eternity and time meet. And then I have a picture of a cement factory, now, in Tibet. With that you can sense the difference between two societies, two architectures, two states of mind—an architecture that gives you an image of spiritual rapture, and an architecture that is absolutely practical, perfectly great for its function. Well, Tibet was in such a state of spiritual rapture that it was way behind in its economic life.

Several years ago, I went to work to help a young Tibetan lama, Rato Khyongla, write his autobiography. It's a marvelous story![4] He was one of the people who examined the Dalai Lama when the Dalai Lama took what you might call his PhD exam for his *geshé* degree.[5] This young man was one of the examiners; he was there in Lhasa the night that the Dalai Lama, after having taken and passed the exam, gave lectures on Buddhism in the Norbulingka, the summer palace, a mile or so outside of Lhasa. My friend then comes back from the Norbulingka to Lhasa, where he learns everybody's in great excitement because the Communist military camp has invited the Dalai Lama to come to a theater production and leave his bodyguard outside.

The whole city of Lhasa poured out between the Norbulingka and the Communist camp so that the Dalai Lama couldn't have gone even if he had wanted to! Meanwhile, the Dalai Lama had begun his escape, and this chap then began his own escape with two old people. The story of these poor Tibetans trying to get out of this with machine gun squads mowing down whole companies of refugees is a fantastic thing; these people pour into India, where they couldn't even take care of their own people.

We finally got the book published under the title *My Life and Lives*. The publisher, Doubleday, cut the guts out of the whole thing and has only the beginning and then the escape, so we've lost the book, but this story of what happened there when the Communists came in was terrible.

Two volumes of reports on what happened in Tibet in 1959 have been published by a group of jurists in Switzerland. I got them when they first came out; you can't buy those books now. In my *Oriental Mythology* (volume 2 of *The Masks of God*), I have a chapter which I call "Buddhism and the New Happiness" on the destruction of these people. It was a terrible thing, a brutal, horrible story.

But these Buddhists are marvelous, with no complaints: this is world process, Buddha process. I've lived with this young man now for years and have never heard a negative word about the Chinese. I learned what religion is from him. This is real love. This is inexhaustible benevolence. This is the wisdom and virtue of the bodhisattva Avalokiteśvara and of Chuang Tzu. You get it from the Dalai Lama as well; he will never say a negative word. They read things positively. It's marvelous!

THE AMERICAN MYTHOS

You have said that "cultures emerge from their mythologies, not from economics,"[6] but wasn't the culture of the United States based from the beginning on the acquisition of material wealth?

I think the impulse for the settlement of Virginia and the South was colonization, property, and worldly goods. This was a more aristocratic group (Sir Walter Raleigh, for example). They were colonizers who came to increase their own properties simply by taking land from the Indians. But they had one terrible time of it, in ferocious religious conflict largely with the colonizing Spanish and French. What those people went through in the way of suffering and disaster! They must have been moved by some terrific drive hardly imaginable today.

But the impulse on the part of those who settled New England was largely religious.

In search of freedom of worship?

For themselves, not for others.

You don't believe they were standing up for principle?

No, I don't. We know why they came over. They were selfish. Those in the North, in New England, came over for their own religious freedom. And each came over with a system of darkness of his own that made it impossible for anyone who differed with them to live where they were—and that is why we have so many little states in New England, each one founded by the members of another religious sect.

The first state in the world, however, not founded on the basis of some religious dogma or other was Rhode Island. Rhode Island would then, perhaps, best represent the kind of thinking that comes out on our dollar bill, where you have not dogma, but a humanistic approach to the problem of people living in decency together.

So the dollar bill *does* represent the American mythos?

I think that in the symbolic engraving on the back of the American dollar bill itself one finds a statement of the ideals on which the nation was founded, the ideals and principles that support the value of the dollar bill—and they are *not* those of crude economic materialism.

What we see represented there are the two sides—the obverse and the reverse—of the Great Seal of the United States. On the reverse, to our left, we see a pyramid, an Egyptian type of pyramid.

How does an Egyptian pyramid end up on the Great Seal?

The imagery of this seal is founded on ideas that have come down by way of the Freemasonry of eighteenth-century Europe. My guess is that the source of the information that supplied the images represented there was the library of Thomas Jefferson, who was a very learned gentleman indeed.

You think the founding fathers had an awareness of these ideas?

Oh, I think that, especially when you read what they have written—Jefferson and Franklin, for example.

These place the creation of the United States in the context of a larger movement?

Absolutely! At least as far as the symbolism on the dollar bill is concerned. This is eighteenth-century Enlightenment. Hence our American sense of a common cause with France; sympathy with the French was right there with these men from the beginning. Benjamin Franklin was in Paris. Jefferson went to Paris, too. The ideas that came out of France were what shaped our Declaration of Independence—independence, that is to say, from England.

What are the mythological associations to this imagery?

The eye at the top of the pyramid within an equilateral, or almost equilateral triangle, emitting a radiant light, is the World Eye. Why should we not call it the World Eye? In India this is known as the Eye of Brahmā the Creator—the Eye of God, which on opening creates the world as its object. It might be today interpreted in more physical terms as the Big Bang of Creation, out of which the universe has spread forth, just as the pyramid opens out below this initiating point. The spreading forth is in a downward direction: the initiating Eye being at the top and the created universe—the pyramid—spreading downward.

If we now count the number of stages represented on this pyramid, we find that they are thirteen. This is a reference to the thirteen original states. Underneath is written, *Novus ordo seclorum* ("A new order of the world"). What we have here, then, is a symbolized *re-creation*, a new creation. The first creation was of the natural order; the second creation is of this particular sociopolitical order, which is in accord with the natural order. For above we read, *Annuit coeptis*: "He has smiled on our undertakings." What we have done, that is to say, has been accomplished in the sense of the original, creative World Eye.

When we look closely at this pyramid, we notice that behind it there is simply a desert, whereas before it there are green sprouts growing, and plants. It is as though there has been a resurrection. This in ancient Egypt was the idea symbolized in the mythology of Osiris: his death, and out of his death, his resurrection. By analogy, out of the death of the old society comes the new, which has been first announced in the founding of the thirteen original states. This is the message clearly symbolized on the reverse of the Great Seal of the United States.

Looking across the bill, we see a reproduction of the obverse of the Great Seal, representing a bald eagle, which is a type of eagle native to North America (the eagle being the classical bird of Zeus, or Jupiter, the ruling Lord of the World). Above this eagle's head is an extremely interesting symbol composed of thirteen stars arranged to form two interlaced or interlocking triangles, one pointing upward, the other downward, in the way of a Solomon's Seal or Star of David. Each of the triangles is constituted of nine stars—nine points, four to each side—with a tenth star in the center.

This is precisely the form of an important, age-old, Pythagorean symbol known as a *tetraktys*, representing the root or source of creation, the nine points surrounding a tenth. When personified as deities, they were to be thought of as the Nine Muses surrounding the god Apollo, by the radiance of whose energy the Muses are motivated in their world-creative, world-sustaining dance. For the Muses represent the creative energy of the god Apollo operative in the field of phenomenality. The same idea is symbolized in Christian iconography in the nine choirs of angels surrounding and celebrating in song the radiant throne of God.

Now, when two such triangles are combined, as here, the upward pointing member is a counterpart of the pyramid shown on the reverse of the Great Seal, and the point or star at its summit or apex is, like the World Eye crowning the pyramid, symbolic of the impulse of the Spirit in the motivating of creation. The downward pointing triangle, then, is symbolic of the material world thus created. But here, too, we have an apex (at the bottom) out of which the world-creative energies likewise proceed. In Pythagorean terms, the single point at the apex of the *tetraktys* stands for the point of the entry into the field of Time of the energy of Eternity. But when this impulse strikes into the field,

it breaks into a duality, a pair of opposites. For everything in the field
of time is understood in Pythagorean thought as one term of a pair of
opposites: the One has thus become Two.

But now that we have everywhere pairs of opposites, there are but
three possible ways for such opposed terms to relate to each other,
namely:

1) Member A dominant over B;
2) Member B dominant over A; or
3) Members A and B in balanced accord.

Thus, the One that became Two has now become Three; and out
of these Three derive all possible relationships whatsoever in the field
of space-time, which field is what is, in the Pythagorean *tetraktys*, supposed to be represented by the Four.

Finally, when the two equilateral triangles are represented interlaced, as in the symbol above the eagle's head, what we have is a structure showing no less than six apexes: one above, one below, and one to
each of the four points of the compass. From all quarters, that is to say,
as well as from below and above, creative energies proceed.[7]

And so now, returning to our pyramid with the Eye of God at its
summit, we remark that the date inscribed in Roman numerals on its
base, when turned into Arabic numerals, is 1776. That is, a date of the
founding of this pyramid. And when we now add 1, a 7, another 7,
and a 6, the sum is 21, which is the year of a child's coming to the "age
of Reason." All of which is to say that in the shaping of this newly created nation, founding a new order of the world, man at last has come
of age. For the first time in human history neither force nor special
privilege, but reason has been the creator of a society in the image
of Man.

How should we understand that?

Translated into political terms, this is the idea of democracy, in contrast to the monolithic image of a single point (the eye of one creator)
at the summit of a monolithic block.

And it is with this multicentered symbol overhead, symbolizing
the new message of which he is the vehicle, that the American bald
eagle descends from the empyrean to this earth. In his talons he holds
the opposed emblems of the only two modes of political action within
this field, composed of pairs of opposites: in his left, thirteen arrows,

symbolic of the way of war; and in his right, a spray of laurel with thirteen leaves, of the way of peace. The bird's head is turned to the laurel spray, but the arrows (thank God!) are in his other fist. So that, whether in peace or in war, the intention of his action is to be ever in the name and spirit of the dual *tetraktys* above his head.

Now, above his head, as well, there is an inscription: *In God We Trust.*

Does this phrase indicate the United States is founded on Judeo-Christian principles?

To appreciate the intended sense of these words, it is necessary to recall that the authors of this composition were not Christians, but eighteenth-century deists who fundamentally rejected the Old Testament mythology of a "Fall" in the Garden of Eden. The mind of Man, according to the deist view, has never been by any such "original sin" made so beclouded that it cannot come to a sufficient knowledge of God directly by way of reason. No special revelation to a chosen people is required, nor in fact has anything of the kind ever been delivered, according to this view. All peoples are capable of the knowledge of God—which is finally why the principle of democracy can be reasonably announced and proclaimed slavery ?

Reason is how we come to know the mind of God—knowledge within reach of each individual—and that's why democracy works?

This is the founding idea: when clarified of those vicious impulses which becloud the mind the moment one descends from the high position of the One to either side of a duality, the gift of reason is man's sole and sufficient medium for knowledge, by reflection, of the Divine Mind.

How did you happen to make these associations to the imagery on the dollar bill?

I had no thought of the symbolism of the dollar until it was brought to my attention during a lecture I was delivering at the Foreign Service Institute in Washington, DC. I was giving a lecture on Hindu political theory as represented in the *Artha Śāstra*, a classical text on the art of politics, which is to say, the art of winning. And I happened to be

standing directly in front of a large reproduction of the obverse of the
Great Seal. Quoting from the *Artha Śāstra*, I held out my two clenched
fists and said: "The ruler must hold, in his two hands, *danda*, the Big
Stick, the means of war, and *saman*, the gentle words of peace, diplo-
macy, and negotiation." At which point everybody laughed, because
directly behind me there was this eagle in the same posture with the
same meaning. I looked back and noticed, not only the double *tetraktys* overhead of thirteen stars, but also the nine feathers of the eagle's
tail, and suddenly I realized that there was something interesting here,
worth learning about.

Couldn't it just be a random arrangement?

Let me give you thirteen marbles and you then arrange them just by
chance in that formation! Think, also, of the nine of the eagle's tail;
thirteen arrows; thirteen leaves of the laurel spray; thirteen stages of
the pyramid, up to the point of the Eye of the Spirit. There can be no
doubt about it. This is an entirely intentional construction.

**I hear Taoist themes in some of the ideas espoused by the founding
fathers—for example, "that which governs best governs least," a concept spelled out by Thoreau but often credited to Jefferson.**

The Taoist principles are the same basically as the Pythagorean. I
think it is in stanza 42 or so of the Tao Teh Ching that we read: "Out
of the *Tao* comes the One; out of the One comes Two; out of Two
comes Three; and out of Three come all things." That is exactly the
tetraktys.

These are all aspects of what has been called the Perennial Philosophy—a common philosophy underlying the ancient West and the
ancient East. Pythagoras and the Buddha, for example, were contem-
poraries, sixth century B.C. The Buddha's dates are generally given as
563 to 483 B.C., and Pythagoras, circa 580 to 500 B.C.

I think it really great to have hit upon this comparison, because,
given the little that I understand about constitutions, this is completely unique—I mean, for that time, for the eighteenth century,
when the Constitution was drafted—this emphasis on the rights of
the individual rather than the rights of groups of individuals.

again, slavery?

Historian Arnold Toynbee identified the inability to react to challenges, whether from within or without, as the primary cause of the collapse of civilizations. Do you think this is true of American civilization as well?

Well, what I would say in answer to that question is that it is one thing to react to a challenge and come out successfully, but it is another thing to react to a challenge and maintain the principle on which your civilization has been founded. And I think that we have not held very well to the principle represented in this image on our dollar bill. *yes /*

With what result?

Well, I think it has put us right back in the desert, behind the pyramid here.

Isn't America reacting to the challenge?

It is certainly good to have a reaction, but this doesn't necessarily get us out of the desert. Every time I open a newspaper there are new disasters in prospect. We are solving things, all right, but not in terms of the ideology represented in this engraving on our dollar bill.

You have to think of a civilization in terms of its dynamic in time: its youth, maturity, age, and old age—and we are in the old age of our culture. It's in a dissolving, disintegrating period. And out of the old comes the new. One has to look and wait for it, and I don't know where to see it. Every time I get a little bit of hope I see more disintegrating old age—people interested in their finances.

There's an awful saying of Oswald Spengler that I ran into in a book of his, *Jahre der Entscheidung* (*Years of Decision*), which are the years we live in now. He said, "As for America, it's a congeries of dollar trappers, no past, no future." When I read that back in the thirties, I took it badly. I thought it was an insult. But what is anybody interested in? And then Lenin says, "When we get ready to hang the capitalists, they'll compete to sell us the rope." And that's what we're doing. Nobody's thinking of what their culture represents. They're wondering whether the farmer in the Midwest will vote for you because you sold their wheat to the Russians, or whatnot. It's a terrible lack of anything but economic concerns that we're facing, and that is old age and death—and that is the end. That's as I see it. I have nothing but negative judgments in respect to that.

And look at what people are reading in the papers. You get into the subways and people are all reading the same thing—this murder, that murder. This rape, this divorce. What topics to be mentating on! This journalistic accent in our lives is murder. Murder.

Can America realign itself with the original inspiration behind the formation of the United States?

I think it is of course possible to get out of this fix. I don't recall who the diplomat was who once said that in our relationships, specifically in the Near East, we should be evenhanded. In my view, that would be the first step to an answer. With evenhandedness, one is back on top of the pyramid again, above the pair of opposites. But on the other hand, we are ourselves so deeply embroiled, right now, as representing one side of the world conflict, that evenhandedness cannot be readily achieved.

War Games

The twentieth century gave birth to a movement to end war, which we've seen expressed in the formation of the League of Nations after World War I, the United Nations at the end of World War II, and the peace movement in the 1960s. Will we see "peace in our time"?

You can't legislate war out of existence unless you can legislate the enemy out of existence. The impulse to conquest is intrinsic to society. Primitive peoples—my god! When you read of the actual war acts of people in, let's say, Polynesia or New Guinea, it's annihilation war! You get a little island with a few thousand people on it and one valley is fighting the next valley all the time! And these are great big husky guys, so what are you going to do with all that if they're not fighting? This is one of the problems.

But the real, or what might be called historic, war style begins in the Near East about 2500 B.C. The first documents of which I have any knowledge are in the period of Sargon I, about 2350 B.C., where he describes overwhelming this city, overwhelming that city, and killing everybody in it and so forth. And the instructions for war in the Old Testament—go in, kill everything in the city, and wipe them out, dogs, cats, even rats if you can kill them all—this is horrendous! It belongs to the first stages of what might be called dynastic civilization.

In certain other periods of war, it is primarily an aristocratic game. This was so throughout most of the history of India; you know, what do you do as a noble except hunting and then war? And in Europe until, I'd say, the time of Napoleon, the wars were largely aristocratic wars—then mass war from Napoleon on. That's the beginning of what we're getting today.

Wars now, of course, are monstrous. What England and the United States did with their aircraft in bombing out the cities of all of central Europe and then, with atom bombs, two cities in Japan—there's been nothing comparable to this ruthlessness in the history of the world.

Is there a mythological dimension to war?

War, like everything else, requires ritual for people's participation. Ritual is a means to enable you to apprehend what it is that you're doing. You usually take it for granted. But realize what's going on here.

The demand on the individual is that he give himself up for his community. That's the mysticism of the warrior life, that he accepts death for himself. And there are rituals, or there used to be, for bringing about that shift of accent in the mind. In fact, during the Second World War, when the Navahos were being drafted into the American army, there was an old Navaho medicine man, Jeff King, who trotted out of the box his warrior initiations, and the boys were initiated into the warrior mentality, which is a different one from daily life.[8] Similarly, the warrior mentality of Odysseus had to be turned back into secular life. My interpretation of what goes on in the *Odyssey*, with respect to the transformation of the consciousness of Odysseus, is that he is being reintroduced, after ten years in the army, to the values, joys, and significance of the relationship of male to female in this world.

War is a ritual; formerly, war used to be quite ritualized. It was only in the First World War that it lost that. Second World War, minimal rituals. Then the Korean thing: nobody knew who was fighting and what or where we were. Were we fighting for the UN or for the United States or what?

But then comes the business of debasing ritual to political aims, which is what Hitler did, and it's easy to do. I have a friend who is a Dutchman; he was in a concentration camp. Hitler came, and the prisoners in the camp had to stand in attendance, and my friend said, "I had all I could do to keep from raising my hand and saying, '*Heil!*'"

This man knew how to do it! The display of glory and power with this funny little man, a strange, mad character seized with some kind of diabolical zeal for what he thought was the salvation of the world— and he made people feel it.

Once that gets going in the world, that's something the sociologists cannot take into account. Sociologists base everything on statistics and all that kind of thing, and then some unique phenomenon like this comes along, with an infusion of energy and power and a genius, and the people around him knowing how to fulfill it for the symbolic display. He went mad—and he wrecked it himself with that turn against Russia.

It's a strange thing, history. You know, these funny little moments that make all the difference between the tide going this way and the tide going that way. You can put your finger on it, some accident—or it looks like an accident, but then destiny shows itself in what look like accidents.

War will then always be with us?

I see that war now, in terms of our contemporary culture, is superfluous. That's not the way to win anything. I think the Japanese have learned that the way to win is to produce useful goods well and be inventive and original in meeting the market.

The Japanese, then, have channeled their intrinsic aggressive nature into more productive activities?

Well, I wouldn't say that the Japanese are intrinsically aggressive. Their period of internecine war, fighting among themselves, belongs to a period of social transformation in the fifteenth, sixteenth, and seventeenth centuries. And that's the counterpart of Europe experiencing in exactly the same centuries the same kind of thing. But they are people of enormous energy, enormous intelligence, and also discipline. They don't mind working hard, and that's better than warcraft.

I live now in Hawaii; also, I was for six months in Kyoto in Japan, and I think I have something of a feel of these very different people from ourselves. They are filled with wonder. But I think with respect to the two nations, the Japanese are working for Japan. They are! The Americans are working for their own income tax—and that makes a big difference. What looks like a field of competition in America, management against labor and all that kind of thing, is a field of cooperation in Japan.

In teamwork, you know, you can't be an individual, and the life of a culture is the life of a team. I don't know what's happened, because when I was a boy (people my age always say, "when I was a boy"), it really was different. The impulse to sheer individual pull-out achievement, and getting on and going home, I don't recognize that as belonging to my early days, and it wasn't that I wasn't aware of what was going on either. I think it's not American. It has to do with the condition of the culture at this time. I see our culture in terrible shape.

We live in an anxious time.

Always. This didn't start with the atom bomb.

All you have to do is read the Old Testament, the Book of Judges and the Book of Joshua, to see what it would have been like to have lived in a little city in the second millennium B.C. A dust cloud appears on the horizon: is that a tribe of Bedouins, or a dust storm? Next morning there is not a person alive in the town.

People have always lived under the threat of death. We are just so used to living in the luxury of a margin of protection that this threat of death comes to us as an exceptional thing. But it's normal throughout history—not only of human life, but animal life as well. Look at the pictures of the animals on the Serengeti Plain when they go to a pond to drink water. The lion is always there.

This is part of life—but we're so afraid of this or that threat which may or may not come. If it doesn't come, so what? If it does, so what? When people *know* that they're going to die in a few months or even weeks, they become so alert and aware of the present—and then they begin to more fully experience it. To live with the anxiety of a future calamity, when all the joys of the present moment are asking to be recognized, seems to me a good way to miss the show.

The Future of Myth?

What kind of mythology do we have today?

I won't say what kind of mythology we have because I don't think we have a generally functioning mythology. There is no general mythology today because our lives are too greatly various in their backgrounds, aims, and possibilities for any single order of symbols to work effectively on us all.

What accounts for that?

The cultural crisis—and this is certainly a period of great crisis—is primarily caused by the very recent coming together and collisions of culture forms, culture ideals, that were in total ignorance of each other one hundred years ago. This is a crucial problem today. Our contemporary world is so heterogenous that few people share the same experiences. Pluralism makes a unifying myth impossible.

Every mythology—and by mythology I include every religion— has grown up within a certain social order. And today these social orders have come into collision with each other. All you have to do is look at what's going on in the Near East now, and it's a horror. There are the three major monotheistic religions of the world creating havoc because each of these units of religion thinks it has all the values on its side and doesn't know how to open up and recognize those are human beings also.

Myths do not export very well, either through time or through space. They grow up in a certain environment, and now these circles have collided and fallen apart. A myth has to work the way a picture works: either you say, "Aha!" or somebody has to explain it to you. And if it has to be explained to you, it's not working.

If a culture has no active, living mythology, so what?

We have seen what has happened to primitive communities unsettled by the white man's civilization. As old myths die, the societies dependent on them disintegrate. Their old taboos discredited, they immediately go to pieces. Today the same thing is happening to us.

Mythological situations refer to the spiritual life; the whole thing becomes a metaphor with a spiritual reference—and in one's life, one is participating in the metaphor. But that doesn't work anymore.

When a society changes, it loses its symbols and has to invent new ones to reflect its current situation. But in modern society there has not yet been a conversion of the conditions of our lives into mythological symbols. Conditions are changing too fast.

Look at what happened in my lifetime! We go from the railroad

train to the airplane to the rocket to the moon. The year I went as a
student to Europe, Lindbergh flew the Atlantic; now we go to the
moon.

This rapid change has made it difficult to convert conditions into
myths. Hence, many people feel rootless. That's why the Hindu gurus
come over here and reap a fortune by telling people to "turn inward."
That is more than a fashion; there's a real movement to meditation in
this country. Our mythology has been wiped out. Christianity isn't
moving people's lives today. What's moving people's lives are the stock
market and the baseball scores. What are people excited about? It's a
totally materialistic level that has taken over the world. There isn't even
an ideal that anybody's fighting for. What runs the world is economics
and politics, and they have nothing to do with the spiritual life.

Can't we just craft a new mythology to address today's needs?

No, because myths don't come into being like that. You have to wait
for them to appear. We cannot predict the next mythology which
is coming, for mythology is not ideology. It is not generated by the
brain, but from those deep creative centers below the human psyche.
But we can predict what it had better be.

Myth has to do with the individual life, with the social life, with
the relationship to the geography, and then to the transcendent. The
relationship to the geography and the society within it is what sepa-
rates this mythology from that.

There are two things that have to happen if you're going to have a
mythology that's appropriate to man today. One is to take the world of
nature as it is known, and *my God*—I've been hearing recently about
some of the things that the physicists and astronomers are finding out,
and it is magical and incredible! That's the ground. It's not difficult to
turn that into a mystical inspiration.

And the second thing is to realize that the society with which you
are involved is not this group or that group, or this social class or that
social class, or this race or that race, but the planet.

**But didn't you just say that mythologies are tied to a specific land-
scape?**

That's right. But when you can fly from New York to Tokyo in a
day, you can no longer say that's an incredible span of consciousness

to include as one unit. The new mythology has to invest the whole planet. There's no doubt about it. What is the group today? It's the planet, linking economically, politically, in a tight net of cultures that were unknown to each other.

We need a global concept if we are to survive, and while that may seem unlikely to happen at present, it is possible if economic need forces it. As long as there are economic interests asking for it, there will be strong pressure for it. This unification of the planet into one society is becoming apparent to everyone as an economic fact; and when it is an economic fact, then it is a fact indeed, as far at least as the public mind is concerned.

well.. this is not happening

But it *is* beginning; it is really beginning. They're importing from Tibet—this could not have happened fifty years ago! Until I went to Europe as a student, I had never seen even a Hindu; there were none in the United States. Now we have Chinese, Hindus, Vietnamese in our classrooms. What's happened academically as a result is very interesting. History studies are out; the vertical history of the group to which you belong is all gone—nobody's interested—and anthropological studies are all over the place. I noticed it, oh, about midway in my teaching career. Suddenly I'd have kids in the class who had been to Africa; they'd been to Nepal; they'd been all over the place. Formerly, I could just make believe I knew something about those places.

So, what is asked of us is this opening to our brothers and sisters around the planet. How do you get on with that man who's on the other side of the fence, has a different psychology from you? How do you get on with him without trying to impose your psychology on him, but through an understanding of the "thou" that's there?

But what is happening, instead, is that people are pulling back. You have all kinds of in-group loyalties, and nobody is loyal to the planet. It's possible to have a mythology of the great cosmos, to have a mythology of the society of the planet, instead of this one of "we're the good ones"—because we're not.

You might say we're pregnant for it. It just hasn't come.

Do you know of any ancient mythologies that were global?

No. There's no ancient mythology that was global. Each one is in a defined horizon, every single one. Oh, there are overlaps—the same themes will occur—but the people in those cultures do not regard themselves as members of a global society.

But now it may be possible?

I think that is possible. That's what I'm interested in.

We're getting tremendous information. It's all I can do to keep up with what's happening every year, pouring in from every quarter—archaeological discoveries, whole new literatures, translations out of languages we've never heard of before, old, archaic, dead languages being rediscovered and then translated and their grammar studied. This is a fabulous period!

But how do we assimilate all that? It's a period of just too much pouring, pouring, pouring in; things are taken for granted today of which we knew nothing fifty years ago—I mean, that there were such people, that there were such thoughts, and so forth. It takes a while to assimilate it all.

But nothing will really straighten out until the sociological image of the planet, rather than of this group or that group, takes over.

Is the emergence of a global mythology inevitable?

Well, this has a very important bearing on mythology because, again, every culture's mythology up to date has grown up within a certain horizon, a horizon of common experience which the members of that culture have all shared. And you go to another horizon you have other experiences, and the mythology will have a different complexion, a different quality altogether.

Now the horizon is the planet.

The only question, and this is a big one, is whether this great new heritage of man will finally dissolve away as the building of the pyramids did when Egypt lost its power. That is to say, is it the Western mind, the Western psyche that supports it? Or, on the other hand, is this something which can be and has been fundamentally assimilated to the consciousness of the global man, if we can call it such, that will continue, and we shall move into a new world phase? Are we entering the phase of no more horizons that I've spoken about, the true post-agricultural phase of human society? This "airport civilization" that's, as it were, putting down its centers all over the world—is that something that's going to fade as the gifts of the British Empire faded? Or is it something that will be carried on? Can these other culture worlds take it in? Do they want to? Are they using it, as Spengler says, simply to smash the West that gave it to them, or is there something there that they truly want for themselves?

How long that next movement will endure is the question that arises out of what we've just been talking about. Is it going to be a phase that will disappear, and then will all these separate cultures go back into their own little boxes again, or is it something that actually represents the beginning of a totally new age of man on the planet?

That's a tall order, transcending national identities.

We're in a period, in terms of history, of the end of national and tribal consciousness. The only consciousness that is proper to contemporary life is global. Nevertheless, all popular thinking is in terms of loyalties to the local communities to which all are members. Such thinking is now out of date.

What we face is a challenge to recognize one community on this earth, and what we find in the face of this challenge is everybody pulling back into his own in-group. I don't want to name the in-groups, but we all know pretty well what they are. In our country we call them pressure groups. They are racial groups, class groups, religious groups, economic groups, and they are all tangling with each other.

For any people to say, "We are it and the others are other"— these are *dangerous* people. And there are religions still doing this. The new thing that is very difficult for people to realize is *our society is the human race.* And our little suburb is the globe. Spaceship Earth.

The tension today then is between a pull toward a more universal perspective and a contraction into tribal, sectarian in-groups.

The one toward more universality is the trend of the century, and the sectarian is the pull of people who are afraid of what is before us. And when you think of this, the number of men who are in fact responsible for the condition of the world right now—I mean in its political life— they could all be contained in this room, and they are acting as though there were no way of common understanding! They are all men of intelligence, but so linked to this system of now archaic desires and fears that the world is in chaos simply as a function of their inability to assume the middle position in a conversation.

Do you believe the human spirit is at a crossroads?

I think the human spirit is developing. I don't take a negative attitude toward what's happening with the human spirit. I take a very negative

attitude with what's happening to our politicians, but that has nothing to do with the human spirit. The chaos in the world today is not a
function of the illumination of humanity today; it's a function of the
bungling of a bunch of self-interested politicians.

But what if we take the wrong road?

Well, I'll tell you—this is a big confession—I'm a minority of one. I
think what's happening is okay. I'm very optimistic. And I tend to like
what's going on. Most of my intellectual friends are superior to it. I'm
not. War? Fine.

Fine?

Well, that—good people killing people in wars—that's the result of
tribalism. But I'm not the one to say this should not have been. There's
a line in Schopenhauer's *World as Will and Idea* where he says, "Life is
something that should not have been." And I think that's what a lot of
people really feel because of the way it goes: it's reprehensible—holo-
causts and other things of the kind, storms that wash California into
the sea.

**You speak with obvious concern about the sort of limited views of the
effect of Western religion on indigenous culture and how the world is
pregnant for a sense of global unity, but then you say you're okay whatever happens. What am I hearing?**

Well, what you're hearing is that this Western religion, which has iso-
lated itself from the rest of the world and has been responsible for
sending out missions in order to make the whole world Christian, is
also the engine that has made this one planet. And so, you know, the
devil is that one which serves the good even though it actually represents evil. I remember somebody asked Ramakrishna one time, "Why
is there so much evil in the world?"

And he said, "Well, that's to complicate the plot."

A basic thing I say is that there are two mythologies in the world.
There's one that says we are to put ourselves in accord with the harmony of nature; that's the point of view of the majority of mankind
over the millenniums. There is another system that began with Zoroastrianism, to the effect that there is a good god, and there is a bad
god. The good god created a good world, and the bad god filled it with

badness (also known as the Fall). The world that we're in is a mixture of good and bad. Consequently, you do not put yourself in accord with nature, which is corrupt. You correct it.

Now, I regard history as part of nature; this is just what happens to be. The human race lives in a way that may not be comfortable to all of us, but this is the way life has proceeded. And for me, I say yes. I don't think the world has to be corrected.

Of course, people who dare to change society are also part of this world that you don't think has to be corrected.

Well, look at the mess they've made, in terms of correction. The very attempt to correct the world is what complicates it. They're part of the problem. But then that's fine. One says, "Yes, that's the way it is."

You ask me if I am an optimist? I'm an optimist. Everything is terrible—and I think it's wonderful.

Even if the world ends?

Personally, I am an optimist with respect to the ability of life to survive. And I think the means are bound to appear for the resolution of this tension. Actually, the tension is hardly more than a century old, and that the answer will come seems to me inevitable. We don't have a mythology for people recognizing the humanity of a person on the other side of the tennis net. So, it'll come, it'll come; but it isn't here. And we had better learn that lesson; we had better find a world mythology because if we can't live together, we will make a rubble field out of earth.

Up to the present, however, one can only be terribly pessimistic. Pessimistic with respect to the present or the day after tomorrow, but optimistic with respect to, let's say, fifty-odd years from now.

So your response to all of this is to do nothing?

Well, I just write my books. I feel that what I have to say is something that suggests the harmony of peoples; it's a symphony of the celebration of mankind that we find in the myths. And I know that what I have written already has made a little bit of a dent.

But you can't turn yourself into Hercules to carry the globe on your back. You've got a little job; do it well. And if you think the thing to do is to reform the world politically, go into politics. Personally, I don't think that's the best way to make a difference, because you know what happens. People step into these roles, and then they find there's a momentum there that they have to carry on. This is a tremendous momentum.

How would you advise ordinary people to participate in this process?

Today, with the economic net knitting us all together and the resulting interdependency, every single one of the in-group mythologies is not only out of date, but dangerous. There's no notion of the global community as the prime unit. What I see as the main problem of mythology today is not what the new myth is going to be. The new myth is going to be one that recognizes the whole planet as our society.

But if you want to know what your mythology is, your personal mythology, ask yourself, To what group do I belong? I would not know my identity if I did not know I was a human being—that would be mine. I'm not a dog or an eagle. I have to know myself as a human being. Well, if the only way you can know yourself is as a Navaho, you have limited your perception.

What has struck me is that when you go to other countries, countries far, far away with types of people that you've never seen before, the human-to-human meeting is joyous and easy and full of friendships. The thing that's pulling people apart is another level of interest that's up there on the political and economic front. The last war was fought over economic problems. Also in teachings of doctrines, the seeing of our doctrine as superior to that doctrine, that's simply got to go. You can't say, you know, in this helpful way, "Yes, indeed, you worship God in your way, I worship God in his."

So, I think that in one's political action and influences, if one can think of oneself as a member of a world community without betraying the legitimate interests of one's local neighborhood, one would be helping the world forward.

And the next breakthrough has to be of the recognition of the planet as the Holy Land.

CHAPTER SEVEN

———•———

"The Course Has Gotten Wider"

CAMPBELL ON CAMPBELL

A STUDENT OF MYTH

You have written many books. Have you ever thought of writing an autobiography, giving your readers a sense of how the lessons you glean from myth have played out in your own life?

Well, the little thing I have suggested for people who are trying to find their way is to follow your bliss. Not instructions. I've followed my bliss, and I'm enjoying life, so that's it. But as for writing an autobiography, I feel so sad and nostalgic every time I look back at any period in my life, I can't bear to do it.

Have you followed the same mythic path all your life?

Yes, but the course has gotten wider. I started as a kid of five or six around 1910. Buffalo Bill used to bring his Wild West Show to Madison Square Garden every year, with a bunch of Indians right off the Plains. They would come in and set up their tepees, and the lights would go down. They'd do dances, and a stagecoach would come in, and they'd raid the stagecoach and shoot it—oh, it was great! That was when I found the Indians.

My brother was one year younger. One day my grandmother was wheeling the baby carriage with my sister in it down Riverside Drive—I guess I was five—and a lady stopped us and said, "You're two nice little boys." And I said, "I have Indian blood in me." She looked amazed. My brother said, "*I* have dog blood." (I didn't know Charlie was interested in dogs!) Finding out about Santa Claus was nothing. But finding out that I could never be an Indian was something else!

On Sundays, Dad would ask us what we wanted to do. We'd choose from the aquarium down in the Battery, the Bronx Zoo, and the Museum of Natural History. And *there*—they have it to this day—in a magnificent room, with really grandiose totem poles, was an enormous Kwakiutl canoe from the Northwest coast, and in it were these dummies of Indians paddling and another, in a bearskin, standing up. So I started reading Indian stories, legends, *The Kalevala*—that's *The Land of Heroes*, a Finnish folk epic by Elias Lönnrot. Those were days when Indians were hot from the warpath and Wounded Knee. And these wonderful books were coming out, very fresh, not contrived for children, just *great* retelling to boys of Indian tales, such as Lewis Henry Morgan's *League of the Iroquois*. One of the most important that I still have on my shelf was George Bird Grinnell's *Blackfoot Lodge Tales*. Reading those stories, I began to become absorbed in American Indian myths and tales.

When I was nine, we moved up to New Rochelle. Our house was right next to a vacant lot. Workmen started digging in the lot. My brother and I helped. When the building was finished, it was the New Rochelle Public Library—*my* building—and I was sitting on the stoop when they opened the door to the children's department for the first time. All these nice little books about Indians.

Within a year I'd read all the American Indian books and was admitted to the stacks of the main library, where I began reading the annual reports of the United States Bureau of Ethnology. The beginning of my real scholarly life had been up there. By the time I was thirteen or fourteen, I was a good little anthropologist on American Indians. That was a delightful period of my life! (We had a dramatic finale: the house caught fire, my grandmother was killed, my father was almost killed, and that was the end of our relationship to New Rochelle, in 1919.)

A young boy's love of Indian lore is the seed from which *A Skeleton Key to Finnegans Wake*, *The Hero with a Thousand Faces*, and so much more has sprouted?

Well, I just got fascinated with anthropology, Indians, the myths, the whole history of the Southwest. One thing led to another. I guess I never quit studying. Then, when I was in prep school, books began coming out—Frederick O'Brien, *White Shadows in the South Seas*, and so forth—about Polynesia, so I became interested in that material. I was being brought up a Catholic, and it didn't take me long to recognize that there were deaths and resurrections, virgin births, floods, and all that in these other mythologies, and my mother again began to become nervous about the whole thing. This was the beginning of my interest in comparative mythologies.

Did your birth faith survive this recognition?

I was a good practicing Catholic until I was twenty-four or twenty-five years old. Every week I would go to confession, and before going to confession I'd examine my conscience. I would think of all the negative things I had been guilty of doing. Why in heaven's name not think of all the great things one has done, and the good things and the lovely things, and *forget* the others? But dragging those up and meditating on them—it turns one into a worm. You're always on your knees, beating your chest—"through my fault, through my fault, through my most grievous fault." Sure, get it off your chest when you've done something, but these little peccadillos, these little tiny things—what in heaven's name! If you do something ghastly, you don't have to go to confession about it—you know what it is and it's hitting you in the face all the time.

When you find that you have lost your faith, you've lost the imagery that really connected your conscious life with the deepest spiritual potentials within you. And so my belief is that one shouldn't throw these things out, but reread them so that they do have valid spiritual rather than impossible historical references. And then it all comes to life again. The Catholic myth, after all, is indeed a rich and beautiful one.

Later, when I was a student at Columbia, I discovered the Arthurian romances where the old motifs came up again, linked to Roman Catholicism of the Gothic period.

You have mentioned elsewhere that after prep school you attended Dartmouth, majoring in biology—until an encounter with Dmitri Merezhkovski's *The Romance of Leonardo da Vinci*.

That book simply overwhelmed me! I realized I didn't know a *goddamned thing* about literature, the arts, or anything like that. Meanwhile, I was totally fed up with Dartmouth. So I left there, and I switched to Columbia. And I switched my whole interest from biology and mathematics to the history of literature, history of art, of music, and so on.

What about extracurricular activities in college?

The courses were so easy I wasn't paying much attention to them. I became interested in playing in a jazz band. I had a family of saxes—C soprano, E-flat soprano (ah, that C melody!), alto, and E-flat baritone—and guitars, ukuleles, and so forth. We had a wonderful little band. Played for fraternity dances and junior proms. We'd augment the band and get it up to twelve pieces—that's *a lot of fun*, playing in a real band like that. The band swung out on those great Jungian melodies "I'll See You in My Dreams" and "Tell Me, Little Gypsy, What the Future Holds for Me."

We'd go down to the New Amsterdam to hear Paul Whiteman, our favorite. And the theater, what theater! Terrific! Every year a new play by George Bernard Shaw and Eugene O'Neill. The Ziegfeld Follies! The Greenwich Village Follies! And every week a whole new sheaf of music for us to play. I'd been brought up in Prohibition, never had a drink in my life. Ask a girl to go to dance, that's as far as we went, and order ginger ale and for ten dollars have a glorious evening. My God! *Jesus.* Ohhh.

Then a whole new interest came into my life. In compulsory "phys ed" at Columbia, you had to run around a track. I've never been able to allow anybody to beat me at anything, so I used to come in first. Lapping kids all the way, all these kids falling down—they'd fall down when they were born, for Christ's sake—I was just lapping people and *passing them again!*

So the track coach, Carl Merner, asked, "Have you ever run?"

"No."

"Would you like to go out for track? You can go a faster mile than anybody we've got in college right now."

"Sure."

I really was devoted to track and to playing in the jazz band—but they didn't go together. Then the New York Athletic Club invited me to run on their team, and I did. I ran my junior and senior years. I've got a box of championship medals that would cover a bed—mostly *gold.*

After graduation you continued on at Columbia. Was this decision driven by your interest in mythic material?

When I graduated in 1925, I'd just been elected captain of the team for the coming year, so I went back to Columbia to graduate school in order to run for another year. Well, what could I *take*? Nothing very serious! I couldn't read German or French that well. Knowing only English, I read for a graduate degree in English. I chose the Romantic period and the Middle Ages.

Well, when I started reading the medieval material, I became *so* excited. There were the old myth motifs again, which I remembered from my Indian days, particularly in the Arthurian stuff. I'd been brought up a Roman Catholic and was having very serious problems with it. Even as a kid, I'd seen the motif correspondences. And now this became something I was really seriously interested in.

So, running, eating up this medieval material, and playing in the band. Playing let me go to dances without getting involved with any particular female. But each year I had a girl I took out to the dances. And then at the end of the year I moved over to another girl, interrupting the continuity in my erotic career.

No serious relationships?

If you invited a girl out three times, then her mother was looking forward to you as the son-in-law. There was that "catch-me" motif. I didn't want to get married! That was the *last* thing I wanted. Really.

Meanwhile, summers, my mother had been taking us traveling. (I had very good parents.) We took a trip across the United States, a boat in San Francisco, down the coast of Mexico, through the Panama Canal and up to Baltimore. Memorable! Brother Charles, Alice (my sister), and my mother. Then she took us to Europe the summer of the 1924 Olympics. A great Olympics—Paavo Nurmi, what a runner! My father met us, and we went to England and Scotland, Holland, Belgium, France, Switzerland, Italy—and gosh, I still remember every one of those cities, every place we went. What a wonderful introduction.

So, I'm on the boat to Europe, a ten-day boat, slow passage, and three deck chairs together were occupied by three dark-skinned young men. When they went off, I looked at the chair names: Jiddu Krishnamurti, his brother Nityananda, and Rajagopal.[1] There was a nice-looking young woman who knew them. I introduced myself to her, in the way of youth, and she introduced me to them, and Krishnamurti and I became very fond of each other on that voyage. The young woman gave me a copy of Edwin Arnold's *The Light of Asia*, and that was my introduction to Buddhism and Hinduism.[2]

What did your father do for a living that allowed your family to afford so much travel?

He was in the hosiery business, importing and wholesale.

You continued with track?

The New York Athletic Club team was invited out to Golden Gate Stadium in San Francisco to run—and we ran away with everything. My roommate, Jackson Scholz, an Olympic runner and winner, told me about Hawaii. Well, I'm in California; why not Hawaii? So I get aboard a boat, full of myself—we had won everything!—and the boat drops anchor about a mile off the island in July. The island flowers are all blooming and the perfume comes a whole mile out: the whole island was a bouquet. Ecstasy. The boat comes in to dock, *Aloha* is being played by the band, there's this crowd, and above them is a staff with a pennant that says "Aloha Joe Campbell!" I thought, "This is little enough for a guy like me!" Track star, you know. But it was Jackson's friend trying to meet me.

Well, fate: I stayed at the Courtland Hotel and, unknown to me, this was within one block of the home of Jean, the girl I married thirteen years later. She was a little thing then, going for dancing lessons, a *child*.

On the boat back I met a girl, we had a light affair, very innocent, none of this heavy necking we have now. She comes back in my life years later. I was invited to go on a trip up the coast to Yakima, Washington, and I was there for the American Indian rodeos. Then back to graduate school.

Focused on Arthurian lore?

My thesis was "The Dolorous Stroke," a motif from Malory's *Morte d'Arthur*. They liked my thesis. At the end of my work on the master's degree I was given a fellowship to go to Europe.

I was absolutely fascinated by this material, and *still* running. I was twenty-two, twenty-three, years old. And the fellowship just came to me, as everything else did: this is a life of serendipity. So I finally dropped track. You can't do serious scholarship and track at the same time. I went to Paris in 1927.

At that time, you were one of the fastest men in the world. Was it difficult to give up running?

I was on the point of making a decision to start into scholarship when I lost one race, and it was the one I really wanted to win. And I'd never lost a race before. I've rerun that race five times a week, you know. If I had won that race, I would not have given up running, and I would have stayed there as a jock for two or three or four years.

The 1928 Olympics were the next year, but I broke off. In 1928 I was in Paris when all my friends were in Amsterdam. After the games they came down and we had a party, but I wasn't there at the Olympics.

Considering there weren't a lot of professional opportunities in sports in those days, had you won that race and run in the Olympics, might you have had a career as a coach or athletic trainer, instead of a mythologist?

Well, something silly like that. And it was the failure at that point that, from the standpoint of a career—I mean, I know the chap who won the half mile at the Olympics that year. I had run against him many times. And you think, "Oh jeez," you know? So I didn't get the Olympics.

Thank God I didn't, is what I'm saying now. I have to see that.

Now, Nietzsche is the one and he's my boy, if you want to know; he says if you fail to affirm everything in your life that has come to you with amor fati ("the love of your fate"), you have unraveled the whole life. Any significant moment in your life, if it had been the least bit different, the whole life is different from there on.

So you said "yea" to losing that race?

If you say no to any detail of your life, you've said no to the whole web because everything is so interlocked. And if you want to get in the way of affirmation, just say no to the failure, the thing that is your most acute shame.

Shame?

I'm speaking about shame, not guilt. Guilt is what Nietzsche calls slave morality. You are guilty because you are disobedient, and you are in fear of punishment. Just think about the religious feeling about guilt: hell is punishment, and guilt is fear of punishment because you have disobeyed an order.

Shame is an aristocratic sentiment. It means failure in performance, and you're ashamed; I've failed in performance, so I commit hara-kiri—that's shame. Guilt: I disobeyed somebody at some duty I should have done; it's put on you. It's a totally different morality. This is a very important psychological distinction between shame and guilt.

So in a heroic sense, how did you say yes to your failure?

Because I've had such a marvelous life.

Up to that point?

No, all the way. I would not have had the life I've had if I had won that race. I know it.

But did you know that then?

No.

So how did you manage to shed the runner and become the scholar?

I had made the decision beforehand that I was going to go into scholarship. But I wouldn't have been able to do it properly if I had continued running. So it made it easier for me really to cut off and give everything I had to my scholarship. See, when I went to Paris, I could have run for the jockey club there, but no.

Then affirming what comes to us "with amor fati" requires a leap of faith that it will in the end be better?

No, no. Not that it would have been better. That it's good. You affirm it. It may be a mess, but you're affirming the mess, too.

There's a very interesting word in English, namely *weird*—as in the three Weird Sisters in *Macbeth*. This is the whole problem of destiny.

In Islam, there's the word *kismet*, which is the destiny put on you by God. Kismet—that's why the real Muslim warriors are so courageous. Nothing can happen to them that's not their destiny. And so they go. If they're to die, they die.

But there's a European word, *werden* in German, "to become." You become what you are potentially to be. And that *werden*, "to become," is at the root of the word *weird*. This is translated as "fate," but it's very different from kismet. It appears in *Beowulf*, the earliest English epic, when Beowulf, as an old warrior, is about to go against the dragon, and he knows he isn't up to it. But it's what his destiny is to do; he's the chieftain, after all, and nobody else can go in on that dragon. There's a line that, to me, is one of the most telling lines in Anglo-Saxon literature: "Wyrd was very near." He's sitting, thinking, pulling himself together to go into this battle. "Wyrd"—the terminal moment of his *werden*, his becoming…Beautiful. Beautiful line!

In Greco-Roman myths, the fates exist apart from and outside us. Is this a way of taking the pressure off—it's not me, it's fate?

Well, fate is a dimension that is not of your person. It's transpersonal. You open up to something that is deeper than your own personal notion of yourself. Even though it's you, it's beyond what you know of yourself. It's experience that's coming *to* you. When I open up like that, it comes to me from down here. And since I know that's where it's coming from, I read it that way. But someone else might read it as coming in from, say, the northwest.

Back to your postgraduate years: you leave your track career behind in the United States, and…

Off to France.

Well, it opened up first in Paris. Everybody was there—Picasso, Joyce, Matisse; I'll never forget the exhibit of the Intransigents out in the Bois de Boulogne. I knew nothing about art; New York knew nothing. I learned about modern art and its relationship to all these myths.

And I discovered Joyce. The whole thing opened up like crazy when I found *Ulysses*, which was forbidden in the States. I had to smuggle my volume in. You went to a bookstore feeling you were doing something pretty far out and said, "*Avez-vous Ulysses?*"

That third chapter of *Ulysses*: "Ineluctable modality of the visible: at least that if no more, thought through my eyes. Signatures of all things I am here to read, seaspawn and seawrack, the nearing tide, that rusty boot." I couldn't understand what I was reading! What the hell's going on here? I went to Sylvia Beach at the Shakespeare and Company Book Shop in indignation: "*How* do you read this?" And she said, "As follows." And gave me a start.

Joyce assumed scholarship. He wrote things only a person with a bit of literacy would know. And he'd been a Catholic who had found a way out without losing his symbols.

The first drafts of *Finnegans Wake* were being published in the avant-garde magazine *transition*, edited by Eugene Jolas. I must say I was totally baffled, as everybody was, but I bought the whole year of *transition* as it came out and studied it closely, realizing there was something there that was meaning a lot to me, and I didn't quite know what it was.

So, by the time *Finnegans Wake* was published in 1938, I was ready for it. I was pulled in. And with that I began to lose touch with my PhD direction. Suddenly *the whole modern world* opened up. With a bang!

While the world was opening up for you, what was happening with your studies?

I was soaking up medieval literature at the University of Paris, studying Old French and Provençal. I read nothing but French, but I found all the basic books were in German. They renewed my fellowship for a year; I went to the University of Munich and studied German and Middle High German.

In Munich I lived with a German family, spoke German, and thought German. I bumped into an American student who was in philology like myself and was working on Sanskrit. So I enrolled in Sanskrit and Buddhist studies with a *wonderful* Professor Oertel at the University of Munich, and then India comes in. I went into Sanskrit for the philological side but got caught up in the philosophy, the mythology, literature, and that was *far, far away* from where I was supposed to be in medieval French. But this thing just grabbed me.

And there I discovered Jung and Freud and Mann. The whole world opened up!

**How did you reconcile that with what you were studying
Columbia?**

I came back to Columbia—no money, no job—in 19⌐,
weekends before the Wall Street crash, and I said, "I don't want to go
back into this little bottle that I started out with; things have been
buzzing out there!"

What? You dropped out of the doctoral program!

I decided long ago I wouldn't do a goddamn thing I didn't want to do.
My father's hosiery business was in very bad condition in the Crash. I
didn't know where I was. The world had blown open. I'm no longer in
the PhD bottle. I don't want to go on with my little Arthurian pieces.
I had *much* more exciting things to do—and I didn't know what they
were. I wanted to write, I wanted to be an anthropologist—I didn't
know *what*! A new wonder was around.

So I said, "To hell with it, Columbia!"

I didn't have a job for five years!

BOHEMIAN INTERLUDE

Looking back, do you wish you had finished the PhD?

Those years, your early twenties, they're when your star is twinkling.
If I were to have put myself under the ceiling of Roger Sherman
Loomis,[3] with whom I had been working, I know where I would have
been; I would have gotten the job at Columbia that was waiting for
me. I know who got the job, and I know what kind of a guy he was.
This is wonderful too: to have seen the fork in the road, to have seen
the one you took, to have seen the guy who took the one you didn't
take. He had a wonderful academic reputation, but you'll never hear
of him again.

My word for young people now who ask me is, follow your bliss.
It will come. Nobody's ever been on that road before, and so, where
you didn't know there were doors, there are not only doors but palaces.

What doors opened for you?

My family had no money; I couldn't finish my academic work, so I
moved up to Woodstock and rented a little shanty to live in. I paid

$20 a year for the house. I was a young man, not yet married, and so I had no trouble. I just went up into the woods for five years and did all I wanted to in the way of reading, pulling all this stuff together. I read and read and read.

I'm writing short stories. I discover American literature—Hemingway, Sinclair Lewis, the whole bunch. Hemingway just knocks me over, those early things of his—*In Our Time, Men without Women, The Sun Also Rises*. Like every callow young author, I wanted to write like him; meanwhile, Joyce was interesting.

Five years, no job! And I was trying to work my way out of a hole with Bertrand Russell and John Dewey, all this garbage I'd got at Columbia. Writing stories nobody would buy. Finally, in desperation, I thought: I'm going away. So Mother let me take the Model A Ford and start across the United States to try to find a job.

That car drive across the States was simply something. A coupe, its maximum speed was sixty, and you felt you were rattling the hell out of it.

Did the job hunt pay off?

Just before this my dad had decided to get the Crash off his mind and said to me, "Let's take a cruise." So we got on a Swedish liner and went down to the Caribbean and Havana. There was an attractive young woman on the boat whom I found *very, very*...well, this is my first American girl after my years abroad...and her name was Adelle Davis.[4] She was a brave kid and had all kinds of ideas about nutrition. When we came back, she decided she couldn't find herself in New York and went off to San Francisco. Two years later I'm out there in my Model A.

Meanwhile, I'd started Russian. But it's 1932—*What am I going to do?* You couldn't go into anything. The world was *stuck*. It's impossible to imagine now. There wasn't a job in the world.

I think, I'd like to find Adelle. I look her name up and she greets me with a couple of parties and helps me realize I'm at the bottom of a well and don't know where the hell I am. She kind of took care of me. A wonderful person, a wonderful woman. She gave me spunk—I was really depressed.

I'd heard about Carmel, the artists. So, driving down, I stop off in San Jose and phone *Idell*, the girl I'd met on the boat coming back from Hawaii, who lived in San Jose. "Oh, Joe!" She told me her sister

Carol had married a chap who was trying to write, too. "Let me drive down to Carmel with you and introduce you to my sister!" She then introduces me to John and Carol Steinbeck, in Pacific Grove. I just fell in love with the pair of them.

I stayed and got a little place in Carmel called the Pumpkin Shell. And again here I am, trying to pass John Dewey and Bertrand Russell, Adelle bringing me vitamins, and Steinbeck and I trying to write. There was a little fellow with a goatee at John and Carol's, Ed Ricketts, who was Doc in *Cannery Row*. His laboratory is the place *Cannery Row* is all about. That was an important moment for me, getting to know him. Ricketts was an intertidal biologist, and I had been interested in biology from my school days. Talking with Ricketts, I realized that between mythology and biology there is a very close association. I think of mythology as a function of biology; it's a production of the human imagination, which is moved by the energies of the organs of the body operating against each other. These are the basis for the archetypology of myth. So I've thought of myself as a kind of marginal scientist studying the phenomenology of the human body, you might say.

Were you able to eventually "pass John Dewey and Bertrand Russell"?

I was in the Carmel library—sort of, "What am I gonna read now?"— and my right hand went up to a book. *That* was the beginning of everything: Spengler's *Decline of the West*. I read the first page and knew I'd found it—Dewey and Russell just *blew away*; I read nothing but that for two years. Two volumes. This was it! It brought back everything I had had in Germany, and added, made sense of it, put it in play in the contemporary situation. From him I went into years of the study of Goethe, Schopenhauer, and Nietzsche, and then I realized Mann, Jung, and Joyce were all saying the same thing.

"The same thing" being what?

A system of archetypal impulses that have moved the human spirit and operated historically and in the religions. It is the synthesis I've been working on ever since.

When I finished volume 1, I gave it to Steinbeck. Well, next I see Steinbeck—he was a ponderous guy, walking around like a bear,

rubbing his side thoughtfully (people thought we were brothers)—
he's rubbing his side and I ask him, "What's wrong, John?"

"Can't read this, can't read this."

"Why not?"

"My art! My art! This thesis that now we're to put down the pen
and paintbrush and pick up the monkey wrench and the law book—
technology and law!"

"John, you can't just shut your eyes to things. You gotta take it
and beat it." So he gave me the book back, and I went on in rapture.

Sounds like idyllic bohemian days.

I'll never forget the miracle of those years when the lights were shin-
ing out in front. A beautiful time; four months of something glorious.
Wonderful people. We were all in heaven. We weren't the dropouts;
the world had dropped out. We were in a halcyon situation, no movement, just floating. Just great.

How did you survive?

I got a little house in Pacific Grove for fifty cents a day. My money
was going down. I had made enough money during my years on the
saxophone at college to support me through this. In fact, I helped Dad
with some of my savings.

I'm coasting along, trying to find where I am, crazy on Spengler.
Ed Ricketts was an intertidal biologist; we'd go out and collect hundreds of starfish, sea cucumbers, things like that, between high and
low tides, furnishing animals for biology classes and schools. Ed made
an arrangement to go to Alaska on a small boat. Great! What else
is there to do? So, we cruised up the Inside Passage from Seattle to
Juneau, collecting specimens.

Well, the Inside Passage was gorgeous! We sat on the stern as
that little launch went out into the waters of Puget Sound, off for six
weeks, much of which we'd spend at an absolutely uninhabited island
gathering animals while Ed made notes. The cost: twenty-five cents a
day for the whole crew. We would pull into port, all the canneries were
closed, the fishing fleets immobilized—they'd *throw* salmon at us. Put
your hand in the water and pull fish out. Just an idyll. The towns were
supposed to be dead, and they were the most *living* things. There's

nothing like living when you're not living with a direction but just enjoying the glory of the moment. *That's what we were doing!*

We arrive in Sitka, Alaska. Ed has an order for fifteen hundred *Gonionemus*—little jellyfish. We lived in a cabin. Every morning I had to deliver our canoe to the folks on the boat, then swim back to shore stark-naked. In ice water! I'd come out congealed.

Then on to Juneau. A very exciting border town, a gold mine there and a lot of men working the gold mine, every other storefront a bar, and the alternate ones pool parlors. Alaska was first Russian, which I now spoke, and many Russians had married Indian women and were hang-overs. They loved food, parties, no end of food! Many were aristocrats who had come out of Russia to escape that trap. These were an adventurous bunch of guys. Working in mines—and they wanted dangerous jobs. They'd go into a mine after an explosion and see that everything had exploded. We'd be having a party and their time would come and they'd be wearing greatcoats like Kazakhs—*We who are about to die salute you!*—and off they'd go into the mine, like giants.

I'd never seen a balalaika, but it's a very easy instrument, strung in the major triad, so I learned to play the balalaika and played with their Russian groups. *Ohhh!*—a ball, a ball!

Where did you go from there?

I'd accepted a teaching post at Canterbury, my prep school. I borrowed my fare from Ed and taught at Canterbury for a year, and Alaska and California dropped *like that* out of my life.

But it had been glorious, with a tension behind it all the time. Where was the next dollar coming from?

Why so short a time teaching?

I had a job for one year at that prep school in the middle of the Depression, and I wouldn't go on with that. I don't ever want to teach boys that age again! I think the male at those years is something else. I had gone through them once myself, so I just quit and went back to the woods.

I was building up my historical studies, based on Spengler, and resuming Sanskrit—a grim year. My father's business was in very bad shape. Then one of my short stories sold! The only story I ever sold,

"Strictly Platonic."[5] My agent sold it for $350. So I retired. I don't know what the magazine was; I took the money and ran back to Woodstock.

Living on nothing, a single young man, always available for dinner—I learned to live on that dinner. A couple with a great big dog named Fritz (a cross between a Doberman pinscher and a police dog, a big, powerful, amusing lunatic of an animal) had built a house in the woods, and they asked me to take care of Fritz and keep the house warm while they lived in New York for the winter. A buster of a winter, so cold! So I was cutting wood and I really just buckled into reading Joyce and Sanskrit, Spengler, Mann, Jung—the whole thing was coming together. And another great passion of mine, Leo Frobenius, a German Africanist whom nobody was supposed to read because his patron was Kaiser Wilhelm. But he was the person who opened up African studies.

I was tremendously excited. Those years were terrific. I was out in the woods—thrown out, you might say, by the collapse of society— and I found my own path. I wasn't interested at all in a job. I could live on nothing and was having a wonderful time. Then it began to be good. I really had no money and found I didn't need it. And I took a vow that I would never work for money.

Did you continue writing fiction?

I wrote a detective story, which a cleaning woman threw out—thank God! And a novel. The novel was contrived and stupid.

I wrote four poems when I was a kid in prep school, and they're still good. With respect to fiction, I'm not basically a fiction writer. A fiction writer has to be interested in the way the shadow falls on your jacket, the quality and the feel of it, and all that. That's not my talent. I'm just too much up here to be visual that way and sensuous that way. My fiction is lousy. I found that everything I did was stiff, and I quit.

I didn't want to write, either. I just wanted to read.

When did that period of your life come to an end?

The Depression was still on. In my mailbox came an invitation to teach at Sarah Lawrence. I drove down. They wanted me. I told them that if I was going to teach, I'd like to give a course on comparative literature that started back with the old epics and came on down the line. They liked the idea. It was very, very nice.

You married one of your students, Jean Erdman. How did that happen?

We gave individual conferences for the students. One day one girl comes in and drops a photograph on my desk. It's me, ten years earlier, on the roof of the Courtland Hotel in Honolulu, playing a ukulele. Well, think of the person I'd become since then! Jesus, the bottom dropped out; I went down three depths. Mortified! That grin. I wasn't the same guy, and here's this picture!

Well, the girlfriend of the guy who took the picture had married and was living in Bronxville; she had given a party for five girls from Honolulu who were students, and they'd found my picture in her album. "Isn't that Mr. Campbell?" And Jean, the young girl I later married, who had lived a block from me in Honolulu, had been at the party. My destiny had dropped a plumb line.

Jean's teacher, René d'Harnoncourt, a wonderful man, had to leave to do something for the American Indians, and Jean decided I was the only person she could go on with in Aesthetics. So she asked to take a course with me. I took her on as a private student.

I'm susceptible to female beauty, so I was in a mild high all the time at Sarah Lawrence, but I realized that some little person somewhere was maybe a notch higher, and that was Jean. She left at the end of her second year to go around the world with her family, then join Martha Graham's dance company—Martha had asked her to dance with her. Jean was a beautiful dancer.

Well, I had a feeling that maybe this was it, but I wasn't sure (I still called her Miss Erdman). What can I do to make sure she'll see me after she graduates? I gave her *The Decline of the West*! I kept in touch with her through the guise of instruction. Ha!

She was crazy about dance. I had a theory about the relationship of aesthetic forms to psychological grounds—it's one that really does work—and she was going to be seeing all these traditional dancers, and I was deep in Oriental studies by that time. I'd give her advice. In the course of this exchange of letters, it became evident to me that I'd been hooked. I cast our two horoscopes and I saw that. That was all!

When Jean came back, 1938, we just got married. Her father was a minister. I was in such disdain of religion that I told myself I wouldn't have what seemed to me a religious marriage. But her father was both a minister *and* her father—it was a kind of *augmented* paternal bless-ing. When it came time to say, "I do," I knew that it was more than a paternal blessing! I think it took.

Do you have a mythological perspective on marriage?

When you see people in roles, it's really something to recognize the mythological. And the best place, the best trial ground for this, is marriage. I'm not kidding. It is really true. Because there you are in the great mythological relationship of the pairs of opposites, and the field of the relationship is where the transformation operation is tak-ing place. Who wants to be transformed? Nobody does. But the whole thing is a transformation field. And when I look at Jean and she's get-ting nasty and all that, I have to say, "I see You there."

You see *who* there?

Woman, the Guide, the Helper. I see *You* there—the Goddess. It's the energy, the power that she represents in relation to my power that's what's important. And the personality between can be experienced either as opaque or transparent. This is something I think comes in marriage. If you can stick it out, then you realize how this mystery has worked. And the thing of the two being one, you know they are. They *are*! It's no myth!

I remember once talking about courtly love and this idea of the two that are one, and one woman in the audience—I guess she didn't have a very happy marriage—raised her hand and said, "Oh, but that's just an image."

I said, "Yes, it's an image, but it's an image of something that *is*." The two *are* one. Just as you and I are here. Only there you really have to experience the deep implications of that. So that's a little word for a greatly maligned institution.

CAMPBELL THE WRITER

Setting aside your forays into fiction, how did your career as a serious writer unfold?

I was teaching a course in Kant, Schopenhauer, Nietzsche, and Thomas Mann at Sarah Lawrence when one of my students said I sounded like her mother's swami. She invited me to meet Swami Nikhilananda, who was the pastor of the Ramakrishna Vivekananda Center uptown. He invited me to visit him in Brant Lake in the Catskills while Jean was off dancing at Bennington with Martha's company, so I went and stayed with the swami. A young man was helping him do a translation of *The Gospel of Sri Ramakrishna*. Monks like to go to bed early and get up early, and I like to go to bed late and get up early, so one evening Nikhilananda handed me a chapter and said, "Before you go to sleep you might like to read this and mark down any suggestions."

When he got the chapter back it looked like a map of the Labyrinth. I could see the shock. So he asked me if I would go through the whole thing, a huge, huge piece of writing, and he would in exchange talk about Vedanta philosophy. This was a *very* fair exchange. I worked on that damn thing for two years, a *huge* job!

In 1944 you coauthored *A Skeleton Key to Finnegans Wake*—the first guide to James Joyce's complex final novel, and the first published work to appear under your name. What led you to write that book?

I wasn't interested in writing it. I was interested in *reading* it.

Well, we were married, I met Nikhilananda, and *Finnegans Wake* was published. I'd been puttering around with early renditions of *Finnegan*—it was then called *Work in Progress*—all these years, so when the book came out, I bought it and read it that weekend, looking for soft spots so I could really go to work on it seriously, for my own pleasure.

My friend Henry Morton Robinson was the one who tricked me into writing a book. He was a real pro; he knew how to write a piece. He'd been a young member of the Columbia faculty, then had resigned and become a freelance writer (he later wrote the bestseller *The Cardinal*). I'd found him in Woodstock; he was a Joyce enthusiast too.

In 1939 *Finnegans Wake* appeared. Rondo came to our place one evening with his wife and said, "How ya doing with *Finnegans Wake*?"

"Fine."

"How about you and me doing a book on it?" We'd talked about Joyce for years; he was a good Joyce scholar, a *very good* Joyce scholar, but I didn't take his idea seriously. We were walking out to dinner at Rochambeau (it's now a Blimpie's), and he argued me into it.

"Somebody has to write a key to it, and it might as well be us." And we started.

Our agreement was Rondo would have all the authority on How to Write a Book, and I'd have final authority on what Joyce was saying. He knew Joyce very well, but if we came to an argument I had last say on interpretation. A perfect arrangement. We ended up better friends than we began. Rondo was fat and a poet, a wonderful man. I *loved* him.

I wrote something like thirty thousand words about the first page, and when I brought this to Rondo he said, "For Christ's sake! Are we gonna do the *Encyclopaedia Britannica*?" So he went at it with a meat-ax, and finally I found a way to do this thing: stretches of narrative, what the real thread of the story was on which all of this had been structured or exploded out of. Worked on it *four years*. There were still cloudy areas we couldn't handle. And when we were finished, he sent it to his publisher, Harcourt Brace. They didn't want it. We thought, *What the hell! Who wants it? Should we publish it ourselves?* We knew it was valuable.

Well, one fine day I read in the paper that Thornton Wilder had a play going, *The Skin of Our Teeth*. I'd done all my theatergoing in the twenties, but somehow I thought I'd like to see that play. We got tickets. First row balcony, center. Hey, one quote after another from *Finnegans Wake*! "Do you have a pencil?" I start copying it down on the program. In the morning, I phone Rondo in Woodstock: *Skin of Our Teeth is Finnegans Wake!*"

Monday, he phones Norman Cousins at *The Saturday Review*. Cousins told us to bring something in writing to them immediately, so we wrote a piece Cousins published as "The Skin of Whose Teeth?" And it really rang a bell all over the country.

Well, the newspaper columnists dive-bombed us. We were just a couple of "micks," and they came down like a pack of wolves on us. Wilder was the great American artist who said the idea had come into his head when he was at the Broadway show *Hellzapoppin* and a turkey fell into his lap. What nonsense was that? He had put things in the play that were signals to let you know it was from *Finnegans Wake*. A wedding ring found in the theater by a scrubwoman at 6:32 p.m.—that's *Finnegans Wake*.

We just waited. Once the play appeared in print, I went through it with a fine-tooth comb. There were at least 320 parallels, including a four-line quote word for word.

Then Cousins said, "Do you guys have anything else?" He liked excitement, you know. We sent him chapter 1 of *A Skeleton Key to Finnegans Wake*. Then Harcourt Brace sent it to T. S. Eliot, who said, "Buy it." They bought the book, the same bunch who'd rejected it. So that's how the *Skeleton Key* got published. That was the first. And then, Simon & Schuster, on Robinson's suggestion, invited me to do a book on mythology. And that was *The Hero with a Thousand Faces*, which they refused. That's how I got started writing. I've been writing ever since.

During this period, you developed a symbiotic relationship with the Bollingen Foundation (which eventually published *The Hero with a Thousand Faces*). How did that come about?

While I was working on *A Skeleton Key to Finnegans Wake*, Heinrich Zimmer came over from Germany with his wife and three little sons. I was already well along in my own teaching career when he arrived. I was helping Swami Nikhilananda with *The Gospel of Sri Ramakrishna*, and I knew people in the Jung Foundation. They all knew of Zimmer's arrival here. I had never heard of Zimmer. I met him first at one of the evenings that Swami Nikhilananda liked to put on where he'd invite people and prepare a curry dinner for them. (He was a really good cook.)

Then I learned almost immediately that Zimmer was about to deliver some lectures at Columbia. It was not Columbia who had invited him. A great Indologist, about fifty, couldn't get a job—the Oriental departments didn't want competition with him. So the ladies from the Jung Foundation, the "*Jungfrauen*," discovered a room on the campus where he could lecture. It was at the top of Low Library—a little museum up there. Having met him at Nikhilananda's, I was eager to hear him.

The first series of lectures he gave was to *four people*. Me, curator Marguerite Block, a little *Jungfrau*, and a Polish sculptress who, when she came in, emitted a perfume that filled the room. Zimmer lectured as if he were lecturing to an auditorium.

The second semester, he had to move into another room, because there were about fifty people this time. I mean, news gets around! (My father had a saying: you can't hide a good restaurant. And Columbia couldn't hide Zimmer.) In the fall, he started a series of lectures.

What an ebullient man! Wonderful! The first person I ever met who was way down the road that I found, interpreting symbols positively, deep in Oriental material. If anybody should ask me who my guru was, it was Zimmer, who really just kicked it; I was just ready for the signal of that man. I was thirty-six, thirty-seven.

When Zimmer came here, the Bollingen Foundation had just gotten started. Mima [Mary] Mellon, who was the cofounder and inspiration of the whole thing, had been trying to get advice from several of the European scholars who were coming over here at that time. And when Zimmer came, obviously he was the one. He was really the initiating scholar of the Bollingen series. They asked him what number one should be. He said that if we were doing this in Germany, he'd try to begin with something *of* the land, thus giving respect to the land, letting the spirit of the land support us. So he selected a Navaho myth and series of pollen paintings that Maud Oakes had brought back from New Mexico. It had to be edited because Maud knew how to collect material—she did it beautifully—but didn't really know how to build a book. They asked Zimmer who should edit it. As I had already given him a couple of books of American Indian myths, he said, "Joe Campbell." And that's how I got started, with *Where the Two Came to Their Father: A Navaho War Ceremonial*, 1943. Full circle! Back to Buffalo Bill.

Then, in the middle of the second year of his lectures, Heinrich Zimmer is suddenly dead! He'd been carrying pneumonia around with him and didn't even know it; he'd been walking around with it for a couple of weeks. A big, strong man, he just thought he had a cold or something like that, and—zing—it took him away. His widow asked if I would edit his American lectures. Meanwhile, *Skeleton Key* is accepted. So now, helping Nikhilananda still, my new myth book [*The Hero with a Thousand Faces*], Zimmer's four volumes of lecture notes—all this had fallen on me. *And* I'm teaching.

Heinrich Zimmer's lectures weren't recorded. How did you manage to turn his talks into those four elegant volumes?

When Christiane asked if I'd edit this material—his American lectures—I thought: a couple of years.

It was twelve years I worked on those notes.

Zimmer lectured as though he were lecturing to an auditorium! He was not a good lecturer in English yet; he couldn't do it right off the top of his head. So he had written out his lectures. I have them all in my files, the ones I turned into those books, on little pieces of paper—about six by four inches, something like that. And he would type out the lines—not in a running prose, but in stroke phrases. And he would underline in red the syllable to be accented in each word. I mean, he *worked* on those things, and the lectures were great. And every now and then when he'd come to the point of telling a story, he'd put the thing down and tell you the myth—always with a wonderful sense of the humor that is the life of myth.

Well, those were stunning lectures (he only lectured about things he believed in). His first series of lectures are the ones I made into the great big two-volume work, *The Art of Indian Asia*, which was the last book on which I worked. That was the first semester.

His second series was a full semester of philosophy; then came the series that I published under the title *Myths and Symbols in Indian Art and Civilization*. That was the first that I brought out. Then I did *The King and the Corpse*, which is based on written material that he had published plus the first chapter of his unfinished translation into German of the Kālikā Purāṇa. But the fourth semester of his teaching was the one that broke off with his death. It was again a semester on philosophy. So when I started on the philosophy volume, I had only a semester and a quarter of his lectures, and that was not the whole story. I found a lot more material in his notes. I phoned Jack Barrett at Bollingen and said, "Look, if you'll give me another two or three years on this book, we can have a killer here." And it is. *The Philosophies of India* is a corker!

Compiling and editing work from someone else's notes, incomplete notes at that, must have been challenging!

There were some very interesting things that happened to me in the course of doing those books. Zimmer used to give his manuscripts to his friends and students just to have them read them over and help him straighten out his prose. So when I would come to certain chapters, they wouldn't be there. There would be a gap. Some little lady would have kept them somewhere in her memory chest.

But Zimmer had a very striking and forceful presence in his presentation; in my memory I could hear him. I would get to the point where pages were missing and a break came; I'd jump the break and pick up again where the thing resumed and do a few paragraphs of that. Then I'd see what the gap was between the two and what had to be covered. I had talked with Zimmer a lot about these things, and I would bridge the gap with four or five questions; I'd ask a question and listen, and he would dictate. The style was his style, more or less. Then when I got into the big book on the art of Indian Asia, I could no longer hear him dictating—that was eleven or twelve years later—and I was finished. There was no way to go on.

You were actually *channeling* Zimmer?

No, those were just bridges, you know; I don't have any sense of that kind of spooky thing. It was my recollection of his manner, of what he had been saying, that is, what I'd hear him say—maybe I had a couple of notes of my own from the lecture.

My technique in handling Zimmer's material was to keep his page at my left hand and write with my right (I don't use a typewriter when I write). I was using his phrases as far as possible, with a correction of some of the verbal choices, and I would try to get that baroque rhythm that he had. I would mark off with a red line down the page whatever I had used, and sometimes I'd jump from the top to the bottom of the page and come back to the middle and so forth. It was all built out of his words and put together with a more naturally English tone and type of prose. I don't know where Zimmer ends and I begin. It was a great inspiration to me—working on that wave of his vitality.

Often when I talked with him, he had Wagner going on the record player full blast. Wagner full blast and Zimmer full blast, and I'd stand there and I'd know the whole answer to the universe is coming at me right now, and I'd wonder if I'm understanding it or getting any particle of it! Some of those moments were really fantastic.

You certainly captured his vitality in those volumes.

Well, yes, I got it, but as I said, I worked twelve years on it. It was hellish hard work, but a real, real delight.

Sometimes I wished he'd written the damn paragraph in German—the English was *just* off. That's the hardest kind of thing to get back on the track with—where it isn't *quite* correct. Also, with his enormous philological knowledge he could make up words! He would put in a word that he thought ought to be an English one, and there wouldn't be anything in English quite like it.

I wouldn't have been able to do the books at all if I hadn't known that Zimmer would have liked the way I was doing it. He was extremely amusing with relation to what we call academic formalities. There was one chapter in *The Philosophies of India*—the whole thing on *satyagrāha*, the Gandhi piece, which I wrote from my notes of his lecture and what I remembered. Somebody had run off with that lecture. Later, when I was in Calcutta, they gave me the newspaper one day, and I opened the thing, and here in a framed box on the front page was some Indian declaring that the Westerner, the white man, just can't understand Gandhi, and that Gandhi's message is as follows. I went on reading, and my God, I was recognizing my own prose! It was this chapter! They were pulling it right out of the book! That was very amusing—and pleasing in a way.

So that initial foray into writing with Henry Morton Robinson ballooned into multiple balls in the air at once!

Believe me, I was sweating it out, working like hell in Woodstock, Jean working on her dances in a studio up there and teaching. Ha, twenty-three volumes! That's not bad. I could do it because Sarah Lawrence had no demand for publish or perish. I didn't have to publish a lot of junk in those official scrap baskets, *Publications of the Modern Language Association* and *Journal of the American Oriental Society*. Who the hell reads 'em?

The big thing that carried *me* into play was not the *Skeleton Key* but *The Hero with a Thousand Faces*. I worked for four years on that book; well, I'd worked for four on the *Skeleton Key*. But this one was where the material was coming in and I could put it together and handle it. There's never been anything like that since in this way of my developing with a book. *The Masks of God* was far more an intellectual stunt, carried on for twelve years!

I think back to the old days when I was writing *The Hero with a Thousand Faces*, and it was all I could think of and all I did think of. I had day after day after day of continuous thinking of that book, and that's impossible now.

Is that why, long after you retired, you eventually moved to Hawaii—to escape the distractions?

I wanted it back. I think that's one of the problems of contemporary life. Things are coming in at so many angles that one can become actually broken up. And that's why it's necessary to cut things out, pull yourself together. For me, I couldn't stand it, I have such a wide range of relativities in relation to my work—you know, things that it relates to. And when I yield, I become terribly scattered, my concentration is totally broken. And then there's no direction in time, no direction in achievement. And I didn't see any reason for that scattering anymore.

In India—well, I should have done it fifteen years before—they go into the forest and drop the world entirely, drop their caste, drop all social affiliations, and turn inward. I don't want to do that. I want to keep what's going. But by now, it's so various in its demands.

You know, what I've found is that as you go through life you set up certain waves, certain influences, and then at a certain time they all come back. It's as if the waves had gone out from the boat and have now come back and are blocking the passage. Commitments, commitments, commitments. And they really were not commitments but statements that have echoed and re-echoed. I had to pull myself together.

Did you see your work suffer in quality?

I'm getting so that I can say things better than I ever said them before. And in that sense, my ability to say what I have to say is improving. But I'm not getting a continuity of statement; I know what I want to do, but I just don't have time to pull it together.

Do you keep to a schedule when writing, to meet deadlines?

I put a timetable up, but I never function according to it. I tell you what happens with these things. Remember those little Japanese things they used to have where you drop them in a cup of tea and they open out into a flower? The books grow like that.

My personal schedule is something else. When I get up in the morning, I sit down and start to write. On the last couple of chapters of *Creative Mythology*, I wrote for thirty-eight hours without a stop, eating coffee pills to keep awake.

Now, out in Hawaii where I'm writing, I have a little schedule. We get up at 6—the birds wake us—and at 7:30 I sit down to write. About a quarter to one, I begin to fold it up to have lunch with Jean. Then I want to do something else, but I don't. I go back to writing.

Who is your audience when you write?

I'm a scholar! And my problem is to communicate my scholarship to a public. And my public are my students and their like. Everyone has to have someone to whom he is addressing himself. I find that there are many who are ready to receive this news, but then comes the problem of how you communicate. There are two modes of communication, and I've worked hard—I wouldn't say as an artist, but as a crafts-man—on both.

One is giving a lecture, and I can give a damned good lecture. Let me add that I have also been building a vast archive of slides. This is one of the most exciting things that has happened to me in this whole business. I have been using slides while lecturing. In that way, the images communicate their own irreducible message to an audience while, at the same time, I provide a general discourse of a discursive kind. A kind of triple play takes place. Image, discourse, and the imagination of the audience interact with each other. In this way, one can begin to approximate the tremendous richness of man's mythological consciousness.

The other is writing. I was interested in writing when I was in prep school, and I had an elegant teacher, and I worked at it. So I started to learn *how* to write long before I learned *what* to write. And I'm applying the techniques, the craft part.

I've been working on this material ever since I was a youngster. It's all in my files. And what I write comes to me as messages from the material itself. I don't go at things with a point of view. I have done so in the distant past and found that the material wrecked the point of view. So now I listen to what the myths say.

How would you describe your writing style?

In my books there are about five different kinds of writing. There's a lot of writing that has to do with just historical fact. And it's very difficult to pull it together and then to make it sing. The rhythm of the prose is at the very center of the problem. I wouldn't know how to instruct anybody, but it's terribly important. And that's why, when some goddamn proofreader turns something around, as they very freely do, the top of my head blows off. I've sweated it out to have it that way instead of the way that it's been corrected to. Often what has been done is to restore a style that I have eliminated already. It may be more rational, clearer, *but there's no music.*

Well, there's that kind of thing, the historical business. You can't imagine the number of facts and from how many places these things come. Then there's the translating. I do a lot of translating—from German, from French, from Spanish, and sometimes other languages too—Sanskrit. And with dictionaries around I can translate from almost anything, except Japanese and Chinese. Then to turn that into my prose—that's another problem.

Then there's the business of taking a myth, which has been recorded by some anthropologist in trite, dead language, what I call "anthropological pidgin." You know, they make believe that primitive people speak this way. They don't! The primitive languages are very complex and carry many meanings in a word, and the "anthropological pidgin" doesn't do it. Well, to turn that back into life, that's another kind of writing you have to do in a book like this. You don't realize it when you're reading along that you're going over watery land, now over dry land, now over swampland.

And then I'm singing along on my own elucidations, and finally, there's the criticism of my colleagues. I try to homogenize it so that it all goes nicely.

I've worked hard on my prose. Most scholars don't. I have found that the difficulty of scholarship is not the material; it's the way these guys write. Really, I've looked at a paragraph and said, "What the hell is this guy really saying, if I want to pull it out?" Some of them are my best friends!

You mentioned the realm of the Muses in relation to _The Hero with a Thousand Faces_. In the preface to _The Mythic Image_, you write, "Finally, in a book of this kind it may be allowed to thank the Muses—of whatever time or place they may have been—who watched over and guided the work throughout, in that wonderful way the spirits have of letting one imagine that the ideas of their inspiration are one's own." How do you envision these mythic figures?

The Muses are the personifications of the energies of that unconscious system that you touch when you sit down as a writer. You just have to find them.

When I'm writing, there are two ways that I write. One is badly, and the other is well. And when it's badly, it's dictated from up here, in the head, and that's the stuff that goes into the scrap basket. There's often a period of trial, pushing around to see where I can get that trapdoor to open. And when I hit it, it's almost physical—the feeling of opening a door, holding it open, not giving a damn for the critics, what they are going to say or think. Meanwhile, I've thought out what's going to be in this chapter. All that has to be planned first.

Sounds a little mysterious.

It's an actual experience, nothing mysterious about it. If you have never hit that level, well, then it's mysterious. But if you have, it's not. The next problem is how to get there, and how to make it serve the program that has been determined for it. In India, Coomaraswamy describes the meditation of the Indian artist.[6] First he studies all the *śastras*, all the textbooks on what the god should look like—say, Śiva—what the weapons are and symbols he's to have in his hand. Then he pronounces the Sikh syllable of Śiva and goes into meditation. And then Śiva shows himself, with those weapons that he already knows should be there. It's not that the stuff is there, it's *how* it's there that makes the thing sing.

Writing is a meditative act?

It is for me. Meditation sounds complicated, but it's just waiting. I try not to publish anything that's from any other center.

The wonderful thing is when I get on a certain beam that hits the level of mythic inspiration. From there on I know about three words ahead what I'm going to say. When the writing's going like that, I know I'm in the groove; it feels like riding a wonderful wave.

But if you're writing only three words ahead in a sentence, you don't know how it's going to come out.

It always comes out.

You're not writing with reviewers in mind?

I was reviewed twice in *The New York Times*. My first book was *A Skeleton Key to Finnegans Wake* (it's *still* getting this little pittance of royalties!). Max Lerner used to teach at Sarah Lawrence College, and he divorced his wife, who was also teaching up there, in order to marry one of his students.[7] But then he had to keep in touch with his wife there for alimony purposes and all this.

So I hadn't seen Max for God knows how long, and I get on the train coming down from Bronxville, and there's Max.

"Oh Max, how are you?"

"Hi, Joe. I haven't seen you in a long time. What have you been doing?"

I said, "I've been writing. Just finished a book on *Finnegans Wake*." I could see him wanting to do the review, because he was the guy who could write about anything, you know—and he could. So I gave him the load of what Joyce was all about and what was in this thing, and I knew damn well he was going to write *The New York Times* and ask to review that book. That was the first and only decent review I ever got in *The New York Times*.

Oh no—then when *The Hero with a Thousand Faces* came out, they gave the book to Max Radin, thinking it was Paul Radin. Well, Max is Paul's brother. Paul Radin was an anthropologist; Max Radin was a specialist in Justinian law. Now, what the hell he knew about what I was writing about was just about zero. They had one column, and two-thirds of the column was saying how boring mythology was, and then the finale was "Campbell's book isn't boring." That was when I stopped reading reviews.

Oh yes—one more! A chap who was at Dartmouth when I was there, Francis Brown, became the book editor for *The New York Times*, and he's a member of the Century Club, as I am. And, um, "Hello, Joe."

"Hello, Frank." And volume 1 of *The Masks of God* comes out, volume 2 comes out, volume 3 comes out, volume 4 comes out, and there's no word of it in *The New York Times*. Well, then, Gerald Sykes says to Brown, "What is it? Campbell's got a four-volume work here, no one's done a history of mythology before, and there's been no mention of it in *The New York Times*."[8]

Brown says (and this I heard from the horse's mouth), "If you can make Campbell intelligible to the readers of *The New York Times*, we'll print it."

Sykes says, "Oh, I think I can do that," and he wrote a review of the whole goddamn thing. It was published in a nice spread in the middle of the *Sunday Book Review*, with a picture of that old German Sun Horse, the horse in bronze pulling a solar disk. Next meeting at the Century Club, Brown comes to me and says, "Hi, Joe! How did you like our review?"

That's the end of Joe Campbell in *The New York Times*.

I gave up worrying about reviews long, long, long, long, long ago. In fact, I don't read them. That's what you mustn't worry about. I have the feeling when I write that my neck is out, and the guillotine is there. And I just say, "Okay. I said it. You can knock it off later." As far as I am concerned, this is the last thing I give a goddamn about. And I don't think you can write well with fear of reviewers. You just can't. That's the beginning of writer's block.

CAMPBELL THE SCHOLAR

How has your work been received in academia? Do you follow an accepted methodology?

I am very much against methodology because I think methodology determines what you are going to learn. For instance, Lévi-Strauss's structuralism. All you can find is what structuralism is going to allow you to find. And an open-ended approach to the facts in front of you is going to be impossible there. He insures himself against illumination, it seems to me. You have to know how to run, walk, stand, and sit down. But if all you know how to do is sit down, then you're limiting your experience.

In the twenties and thirties, functionalism was in fashion. You could not make cross-cultural comparisons; you had to interpret everything in terms of what you knew about the local culture. That would be like examining the appendix in the body to determine the condition of modern man. You have to follow it back and find out what its use was in earlier times.

Similarly, many of the elements in a culture are vestigial of earlier uses, earlier functions. And these men—for instance, Radcliffe-Brown in his volume (and I think it is a splendid volume) on the Andaman Islanders just fails to interpret the myths.[9] Here they are all in front of him, and his approach doesn't answer the questions. All one has to do is make a bit of a comparison, and one finds that the interpretations come out. Stuck to one method, he so limits his vision that he fails to interpret the culture.

Then there is the problem of what's known as the generalist

against the specialist. Just as in medicine, sometimes it's better to go
to a generalist than to a specialist—depends on what your problem is.
A specialist can come up and say, in all seriousness, "The people in the
Congo have five fingers on their right hand." If I say, "Well, the people
in Alaska have five fingers on their right hand," I'm called a generalist.
And if I say that the people in the caves in 30,000 B.C. had five fingers
on their right hand, I'm a mystic!

I try to hold the position of a scholar who knows this stuff, and
I'm not telling you what to do with it—I'm not giving it to you. I'm
not directing anybody. My idea of a top scholar in this field is Mircea
Eliade at the University of Chicago. He is magnificent. I don't know
how much influence he has on young people. His address is more to
the scholarly community. I feel almost that he and I are standing in
the same place back-to-back, I facing a popular community and he
the academic community. He has enormous respect in the academic
world. And properly so.

Are you a mystic?

I'm not a mystic, in that I don't practice any austerities, and I've never
had a mystical experience. So I'm not a mystic. I'm a scholar, and
that's all.

I remember when Alan Watts one time asked me, "Joe, what yoga
do you practice?"[10] I said, "I underline sentences." And that's all I'm
doing. My discipline is taking heavy notes and correlating everything
I read with everything else I've read. I have nine drawers full of notes,
and I have four more packed down in the cellar that I can't get another
piece of paper in. For forty years I've taken notes on these materials
that seemed to me to be opening the picture to my mind.

Do you meditate?

No. Well, I swim, and I had a problem counting laps. I found the
best way to remember the laps I was swimming was to remember the
tarot cards. I swim forty-four laps and think on the twenty-two honor
cards, one card for every two laps.

I'm no guru or anything of the kind. I've just had the great good
fortune to find this golden world of myth, and I was also well trained
in how to write a book.

In the crazy period of the sixties, young people were throwing themselves out of the culture. I had been thrown out years before and was out there for five years mooching around and discovered this wonderful stuff. It gave life to my life. It gives life today. Since I retired from teaching, I've been lecturing at human potential places: Esalen (the California oasis), in Chicago, and elsewhere. I'm running into people in their thirties and forties, and I see the things I have been working on working on them—the world of the Muses, the place out of which imagination and inspiration come. It helps them shape their lives.

All I've done is gather what has excited me into my books, and by God, it works for other people just as well as it worked for me! What I like to do is throw out the marvelous ideas which I have simply gathered because I have done a lot of reading. Those that are ready to grab them, grab them. Those who don't, well, that's all right, too.

Many of the people you count as friends and colleagues—Stanislav Grof, Alan Watts, Huston Smith, Albert Hofmann, and the Grateful Dead, among others—have used LSD and/or various teacher plants (mushrooms, peyote, ayahuasca, etc.) as a doorway into spiritual realms. Others seek out teachers and gurus. Which, if either, would you recommend?

I prefer the gradual path—the way of study. My feeling is that mythic forms reveal themselves gradually in the course of your life if you know what they are and how to pay attention to their emergence. My own initiation into the mythical depths of the unconscious has been through the mind, through the books that surround me in this library. I have recognized in my quest all the stages of the Hero's Journey. I had my calls to adventure, guides, demons, and illuminations. In the conflict between the Celtic-Arthurian and the Roman Catholic myths, I discovered much about the tensions that shaped my past. I also studied primitive myths and Hinduism and later Joyce, Mann, Jung, Spengler, and Frobenius. These have been my major teachers.

This, I think, depends on how good a reader you are. Because, when you are reading a book, you are being initiated by its author. Is that not so? The writer who has written the book is initiating you through his book.

Whether a heightened degree of the experience of initiation is gained through a person-to-person relationship, I do not know and cannot say. I'm in no position to judge. Of course, according to the gurus of India, the individual initiator is absolutely necessary. In my own experience, I feel that I have been initiated, perhaps not into the highest but at any rate into certain transformations of my mentality, and I know when these occurred and what they were. Mostly, they were derived through reading. But I have also had two or three personal encounters with really great and wise people, and these have done more to confirm my reading than any book by itself could have done.

Should we seek initiation, or will initiation find us?

What I think is that when we are ready for an initiation, something in the environment will initiate us. It may be a person, or it may be an event, but if we are ready, it is going to happen. This is the whole mystery of what is known as sudden illumination. The story of Hui-neng, the great Zen master, or rather Ch'an master, in China: as a boy delivering wood, he was standing at the door of a home, waiting for them to answer his call, when from inside he heard someone reciting the Diamond-Cutter Sutra, and suddenly he was illuminated.

Is there ever an end to initiation? Do we ever reach Ithaca, or does the journey go on forever?

Not being a fully initiated Wise Man, I am in no position to answer that question finally. But in my view, it goes on, and on, and on, and on, and on, perhaps because I have never been really initiated. But initiation is also something you can lose. That is why people have certain assigned meditations to practice, certain mantras to recite, which keep them on the line. The world is so much with us, you know, and circumstance can be so compelling, so overwhelming, that you may lose your Ariadne thread—that is to say, of course, if you are simply a human being, and not a fully illuminated sage.

Reading, for you, proved more profound than the college experience?

I was six years in the universities here and then two years in Europe. And of my six years here I can remember three professors. Those are the only ones whose names I remember. And I guess that's a pretty good average. But they were great. They were the ones that gave me courage to follow my own dynamics in my studies and not just what the university was telling me I had to do. And here are these machines, these universities; they are scored to take care of everybody, and so they can't take care of anybody really. You have to go in and find your own way.

I don't think it helps to be cantankerous and resentful. You go into a restaurant, you take what's on the menu and make your choice and eat one meal, and the rest is not what you're eating. So it is with these people. Similarly with the books you read.

When I was teaching my course, I would suggest many more books than I knew that students were going to read or be able to read, without the requirement that they should read any single one, but that they should have that list of books that meant something to me on hand.

I think the best thing is to read what you really like, not what your friends say you ought to be reading. When you find someone who really is talking to you, stay with him or with her and read everything that person has to give. One finds one's guru, so to say, one's literary guru, this way. And then that person will wear out after a while.

When you find a book you like, look at the footnotes. See what the books were that influenced that fellow. Look in the bibliography. And cull out your own books that way. You never have to ask anybody what to read if you want to find the person who can lead you on and then try to see what you read operating in your own life.

I've had sessions of interpreting my own life in terms of the clues given to me by the great poets and artists of my interests. The ones I went to when I was trying to build myself were Spengler and Mann and Jung and Joyce. Those are the main ones. Now I have more or less gone off on my own a little bit. But I learned from what seemed to me to be great minds. They gave me clues to how to read my own existence. The religious tradition that I was brought up in seemed to me to be not adequate. These poets, philosophers, and psychologists helped. That bubbling, the inspiration that came out of that, was an inspiration for my life for those years, and I wrote on it.

I'm very much against newspaper headlines, newspaper reviews and reviewers, bestseller lists, and all that kind of thing. I mean, you can scatter yourself out and have cocktail party talk forever. But that's not what makes the thing really cook inside. My secret was—and I've seen it in my students that come through—find the one to read who talks to you, stay with it, build out the circle around about, and it'll be great.

Do you miss not having taught at the University of Chicago (like Eliade), or any other traditional academic institution, where you would have had graduate students carrying on work under your direction, developing a school of Joseph Campbell scholars?

Well, I will answer that with what I regard as the advantage I had in teaching at Sarah Lawrence. That would be the alternate to the University of Chicago experience. (And I know plenty of University of Chicago people. Mircea Eliade I know as well as I know my brother.) It was wonderful. You had to have interviews, or tutorials, with your students every week, and that was challenging. Teaching women was so different. Men thought about theory—where does this idea fit into the overall network?—things like that. My students approached it entirely differently: How will it affect me? What will this do for my life? It was a totally new insight for me. All this history and anthropology and mythology took on another dimension. They wanted to know what a myth might mean to *them*, a certain relevance to life—whereas, with the graduate students and all, I'd be investigating historical relationships here, or special details here and there, which would not necessarily be relevant to us here, but relevant to, say, the Eskimo in Alaska three hundred years ago or something like that.

With this inspiration, I was held to the *life* of my subject, and this is the thing that built whatever it is I have had as a career, which I think has been a pretty good one. That's why I don't have the same public that others do who are writing for, and in the context of, the academic scholarship community. Mine is maverick, and outside.

With nearly four decades at Sarah Lawrence, have you noticed significant differences from one generation of students to the next?

The big change had to do with TV. When the TV generation came with twenty thousand hours of television viewing before they opened a book, a very interesting change in student interest took place. In my course in mythology, I had a core reading list, but then each student was allowed to choose what her interest would be. Some would choose to do Thomas Mann or James Joyce, or Hindu art, or Greek philosophy, or this, that, or the other thing. When the TV generation began coming in, there was not the same individual choice. They all began wanting the same thing.

Of course, it simplified things for me because I didn't have to be teaching Joyce this minute and then Indian art the next and Freud the next and so forth. But they were all wanting the same thing. And another thing that happened was that any opinion that differed from that which was in circulation was *out*. You couldn't have an opinion that wasn't that of the press this year.

There's a kind of unreality about TV which disengages you from the things it's talking about...

You are no fan of television?

You know those television competitions—if you guess the name of so-and-so, you get something? Every now and then the phone rings and it's one of those, and I say, "I don't have a television set. I don't look at television." And the voice on the other side says, "What do you do with your time?" *(Laughter)*

We don't know what's going to happen in television. It's a very young art form. And it's not an easy form for people to get into. And I think it's inevitable that, in due time, there will be artists functioning there.

Switching gears, as our culture changes, might it be time for our traditional sexual patterns to die, to make way for the birth of something new and more appropriate?

Well, I suppose, um, test tube babies and things of that sort would help us along.

Oh, no—I'm not proposing we get rid of sex!

Oh, what are you gonna do with your time? *(Laughter)*

LETTING GO

As the old form dissolved for you, after nearly forty years teaching at Sarah Lawrence, was it difficult to adjust to retirement?

When it came my time to retire, the day after my last conference with a student, I boarded a plane with my wife to a conference in Iceland on altered states of consciousness. I didn't even attend graduation that year. I just said, "I'm going to plunge into something else." And something caught fire immediately.

Would you recommend that abrupt a break for everyone?

The whole crisis that you're facing is that of retirement. What one has to do is have an honest interest, which is well to try to develop even while you're attending to your role. More than a hobby—something that engages you and in which you're learning something. And then when the time comes, you can plunge into that.

Even just taking art courses, you know—or if your religion has meant a lot to you, you can begin to do something in relation to that. *Not* in the way of service outside; in the second half of life your service is inside. It's to you. So it's about time you began thinking of your own inner buzz machine down there. It's impossible that a person of any maturity of experience should not have something like that to jump into.

The real violent break is the best kind because then there's a lot of energy in play and it throws into the new thing, and you move right into it. It may change fast, but follow the changes and it's like a whole new life opening up. It's a fulfilling thing. But it has to be out of something that was already of significance to you.

That is the problem of the second half of life, the inward way. You've done your service; now find the noise inside. That would be my point there. I can say for me it worked. I wouldn't go back. People say, "Would you like to be young again?"

"Well, I wouldn't mind being seventy-two."

Hawaii must be quite a change after life in Greenwich Village.

It certainly is. We lived in the same apartment on Waverly Place more than forty-five years. But my wife was born in Hawaii, and we thought it would be nice to go back there now. My first trip to Hawaii was in 1925. And since my wife and I were married in 1938, we have been back many times to visit her family, and we've made many friends. So it's no problem moving there. And I love it. We go down one flight of stairs to swim in the ocean. It couldn't be better. It's peaceful. Where we live there is an old set of people; they're all about our age, and it's lovely to be with people who have weathered it out—you know, couples that are loving each other and have had a good life.

Still, you have kept busy in retirement.

After I retired from teaching in '72, I have been lecturing four or five times a week. In fact, I'm quitting right now just because I can't take it. It's too much. My last two lecture tours knocked me out; I've canceled the whole fall. I'm going to spend the whole month of November in Esalen, but that's easy, chewing the fat and talking with my friends and so forth; it's not standing up lecturing.

Who comes to your lectures?

I find an enormous interest wherever I go—I've seen an increasing, very serious interest in the powers of mythology, and the powers of the imagery of religion. On campuses or in growth centers, or just lecturing in bookstores, the public has to be turned away. So many people want to hear about this—that's because my treatment of the material is relevant to human experience and need today.

I think the payoff for me, really a beautiful dividend, is first, wherever I go, people look at me and say, "Your books have changed my life." This is big; it really, really is! And then the second, and it's really exciting to me, is how many artists have been influenced and inspired by my work.

Martha Graham, I know, is very strongly influenced. When I married Jean, an artist and a dancer, she was working with Martha Graham. When we were at Bennington, Martha was planning a work on the Brontë sisters. At that time I told her about the women of the *Sidhe*, the Fairy Hills, and the mythology of the Celtic lore. Her eyes opened, and from that moment on she was on a mythological beam. It influenced all of her work. She would be the first to say that this was the moment and that this moment opened up all of these issues to her. The amplification was spectacular.

The literary crowd I seem not to have touched (I mean the literary critic crowd). The literary people who *have* been influenced by me are the ones who write creative works. And artists, and young people wanting something to live by—I've seen it at work in the world of artists.

You've lived a long, full life and are enjoying an active retirement. Are you at all apprehensive about the impending end?

No, I don't see anything to be afraid of. I feel a little like Woody Allen when he said, "I'm not afraid to die—I just don't want to be there when it happens." But that's not the death problem; that's the *dying* problem. The mystical problem is what you identify yourself with: your consciousness, or your body, which is a vehicle of consciousness.

There comes a time, and I think it comes naturally in people as they reach later ages, of shifting the identification from the vehicle to the consciousness. You begin to see the body as a frail vehicle; you think of all it's missing. Once you've got that idea, you can drop off the vehicle; the consciousness isn't worried.

To talk personally, I've had a very, very rewarding life. I've had what the Indians call the fruits of my life. So the end—it's the end. I haven't lived *tremendously*, but I've had, to me, a lovely life, with rich experience. And I've learned, I think, what I was meant to learn.

And what were you meant to learn?

I had a sense long, long, long ago that there were certain mysteries I had to come to conclusions about. And I've come to conclusions about them. It's all very gratifying. And so—fine. That's it.

ENDNOTES

EDITOR'S FOREWORD

1. Joseph Campbell, *Primitive Mythology: The Masks of God, Volume 1*, Collected Works of Joseph Campbell (1959; repr., Novato, CA: New World Library, 2022), 11.

CHAPTER ONE: "THE ABCDS OF MYTHOLOGY"

1. Sumerian cuneiform on a badly damaged fragment of baked clay, one of thousands excavated at Nippur in 1895 to 1896, filed away at the University of Pennsylvania Museum under the title "Incantation 10673" (III Exp. Box 13), deciphered by Professor Arnold Poebel in 1912.

2. The Sumerian name Ziusudra translates in Akkadian to Utnapishtum, the flood hero of the later Epic of Gilgamesh.

3. John 3:5.

4. Joseph Campbell, *The Flight of the Wild Gander* (1969; repr., Novato, CA: New World Library, 2002), xv.

5. John G. Neihardt, *Black Elk Speaks* (New York: William Morrow, 1932).

6. Karl Friedrich Alfred Heinrich Ferdinand Maria Graf Eckbrecht von Dürckheim-Montmartin (1896–1988) was a German diplomat, psychotherapist, Zen master, and author.

7. Heinrich Zimmer (1890–1943) was a German Indologist, linguist, and historian of South Asian art, best known for four posthumous volumes in English edited by Joseph Campbell. See pages 227–31 in chapter 7.

8. Claude Lévi-Strauss (1908–2009) was a French anthropologist, ethnologist, and key theorist of structuralism; Ernst Cassirer (1874–1945) was a German philosopher best known for his *Philosophy of Symbolic Forms* (1923–1929).

248 MYTH AND MEANING

Chapter Two: "An Outline of Everything"

1. Joseph Campbell, *The Masks of God*, 4 vols. (New York: Viking Penguin, 1959–1968; repr., Novato, CA: New World Library, 2021–2024).

2. Campbell completed only the first two of four planned volumes of *Historical Atlas of World Mythology* (*The Way of the Animal Powers* and *The Way of the Seeded Earth*) before his death in 1987.

3. See Joseph Campbell, *The Inner Reaches of Outer Space* (1986; repr., Novato, CA: New World Library, 2002), 9–12; and Joseph Campbell, "The Mystery Number of the Goddess," in *The Mythic Dimension* (1997; repr., Novato, CA: New World Library, 2007), 115ff.

4. Circa 20,000–15,000 B.C.

5. Hierakonpolis Tomb 100 ("The Painted Tomb"), discovered by English Egyptologist Frederick W. Green (1869–1949).

6. Henri Frankfort, H. A. Frankfort, John A. Wilson, and Thorkild Jacobsen, *Before Philosophy: The Intellectual Adventure of Ancient Man* (London: Pelican Books, 1946).

7. The term *cult*, as used in anthropology, comparative religion, history, mythology, and related fields, does not carry the pejorative connotations of contemporary popular usage and instead refers to a particular system of religious worship, especially in reference to its sacred rites, symbols, and ideology.

8. The battle between the goddess Durga and the buffalo demon Mahishashura, from the *Devī Māhātmya*. For a detailed account, see Heinrich Zimmer, *The Art of Indian Asia*, vol. 1, Bollingen Series 39, ed. Joseph Campbell (New York: Pantheon Books, 1955), 96–107.

9. Circa 8000–6000 B.C.

10. Remains of domesticated pigs have been found on Cyprus dating to 11,400 B.C., indicating they had been domesticated earlier on the mainland.

11. 2 Kings 5:15, also cited on page 86 in chapter 3.

12. For more detail, see Joseph Campbell, *The Flight of the Wild Gander* (1969; repr., Novato, CA: New World Library, 2002), 110ff.

13. Also referenced on page 110 in chapter 4.

14. Elaine Pagels, *The Gnostic Gospels* (New York: Random House, 1979).

15. James M. Robinson, ed., *The Nag Hammadi Library: The Definitive Translation of the Gnostic Scriptures* (Leiden, The Netherlands: E. J. Brill, 1988).

16. Thomas Merton (1915–1968) was an American Trappist monk and mystic who authored over fifty books.

17. Philippians 2:6–8; also cited on pages 93–94 in chapter 3.

Chapter Three: "A Mythology Taken Seriously"

1. This concept appears again on page 122 in chapter 4.

2. *Superstition* comes from the Latin *superstare*.

3. John 10:30.
4. Richard N. Bolles, *What Color Is Your Parachute?* (Berkeley, CA: Ten Speed Press, 1972).
5. See page 60 in chapter 2 where Campbell references this passage.
6. Daisetz Teitaro Suzuki (1870–1966) was a Japanese Zen scholar, Kegon expert, and prolific author. Eranos, derived from the ancient Greek word for "a banquet to which the guests bring contributions of food," was the name given by Olga Fröbe-Kapteyn (1881–1962) to the intellectual Round Table salon she founded, on the shores of Lake Maggiore in Switzerland, to discuss humanistic and religious studies along with the natural sciences. Scholars who have shared their work at Eranos include Carl Jung, Karl Kerényi, Henry Corbin, Mircea Eliade, and Joseph Campbell.
7. Jacques-Paul Migne (1800–1875) was a French cleric and publisher of theological works.

Chapter Four: "Yes All the Way!"

1. Oswald Spengler (1880–1936) was a German historian who argued that all cultures are organic, with limited and predictable lifespans.
2. Oswald Spengler, *The Decline of the West*, 2 vols. (New York: Alfred A. Knopf, 1926 and 1928).
3. Abraham Hyacinthe Anquetil-Duperron (1731–1805) was France's first professional Indologist.
4. This quote also appears on page 63 in chapter 2.
5. The formula for the velocity of a falling object, which accelerates at a rate of 32 feet per second, every second.
6. The four Joseph novels are *The Stories of Jacob, Young Joseph, Joseph in Egypt*, and *Joseph the Provider*.
7. Skira was a Swiss publishing house founded in 1928 by Albert Skira.
8. Compare with page 70 in chapter 3, where this concept is discussed.
9. M. H. "Papi" Göring was cousin to Reichsmarschall Hermann Göring.
10. A Tibetan Buddhist painting on cotton or silk, depicting a Buddhist deity, scene, or mandala.
11. C. G. Jung, *Psychology of the Unconscious*, trans. Beatrice M. Hinckle (London: Kegan Paul Trench Trubner, 1912), revised by Jung and reissued in English as *Symbols of Transformation* (vol. 5 in the Collected Works of C. G. Jung), ed. and trans. Gerhard Adler and R. F. C. Hull (New York: Pantheon, 1952).

Chapter Five: "An Inward Turn"

1. Joseph Epes Brown, *The Sacred Pipe: Black Elk's Account of the Seven Rites of the Oglala Sioux* (Norman: University of Oklahoma Press, 1989; originally

published in 1953); and John G. Neihardt, *Black Elk Speaks* (New York: William Morrow, 1932).

2. Leo Frobenius (1873–1938) was a German ethnologist and archaeologist credited as one of the first Europeans to take African culture, myth, and history seriously. In his later years, his work took a speculative and controversial turn.

3. Henry Morton "Rondo" Robinson (1898–1961) was an American novelist best known for writing *The Cardinal* (1950).

4. Carlos Castañeda (1925–1998) was an American author who wrote a series of popular semi-autobiographical works portraying shamanic initiations.

5. Campbell is referring to the slaying of Congressman Leo Ryan and the mass murder-suicide of 918 members of the Peoples Temple cult in Jonestown, Guyana, in 1978.

6. *Japa* is the repetition of a mantra or divine name, a practice found in Hinduism, Buddhism, Jainism, and Sikhism.

7. Sam Keen (b. 1931) is an American author, professor, and philosopher who spent twenty years as a contributing editor at *Psychology Today*.

8. Robinson Jeffers (1887–1962) was an American poet who wrote in narrative and epic form. His work reflected a belief that humans in general are too self-centered to perceive the "astonishing beauty of things."

9. Giorgio de Chirico (1888–1978) was an Italian artist and writer whose work influenced the surrealist school.

CHAPTER SIX: "TO COMPLICATE THE PLOT"

1. Erwin Schrödinger, *My View of the World*, trans. Cecily Hastings (Cambridge: Cambridge University Press, 1964), 20–22.

2. Nikolai Ivanovich Vavilov (1887–1943) was a Soviet agronomist, botanist, and geneticist best known for having identified the centers of origin of cultivated plants.

3. Karl Marx, *Das Kapital* (Hamburg: Verlag von Otto Meisner, 1867).

4. Rato Khyongla Nawang Losang, *My Life and Lives: The Story of a Tibetan Incarnation* (New York: Dutton, 1977).

5. Clerical academic degree for monks and nuns in the Gelug order.

6. See page 1 of this book.

7. See Joseph Campbell, *The Inner Reaches of Outer Space* (Novato, CA: New World Library, 2002), 94–100, for more detail.

8. See Jeff King and Maud Oakes, *Where the Two Came to Their Father*, ed. Joseph Campbell (New York: Pantheon, 1943).

CHAPTER SEVEN: "THE COURSE HAS GOTTEN WIDER"

1. Jiddu Krishnamurti (1895–1986) was selected and trained as a youth by leaders of the Theosophical Society to be the vehicle of the coming World

Teacher. In 1929 Krishnamurti renounced his messiahship and parted ways with theosophy but remained a significant spiritual teacher for the rest of his life.

2. Campbell is referring to Rosalind Williams, who later married Krishnamurti's friend and editor, Rajagopal.

3. Roger Sherman Loomis (1887–1966) was a noted Arthurian scholar and Campbell's adviser at Columbia.

4. Adelle Davis (1904–1974) was an American nutritionist and popular author.

5. Originally published in *Liberty Magazine* in 1933, "Strictly Platonic" is included in Joseph Campbell, *Mythic Imagination* (Novato, CA: New World Library, 2012), a collection of Campbell's short stories.

6. Ananda K. Coomaraswamy (1877–1947) was a Sri Lankan Tamil historian, philosopher of Indian art, and interpreter of Indian culture.

7. Max Lerner (1902–1992) was a Russian-born American journalist, author, and educator.

8. Gerald Sykes (1904–1984) was an author, philosopher, and critic.

9. Alfred Radcliffe-Brown, *The Andaman Islanders: A Study in Social Anthropology* (Cambridge: Cambridge University Press, 1922).

10. Alan Watts (1915–1973) was a philosopher, author, and lecturer who popularized Zen Buddhism and other Eastern traditions. Watts and Campbell often reviewed each other's work and enjoyed a close personal friendship.

SOURCES

———————•———————

Abrams, Gary. "Conversation with Joseph Campbell on Mythology: Scholar to Attend Hero's Journey Benefit for Hermes Society." *Los Angeles Times*, May 27, 1987.

Auchinloss, Douglas. "On Waking Up." *Parabola*, January 1982.

Ballas, Costis. Unpublished interview with Joseph Campbell, September 27, 1985 (Box 93, Folder 24, Joseph Campbell Papers, Manuscripts and Archives Division, New York Public Library).

Bourantinos, Emilios. Unpublished interview with Joseph Campbell, September 30, 1985 (Box 93, Folder 25, Joseph Campbell Papers, Manuscripts and Archives Division, New York Public Library).

Bruckner, D. J. R. "Joseph Campbell: 70 Years of Making Connections." *New York Times Book Review*, December 18, 1983.

Carlin, Margarite. "A Case of Pneumonia and Mythology." *Rocky Mountain News*, January 23, 1984.

Campbell, Joseph. Discussion group. Skowhegan School of Painting and Sculpture, Madison, Maine, July 22, 1987.

———. "Explorations: Aim of the Hero's Journey." Esalen, Big Sur, California, November 8, 1983. Joseph Campbell Archives L1185.

———. "Explorations: The Hero's Journey." Esalen, Big Sur, California, November 7, 1983. Joseph Campbell Archives L1183.

———. "Explorations: The Hero's Journey (Woman's Perspective)." Esalen, Big Sur, California, November 8, 1983. Joseph Campbell Archives L1184.

———. "Metaphor as Myth and Religion," audience Q & A. Joseph Campbell Archives L0917.

———. "Mythos: Hinduism/Buddhism," Q & A from session on Hinduism. January 22, 1983.

———. "Mythos: Mann Lectures," Q & A.

———. "Mythos: Psyche and Symbol," Q & A.

———. "Odysseus," Q & A. Joseph Campbell Archives L0604.

————. Radio interview with unknown male and female interviewers. Joseph Campbell Archives L121.

————. "What Is Spirituality?" audience Q & A with Joseph Campbell, Fritjof Capra, and Sogyal Rinpoche, Esalen, Big Sur, California. Joseph Campbell Archives L0835.

Clarke, Gerald. "The Need for New Myths." *Time*, January 17, 1972.

Collins, Tom. "Mythic Reflections: Thoughts on Myth, Spirit, and Our Times." *In Context: A Quarterly of Humane Sustainable Culture* (published by Context Institute), IC #12 (Winter 1985/1986): 52.

"A Conversation with Joseph Campbell." *U.S. News & World Report*, April 16, 1985.

Goodrich, Chris. *Publisher's Weekly*, August 23, 1985.

Graham, Lee. Episode 32. *The Asia Society Presents*, WNYC-AM, 1970. Joseph Campbell Archives L0214.

Jones, Gerard. "An Inward and Outward Journey through Central America." *San José State University Weekly*, December 5, 1979.

Keen, Sam. "Man and Myth." *Psychology Today*, July 1971.

Kisly, Lorraine. "Living Myths." *Parabola*, Spring 1976.

Lawhead, Terry. "The Original Jedi Master." *Honolulu Star Bulletin*, January 7, 1987.

Lobell, John. Interview with Joseph Campbell in Campbell's apartment, October 31, 1983. Joseph Campbell Archives L0832–L0834.

————. Interview with Joseph Campbell. *Natural Living with Gary Null*, WBAI Radio, December 28, 1983. Joseph Campbell Archives L0839.

————. Interview with Joseph Campbell. *Natural Living with Gary Null*, WBAI Radio, July 2, 1984. Joseph Campbell Archives L0845.

————. Interview with Joseph Campbell. *Natural Living with Gary Null*, WBAI Radio, n.d. Joseph Campbell Archives L084.

Marler, June. "Joseph Campbell: The Mythic Journey." *Yoga Journal*, November/December 1987.

McDermott, Gerald. "An Interview with Joseph Campbell." *New Boston Review* vol. 1, no. 2 (Fall 1975): 3–5.

McKnight, Michael. "Elders and Guides." *Parabola*, February 1980.

Miller, Walter James. *The Reader's Almanac*, WYNC, September 24, 1978. Joseph Campbell Archives L0581.

Miodini, Cate. "Myths of the Universe." *Anima Magazine*, Fall 1986.

Mishlove, Jeffrey. "Understanding Mythology with Joseph Campbell." In *Thinking Allowed: Conversations on the Leading Edge of Knowledge and Discovery* (San Francisco: Council Oak Books, 1998).

Newlove, Donald. "The Professor with a Thousand Faces." *Esquire*, September 1977.

Nigg, Joe. "An Interview with the Master of Mythology." *Bloomsbury Review*, April/May 1984.

Romano, Carlin. "Tracking the Origins of Man and Myth." *Philadelphia Inquirer*, January 8, 1984.

Rumley, Larry. "Man and Myth." *Seattle Times/Post-Intelligencer*, January 8, 1984.

Sowers, Leslie. "Cultures Linked by Man's Ideas." *Houston Chronicle*, November 10, 1986.

Terkel, Studs. "Joseph Campbell Talks with Studs Terkel." WFMT Chicago, January 31, 1973.

Unrau, Norman, et al. "Interview with Joseph Campbell." *Goddard Journal*, June 1968.

ZBS Media. "Interview with Joseph Campbell." December 13, 1972.

A JOSEPH CAMPBELL BIBLIOGRAPHY

———————●———————

Following are the major books authored and edited by Joseph Campbell. Each entry gives bibliographic data concerning the first edition or, if applicable, the original date of publication along with the bibliographic data for the edition published by New World Library as part of the Collected Works of Joseph Campbell. For information concerning all other editions, please refer to the Complete Works of Joseph Campbell on the Joseph Campbell Foundation website (www.jcf.org).

AUTHOR

Where the Two Came to Their Father: A Navaho War Ceremonial Given by Jeff King. Bollingen Series I. With Maud Oakes and Jeff King. Richmond, VA: Old Dominion Foundation, 1943.

A Skeleton Key to Finnegans Wake: Unlocking James Joyce's Masterwork. With Henry Morton Robinson. 1944. Second edition, Novato, CA: New World Library, 2005.*

The Hero with a Thousand Faces. Bollingen Series XVII. 1949. Third edition, Novato, CA: New World Library, 2008.*

The Masks of God, 4 vols. New York: Viking Press, 1959–1968. Vol. 1, *Primitive Mythology,* 1959. Third edition, Novato, CA: New World Library, 2021.* Vol. 2, *Oriental Mythology,* 1962. Third edition, Novato, CA: New World Library, 2021.* Vol. 3, *Occidental Mythology,* 1964. Third edition, Novato, CA: New World Library, 2021.* Vol. 4, *Creative Mythology,* 1968.

The Flight of the Wild Gander: Explorations in the Mythological Dimension—Selected Essays 1944–1968. 1969. Third edition, Novato, CA: New World Library, 2002.*

Myths to Live By. 1972. Ebook edition, San Anselmo, CA: Joseph Campbell Foundation, 2011.

The Mythic Image. Bollingen Series C. Princeton, NJ: Princeton University Press, 1974.

The Inner Reaches of Outer Space: Metaphor as Myth and as Religion. 1986. Reprint, Novato, CA: New World Library, 2002.*

Historical Atlas of World Mythology:
> Vol. 1, *The Way of the Animal Powers.* New York: Alfred van der Marck Editions, 1983. Reprint in 2 pts. Part 1, *Mythologies of the Primitive Hunters and Gatherers.* New York: Alfred van der Marck Editions, 1988. Part 2, *Mythologies of the Great Hunt.* New York: Alfred van der Marck Editions, 1988.
> Vol. 2, *The Way of the Seeded Earth,* 3 pts. Part 1, *The Sacrifice.* New York: Alfred van der Marck Editions, 1988. Part 2, *Mythologies of the Primitive Planters: The Northern Americas.* New York: Harper & Row Perennial Library, 1989. Part 3, *Mythologies of the Primitive Planters: The Middle and Southern Americas.* New York: Harper & Row Perennial Library, 1989.

The Power of Myth. With Bill Moyers. Edited by Betty Sue Flowers. New York: Doubleday, 1988.

Transformations of Myth Through Time. New York: Harper & Row, 1990.

The Hero's Journey: Joseph Campbell on His Life and Work. Edited by Phil Cousineau. 1990. Reprint, Novato, CA: New World Library, 2003.*

Reflections on the Art of Living: A Joseph Campbell Companion. Edited by Diane K. Osbon. New York: HarperCollins, 1991.

Mythic Worlds, Modern Words: On the Art of James Joyce. Edited by Edmund L. Epstein. 1993. Second edition, Novato, CA: New World Library, 2003.*

Baksheesh & Brahman: Asian Journals—India. Edited by Robin Larsen, Stephen Larsen, and Antony Van Couvering. 1995. Second edition, Novato, CA: New World Library, 2002.* [Reissued in paperback, together with *Sake & Satori,* in 2017; see *Asian Journals* entry below.]

The Mythic Dimension: Selected Essays 1959–1987. Edited by Antony Van Couvering. 1997. Second edition, Novato, CA: New World Library, 2007.*

Thou Art That. Edited by Eugene Kennedy. Novato, CA: New World Library, 2001.*

Sake & Satori: Asian Journals—Japan. Edited by David Kudler. Novato, CA: New World Library, 2002.* [Reissued in paperback, together with *Baksheesh & Brahman,* in 2017; see *Asian Journals* entry below.]

Myths of Light. Edited by David Kudler. Novato, CA: New World Library, 2003.*

Pathways to Bliss: Mythology and Personal Transformation. Edited by David Kudler. Novato, CA: New World Library, 2004.*
Mythic Imagination: Collected Short Fiction. Novato, CA: New World Library, 2012.*
Goddesses: Mysteries of the Feminine Divine. Edited by Safron Rossi. Novato, CA: New World Library, 2013.*
Romance of the Grail: The Magic and Mystery of Arthurian Myth. Edited by Evans Lansing Smith. Novato, CA: New World Library, 2015.*
Asian Journals: India and Japan. Combined paperback reissue of *Baksheesh & Brahman* and *Sake & Satori.* Book I: *Baksheesh & Brahman*—edited by Robin Larsen, Stephen Larsen, and Antony Van Couvering; book II: *Sake & Satori*—edited by David Kudler. Novato, CA: New World Library, 2017.*
The Ecstasy of Being: Mythology and Dance. Edited by Nancy Allison, CMA. Novato, CA: New World Library, 2017.*
Correspondence: 1927–1987. Edited by Evans Lansing Smith and Dennis Patrick Slattery. Novato, CA: New World Library, 2018.*

* Published by New World Library as part of the Collected Works of Joseph Campbell.

EDITOR

Books edited and completed from the posthuma of Heinrich Zimmer:
Myths and Symbols in Indian Art and Civilization. Bollingen Series VI. New York: Pantheon, 1946.
The King and the Corpse. Bollingen Series XI. New York: Pantheon, 1948.
Philosophies of India. Bollingen Series XXVI. New York: Pantheon, 1951.
The Art of Indian Asia. Bollingen Series XXXIX, 2 vols. New York: Pantheon, 1955.

Other books edited:
The Portable Arabian Nights. New York: Viking Press, 1951.
Papers from the Eranos Yearbooks. Bollingen Series XXX, 6 vols. Edited with R. F. C. Hull and Olga Froebe-Kapteyn. Translated by Ralph Manheim. Princeton, NJ: Princeton University Press, 1954–1969.
Myth, Dreams, and Religion: Eleven Visions of Connection. New York: E. P. Dutton, 1970.
The Portable Jung. By C. G. Jung. Translated by R. F. C. Hull. New York: Viking Press, 1971.
My Life and Lives. By Rato Khyongla Nawang Losang. New York: E. P. Dutton, 1977.

INDEX

abyss, the, 114, 130–31, 157
Adam and Eve myth, 94, 101. *See also*
 Fall, the
Adams, Richard, 157
Adler, Alfred, 126
adolescence, 11
Adonis, 56, 57, 67, 96
adulthood, 10, 11
Adventure (Hero's Journey aspect),
 147–50
advertising art, 170
Aeschylus, 60, 63, 84
Aesop's fables, 53
aesthetic arrest, 23, 168, 169, 171
aesthetics, 168
affect symbols, 27
Age of the Sun God, The (Frobenius),
 143
Agni, 132
agriculture, 39, 42, 45, 61. *See also*
 planting cultures
aham, 134
ahamkara, 77–78
Ahura Mazda, 64
air (element), 87
"airport civilization," 201
Alaska, 220–21
alchemy, 24, 159–60
Alexander the Great, 63
Alexandria (Egypt), 63
Algonquin Indians, 76

Allah, 24
Allen, Woody, 245–46
Amaterasu, 43
American Graffiti (film; 1973), 158
American Indian mythology, 208,
 211, 228
American Indians, 3; Campbell's
 interest in, 208, 211; God
 personifications of, 76; losses of
 mythology, 139–40; nature and,
 38–39. *See also* Navaho Indians;
 Sioux Indians; *specific tribe*
American literature, 218
American Oriental Society, 231
amor fati, 213, 214
Amorites, 50
Amsterdam (Netherlands), 213
analysis, 161–62
ananda (bliss), 162
Ānanda (Buddha's body servant), 155
Ancient Society (Morgan), 37
Andaman Islanders, The (Radcliffe-
 Brown), 237, 251n9
Andaman Islands, 4, 237
angels, 132, 189
Anglo-Saxon literature, 215
Angra Mainyu, 64
animal domestication, 40, 56, 58,
 248n10
animal husbandry, 51
animal masters, 37

community, 205
comparative mythology: Campbell's
course in, 116, 143, 222–23;
Campbell's interest in, 69, 209;
Campbell's writings and, 33;
multiculturalism and, 14–15;
religion and, 85
compassion motif, 119, 121, 155
Confucianism, 29, 62
Confucius, 60
Congo, the, 2
consciousness: body and, 246; death
and, 11, 15, 16, 246; dream consciousness, 18, 90, 135; dreams
and, 89; ego-oriented, 70,
102–3, 124, 134; four stages of,
90; Hindu concept of, 134–36;
identification with, 82; one-
ness with, 113; transformation
of, 160, 195; undifferentiated,
90–91. *See also* Buddha consciousness; unconscious
Cooke, Terence James, 91
Coomaraswamy, Ananda K., 235,
251n6
Cooper Union, x
Copernicus, 8
Corbin, Henry, 249n6 (ch. 3)
cosmic rhythm, 41
cosmology, 7–9
cosmopolis, 140
councils, religious, 101
counterculture, 238–39
Courtland Hotel, 223
Cousins, Norman, 226–27
creation: God and, 78; special-
species, 9
creation myths, 59–60
creative imagination, 14
creative movement, xii
Creative Mythology (Campbell), 33,
232
Crete, 45
Critique of Pure Reason (Kant), 107–8
Cro-Magnon man, 35, 37

crucifixion, 67, 93–94, 101
cryptomnesia, 114
Cuba, 218
cult directions, 56
cults: fertility, 50; metaphor and, 24;
mystery, 140; peyote, 140; use of
term, xii, 248n7
cultural crisis, 198
culture: assimilation in, 48; -bounded
mythological systems, 14–15;
collapse causes, 193; mythological functions in, 6–11;
mythology and, 1–2, 20–21; in
transition, 198–99, 243; uniqueness of, and universal images, 6;
Western, 141
cuneiform, 47–48
cyclic myths, 41–43, 61
Cyprus, 63, 248n10
Cyrus the Great, 64

Dadaism, 174–75
daemon, 132
Dalai Lama, 91, 185–86
Dalí, Salvador, 120, 175
Dante, 7, 105
Darius the Great, 64
Dartmouth College, 209, 236
Davis, Adelle, 218–19, 251n4
Dead Sea Scrolls, 64, 65
death: Campbell and fear of, 245–46;
experience of, in Hero's Journey,
144–45; inward turn and, 11;
mythic thinking originating in,
15–18; rites of passage and, 10,
11; war and threat of, 197
death and rebirth, 39–40, 56, 61, 67,
73, 189, 209
Death in Venice (Mann), 117
De Chirico, Giorgio, 175, 250n9
Declaration of Independence (US),
188
Decline of the West (Spengler), 107,
219, 223
deism, 191

Nicolaus Cusanus, 2

Nietzsche, Friedrich: on Apollonian
vs. Dionysian principles, 113;
Campbell and, 107, 213, 219,
224; on casting out devils, 130;
on good/evil, 109–11; on guilt,
214; on man as "sick animal,"
133; Mann influenced by, 114–
15; Naziism and, 109; Occiden-
tal/Oriental coordinated in, 105,
108–9, 113–14; Schopenhauer
and, 107, 108; Spengler and,
107; "superman" as portrayed by,
112; symbolic thought unlocked
by, 114

Nikhilananda, Swami, 225, 227, 228

Nile River, 47

nirvana, 92, 93, 100

Noah's ark story, 3, 5

nomadic herding cultures: bull
sacrifices and, 58–59; invasions
of, 44–45; male gods of, 48–49;
planting cultures vs., 51–52. *See
also* Indo-Europeans; Semites

Norbulingka (Lhasa, Tibet), 185–86

Normans, 153–54

Norse mythology, 41

Northern Europe, 45

Notre Dame Cathedral (Paris,
France), 53

nudes, 174

numbers, 115–16

Nurmi, Paavo, 211

Oannes, 5

Oasis (Chicago, IL), 165

object, crisis of the, 175

O'Brien, Frederick, 208

Occident: Orient coordinated with,
105; social aspects of, 154–55;
use of term, xii–xiii

Occidental Mythology (Campbell), 33

Oceania, 39

Odysseus, 195

Odyssey (Homer), 195

Oedipus complex, 123, 128

Oedipus the King (Sophocles), 99

Oertel, 216

old age, 10

Old Man, 3

Old Testament: Bronze Age traditions
inverted in, 44–45; deist rejection of, 191; Goddess opposed
in, 50, 53; God of, 85; infighting
in, 66; Islam vs., 25; Jesus and
transcendence of, 68; nature as
corrupt in, 97; planting cultures
vs. herding cultures in, 51–52;
rules of behavior in, 56; war style
in, 194, 197. *See also* Genesis,
Book of; *specific book*

Olson, Bradley, vii

Olympic Games (Amsterdam, Netherlands; 1928), 213

Olympic Games (Paris, France; 1924),
211, 213

1132 (number), 115–16

O'Neill, Eugene, 210

opposites: Christ's crucifixion and,
73–74; in Hero's Journey, 147;
Hinduism and, 85; inward turn
and, 160; Judeo-Christian tradition and, 94; Mahāyāna Buddhism and, 92–93; marriage and,
224; in Pythagorean symbology,
189–91; *tat vam asi* and, 81; US
and, 194

Orenda, 76

Orient: bowing in, 80–81; Occident
coordinated with, 105; religious
texts in, 74; social aspects of,
154–55; use of term, xiii

Oriental mysticism, 100

Oriental mythologies, 92

Oriental Mythology (Campbell), 33,
186

Oriental philosophy, 6, 113, 135–36

original sin, 95, 101–2

Orphic tradition, 68, 91

Osiris, 52, 57, 63, 67, 189

poetry, 164
polis, mythology of, 140
politics: art vs., 70; going into, 204–5;
  human spirit and, 202–3; ideologies of, 173, 184; Indian classical
  text on art of, 191–92; modern
  society and, 70, 159, 177, 199;
  mythology and transcendence
  of, 1–2
Politics of Experience, The (Laing), 90
Polynesia, 30, 194, 208–9
pork, bans on, 56, 57
pornography, 169–71, 173–74
· *Portrait of the Artist as a Young Man, A*
  (Joyce), 171–72
Poseidon, 77
pottery, 61
Pound, Ezra, 118
pranayama, 88
priesthoods, 40, 41, 46–47
primal mythologies, 239; global, lack
  of, 200; of hunting/gathering
  cultures, 35–39. *See also* myth/
  mythology—historical manifestations
Prima materia, 159
"primitive," use of term, xiii
Primitive Mythology (Campbell), ix,
  33, 157
Princeton University Press, 125
Prohibition Era, 210
*Prolegomena to the Study of Greek
  Religion* (Harrison), 58–59
Prometheus, 84–85, 149
Prometheus Bound (Aeschylus), 84
Promised Land, 24, 169
propaganda, 169–70
Protestantism, 74
psyche, 69–70, 121–22
psychedelics, 141–42, 239
psychoanalysis, 130
psychology, xii, 6; Campbell's writings
  and, 33; mandalas and, 61–62;
  mythic images and, 120–21;
  religion and, 80, 179; spirituality

and, 121; yoga and, 89. *See also*
  Freud, Sigmund; Jung, Carl G.
"Psychology of So-Called Occult
  Phenomena, The" (Jung), 124
Psychology Today, 250n7 (ch. 5)
psychosis, 124, 130
*Publications of the Modern Language
  Association*, 231
Pueblo Indians, 20
Puget Sound, 220–21
Purāṇas, 229
Puritanism, 53
Pygmies, 37–38, 75
pyramids, 187–88, 201
Pythagoras, 60, 192
Pythagoreanism, 189–90, 192

questing, 154–55, 156
Qumran community, 65

racial unconscious, 127
Radcliffe-Brown, Alfred, 237, 251n9
Radin, Max, 236
Radin, Paul, 236
Raleigh, Walter, 187
Ramakrishna, 54, 203
Ramakrishna Vivekananda Center
  (New York, NY), 225
Rank, Otto, 126
Rasmussen, Knud, 35–36
Rato Khyongla, 185–86, 250n4
  (ch. 6)
reason, 182–83, 190, 191
rebirth, 5, 39–40
Red Sea, 103
Refusal of the Call (Hero's Journey
  aspect), 146, 147
reincarnation, 16–17, 99
religion: American mythos and, 187;
  art and, 176–77; basic problem
  of, 110; of birth, 85; Campbell's
  view of, 74, 223; Campbell's
  writings and, 33; creedal, 85;
  dogmatic, 71; ethically-based,
  63–64, 109–10; German

myths = cultural universals

mythology as validation of inner experience
spiritual

art → aesthetic arrest

themes: awaken your inner, spiritual life

nature vs facts

inward journeys — the universe is in us
divinity, mystery
eternal life
are inside

follow your bliss

say yes to beauty + cruelty in nature

religions of exclusion (west)
vs religions of nature (orient)

rituals as enactments of myth

what would he say about AI,
machine learning
→ Star Wars
2001 Space Odyssey
→ heroe's journey

religions wars as failure of abstraction
concrete, they lose the metaphors

David White — The heart aroused
→ Beowulf 6/18 4pm

two main mythologies
① harmony in nature
② good God vs bad God
nature has to be corrected

Eat
Pray
Love

The origin
of paternal

ABOUT JOSEPH CAMPBELL

JOSEPH CAMPBELL was an American author and teacher best known for his work in the field of comparative mythology. He was born in New York City in 1904, and in early childhood became interested in mythology. He loved to read books about American Indian cultures and frequently visited the American Museum of Natural History in New York, where he was fascinated by the museum's collection of totem poles. Campbell was educated at Columbia University, where he specialized in medieval literature, and, after earning a master's degree, continued his studies at universities in Paris and Munich. While abroad he was influenced by the art of Pablo Picasso and Henri Matisse, the novels of James Joyce and Thomas Mann, and the psychological studies of Sigmund Freud and Carl Jung. These encounters led to Campbell's theory that all myths and epics are linked in the human psyche, and that they are cultural manifestations of the universal need to explain social, cosmological, and spiritual realities.

After a period in California, where he encountered John Steinbeck and the biologist Ed Ricketts, Campbell taught at the Canterbury School, and then, in 1934, joined the literature department at Sarah Lawrence College, a post he retained for many years. During the 1940s and '50s, he helped Swami Nikhilananda to translate the Upaniṣads and *The Gospel of Sri Ramakrishna*. He also edited works by the German scholar Heinrich Zimmer on Indian art, myths, and philosophy.

In 1944, with Henry Morton Robinson, Campbell published *A Skeleton Key to Finnegans Wake*. His first original work, *The Hero with a Thousand Faces*, came out in 1949 and was immediately well received; in time, it became acclaimed as a classic. In this study of the "myth of the hero," Campbell asserted that there is a single pattern of heroic journey and that all cultures share this essential pattern in their various heroic myths. In his book he also outlined the basic conditions, stages, and results of the archetypal hero's journey.

Joseph Campbell died in 1987. In 1988 a series of television interviews with Bill Moyers, *The Power of Myth*, introduced Campbell's views to millions of people.

Papi's favorite show war
"Los genios"
Shorty Castro played the part of Angel Guardian

ABOUT THE
JOSEPH CAMPBELL FOUNDATION

———————•———————

THE JOSEPH CAMPBELL FOUNDATION (JCF) is a not-for-profit corporation that continues the work of Joseph Campbell, exploring the fields of mythology and comparative religion. The Foundation is guided by three principal goals:

First, the Foundation preserves, protects, and perpetuates Campbell's pioneering work. This includes cataloging and archiving his works, developing new publications based on his works, directing the sale and distribution of his published works, protecting copyrights to his works, and increasing awareness of his works by making them available in digital formats on JCF's website.

Second, the Foundation furthers his pioneering work in mythology and comparative religion. This involves promoting the study of mythology and comparative religion, implementing and/or supporting diverse mythological education programs, supporting and/or sponsoring events designed to increase public awareness, donating Campbell's archived works to the New York Public Library and his personal library to OPUS Archive & Research Center, and utilizing JCF's website (www.jcf.org) as a forum for mythologically informed cross-cultural dialogue.

Third, the Foundation helps individuals enrich their lives by participating in a series of programs, including our global, Internet-based Associates program; our local international network of Mythological Roundtables; and our periodic Joseph Campbell–related events and activities.

For more information on Joseph Campbell
and the Joseph Campbell Foundation, contact:
Joseph Campbell Foundation
www.jcf.org